Prospects for Reconciliation: Theory and Practice

Proceedings of the International Workshop, Yerevan, 27 November 2010

Published by:

Institut für Internationale Zusammenarbeit des Deutschen Volkshochschul-Verbandes (*dvv international*)

Proof-reading: Richard Giragosian
Design & Layout: Haroutiun Samuelian
Cover photo: Sergey Parajanov, Three-dimensional collage "Irises" (1986) © Parajanov Museum Yerevan
Print: Printinfo JS LLC

dvv international
Obere Wilhelmstraße 32-53225 Bonn
Federal Republic of Germany
Tel: +49/228-975 69-0
Fax: +49/228-975 69-55
info@dvv-international.de
www.dvv-international.de

For further information please also see
www.speakingtooneanther.org

ISBN 978 - 3 - 942755 - 01 - 6

© 2011 *dvv international*

Prospects for Reconciliation: Theory and Practice

Proceedings of the International Workshop, Yerevan, 27 November 2010

Edited by Hranush Kharatyan-Araqelyan and Leyla Neyzi

Content

Introduction

Leyla Neyzi

The workshop "Prospects for Reconciliation: Theory and Practice" took place on November 27, 2010 in Yerevan, Republic of Armenia. It was organized under the auspices of the two-year project "Adult Education and Oral History Contributing to Armenian-Turkish Reconciliation," funded by the German Federal Foreign Office and implemented by *dvv international*, Anadolu Kültür (Turkey) and "Hazarashen" Armenian Center for Ethnological Studies (Armenia).

As part of this project, university students from Armenia and Turkey attended a summer camp in Dilijan, Armenia, where they were trained in the methodology of oral history and became acquainted with one another's society and culture. Students then took part in an oral history research project in Turkey and Armenia on memories of a shared but painful past, the results of which were published in a book entitled, "Speaking to One Another: Personal Memories of the Past in Armenia and Turkey," co-authored by Professor Leyla Neyzi from Sabancı University in Istanbul and Professor Hranush Kharatyan-Araqelyan from Yerevan State Linguistic University. This research also resulted in a traveling exhibition curated by Önder Özengi from Turkey and Taron Simonyan from Armenia, which traveled to several cities in Turkey and Armenia. The project included a camp in Antakya, Turkey, where students developed joint projects with the aim of contributing to reconciliation. Students from Armenia and Turkey also traveled for a study trip to Berlin to learn from Germany's experience in dealing with the past.

The main objective of the international workshop was to share the results of the project, to discuss the contribution of adult education and oral history to Turkish-Armenian reconciliation, and to make possible an exchange of experiences among Armenian, Turkish and international academics and practitioners in the fields of reconciliation, oral history and adult education. The workshop was planned so as to make the proceedings available in book form.

This international workshop was extremely timely: in the past few years, there has been an immense change in relations between Armenia and Turkey, with a deepening rapprochement between the two societies. While the Armenian Genocide was publicly silenced in Soviet Armenia, it remains officially unrecognized in contemporary Turkey. While these events occurred nearly one hundred years ago, their memory continues to be transmitted from generation to generation and continue to affect the present in both societies. After a silence of over eighty years, the events of 1915 have become both a topic of international political and social discourse and the core issue in political negotiations between Armenia and Turkey. However, while the last decade has been witness to a number of initiatives that aim to normalize Armenia-Turkey relations, the suspension of the protocols has slowed down the rapprochement process. The differences in the approaches of multiple stakeholders to the past and the present are widely known. Although the will to start a dialogue is much appreciated, it remains difficult to find a common ground by which to address the past and discuss the present.

In the absence of a solution on the level of national politics, the workshop sought to determine if and how reconciliation could be achieved on the societal level. Given a long history of violent conflict and a lack of communication, the peoples of Armenia and Turkey have different perceptions of one another and different expectations concerning reconciliation. How have the steps towards rapprochement and civil initiatives in particular, affected the relations between the two neighboring societies? In our oral history research, we have been particularly interested in how local communities, families and individuals remember (and forget), narrate, and interpret the past in the context of the present, and how oral history and memory studies can contribute to dialogue and reconciliation between Armenia and Turkey. The participants of the workshop explored what role memories of the shared past and of violence play in both societies, how a dialogue about the past can contribute to a process of reconciliation between the two countries, and by what means such a dialogue can be conducted in practice.

The first panel of the workshop, "Between the Past and the Present," dealt with more theoretical issues including analytical concepts and questions of context. It broadly centered on four topics: the role of the past for reconciliation; the concept of truth; options for establishing a shared account of the past; and the political climate within and between Armenia and Turkey in which such processes are taking place. How to acknowledge suffering and injustice was a central theme. However, it was also deemed worthwhile to look at the positive aspects of the common past, which spanned centuries. The main questions/topics for the panel included the following: How does the state "silence" history? How does this affect the ways the past is remembered? How does silence, forgetting and fear affect the discussion of conflict resolution? How should historiography and oral history/memory studies be included in the reconciliation process? How is it possible to acknowledge (conflicting) public opinion without recreating hostilities? How may different societies construct history, the present and their relations to one another differently? How may reconciliation processes proceed in tandem with democratization?

Apart from governmental initiatives and the work of the private sector, a number of projects have been carried out by civil society organizations in order to foster Armenian-Turkish reconciliation. The second panel of the workshop, "Civic Initiatives," aimed at sharing the experiences of organizations from both countries, as well as other examples from different parts of the world. The discussions were structured around ongoing and completed reconciliation projects, with specific attention given to targeting and incorporating young people. The participants presented their experiences in regard to the following issues: How is the experience of the two peoples with memories of a violent past expressed in various cultural products? How do these cultural products shape public discourse? What are the main challenges Turkish-Armenian projects face during the collaboration process? What is their main contribution to the reconciliation process, and what new issues and/or questions do they pose? How can recent and ongoing projects on Armenian-Turkish reconciliation learn from the experiences of other countries/projects?

The international workshop, "Prospects for Reconciliation: Theory and Practice," fulfilled its aims by bringing academics and practitioners together to share the results of the project "Adult Education and Oral History Contributing to Armenian-Turkish Reconciliation," to discuss current theoretical challenges within the field of reconciliation, the contribution of oral history and adult education to Armenian-Turkish reconciliation, and the experiences of various civic initiatives implemented in Turkey, Armenia and other settings.

**German Ambassador
Hans-Jochen Schmidt**

Summary of Remarks Made at the Opening of a DVV-Conference Dedicated to "Adult Education and Oral History Contributing to Armenian-Turkish Reconciliation"

Mr. Hans-Jochen Schmidt is Ambassador Extraordinary and Plenipotentiary of the Federal Republic of Germany in Armenia. He studied Law and entered the Foreign Office (Auswärtiges Amt) in 1977. He held different positions at German Embassies in different countries and the German Foreign Office.
Before being nominated as Ambassador to Armenia he was Head of the OSCE Office in Minsk, Deputy Head of Mission in Kiev, Deputy and Acting Consul General in St. Petersburg and Atlanta. Mr. Schmidt served also in the German Embassies in Kinshasa and Cairo.

The conference "Speaking to One Another" is a splendid opportunity to discuss ways and means of how to cope with a difficult past, of how to overcome a deadlock or a stalemate. With great interest the German Embassy has been following the endeavor undertaken by the Institute for International Cooperation of the German Adult Education Association (*dvv international*) in partnership with Anadolu Kültür and the Armenian Center for Ethnological Studies "Hazarashen" to contribute to the Armenian-Turkish reconciliation process by initiating an open dialogue through professional oral history research as well as by serving as a forum for meetings and encounters between representatives of different strata of both societies.

The aim of the project has been to create a better understanding of history and political developments among younger people of both societies. The dvv-project has to be seen against the background of activities promoted by other non-governmental organizations to prepare the ground work for a better understanding of each other's history by organizing thematic seminars and creating media-relevant platforms.

To overcome a political stalemate by the breaking down of prejudices and enabling both societies to develop cross-frontier contacts and – ultimately – ties: a prerequisite for such an undertaking is the recognition of which has happened.

It took the German people a long time to bring about genuine change in its relationship with France as well as with Poland, but ultimately, strong-willed and far-sighted politicians determined the political course for reconciliation. Referring to the holocaust and the difficulties for post-war Germany to deal conscientiously with its horrible past it took at least one generation for most of the Germans to come to terms with its history.

The German couple Mitscherlich (sociologist and psychologist) published in 1964 the landmark book, "Inability to Mourn: Principles of Collective Behavior," a book stirring up the emotions of the parent's generation confronted by merciless questions of their children why they admitted such crimes.

Without a deep analysis and an understanding what and why such things like holocaust occurred or the systematic extinction of a people or a race is undertaken: it is difficult to overcome psychological prevailing barriers caused by traumatic crimes with a seemingly never ending impact on the memory and the feelings of a people.

Reconciliation is only possible by acknowledging what happened. The dvv-project whose actual work had been centering on Oral History (History and Identity-Building Bridges for Dialogue and Understanding) will hopefully enable both societies in the future to restructure their relations by, on the one side, not forgetting the horrible haunting and terrible past but by also creatively working on a brighter future to the benefit of both nations as well as their societies (and taking duly into consideration the wounds caused by a state and parts of its society against another people).

Elazar Barkan

Reconciliation beyond Subjective Histories: Comments on Historians and Conflict Resolution

Mr. Elazar Barkan is professor of International and Public Affairs at Columbia University, is the Co-Director of the Human Rights Concentration at SIPA, and is founding Director of the Institute for Historical Justice and Reconciliation at the Salzburg Seminar. Professor Barkan specializes on the role of history in contemporary society and politics, with particular emphasis on the response to gross historical crimes and injustices, and human rights. His recent books include The Guilt of Nations: Restitution and Negotiating Historical Injustices (2000); Claiming the Stones/Naming the Bones: Cultural Property and the Negotiation of National and Ethnic Identity, (an edited volume with Ronald Bush, Getty, 2003); Taking Wrongs Seriously: Apologies and Reconciliation (an edited volume with Alexander Karn, Stanford University Press, 2006).

1. Conflict Resolution

It has long been recognized among conflict resolution professionals that ethnic and religious conflicts are the most difficult to mediate. Less frequently, it has also been noted that progress necessitates addressing the root historical causes. One view is that it should be based on "a process of transactional contrition and forgiveness between aggressors and victims" to establish "mutual acceptance and reasonable trust." "This process depends on joint analysis of the history of the conflict, recognition of injustices and resulting historic wounds, and acceptance of moral responsibility where due" (Montville 1993). I want to reserve judgment about the question of forgiveness, but there is little doubt that a "joint analysis of the history of the conflict" is a foundational requirement. I shall return to this.

Reciprocal historical understanding is required because most conflicts involve competing notions of victimization, mutual real or imagined fear, and a memory of catastrophe. This leads to the recognition of the need for acknowledgement. Ordinarily, this translates into facilitating mechanisms for communication between "representatives" of the groups in order to change political attitudes. The focus is on the personal trust building, interaction, and acknowledgement. Indeed in the field of informal diplomacy, what is generally known as "track two," or multi-track diplomacy, the goal is to change political attitudes through such personal interaction. Through these special contacts, it is argued that participants can delegitimize stereotypical views by introducing new data and encouraging the stakeholders on each side through establishing a working trust to reexamine their views.

What is the role of history in this process? One view is to "to elicit specific grievances and wounds of the groups or nations in conflict which have not been acknowledged by the side responsible for inflicting them. Only the victims know for certain which historic events sustain the sense of victimhood and these become cumulatively the agenda for healing" (Montville 1993). However, the challenge is that while the victims' perspective of the suffering and the grievances is essential, the victims' view does not necessarily reflect a valid history. Moreover, it may collide with legitimate views by other stakeholders. Unfortunately, when it comes to a conflict resolution mechanism, too often attention is devoted to the interaction itself and positive social and psychological rapport among the participants, and too little on the product that will provide the material for wider dissemination.

Indeed, if the process is primarily psychological, and the goal is to enable the patient to recognize his/her source of suffering and come to terms with it, the conflict resolution process faces the challenge of validation and recognition; the mere recognition of grievances establishes the framework, not the resolution. It is necessary to match the grievances with the external perspective, and move beyond the myth of subjective memories. Transforming the victimhood psychology requires the negotiation of a new political framework between the sides, and the question is what can be added to the tool kit to achieve this?

Since the identity of all stakeholders is informed by historical narratives, historians and scholars can contribute towards conflict resolution by impacting the perspectives through a rigorous analysis of the causes and contexts of the narratives of the conflicting parties. This can be done independently or jointly, and be included in the informal or official negotiations. Serious historical research and writing of historic grievances need not depend entirely on the existence of a problem-solving workshop. Unilateral efforts at a balanced review might stimulate the attention and response of "the other" to previously unknown or ignored aspects of history of violence and aggression which will provide the historical base upon which trust can be built.

2. Scholarly Civic Involvement

How does the desire of scholars and historians to be involved in and be relevant to contemporary society and politics be assimilated with professional integrity and the need of conflict resolution processes to counter nationalist mythologies? The overwhelming political need is to develop a discourse to engage and counter public misconceptions and ignorance that serve as fodder for ethnic and national conflict, thereby opening the space for a better understanding of the 'other'. This dual goal is attainable by explicitly adhering to a separation between 1) the politics of advancing non-confrontational history, and 2) writing a professional history that is not directly shaped by political needs. For a historical discourse to be effective, and not manipulative, it has to represent first-rate professional history.

The need for reparatory history emerges most clearly in cases where there is an urgent need to amend past wrongs, or where the demand for historical redress continues to fan violent conflict. Reparatory history is increasingly being viewed as a right for redress, and has become a wide-ranging aspirational goal of the politics of transition as well as a tool of conflict resolution. The scope of possible redress includes retributive justice (courts, tribunals, Truth Commissions, etc.) restorative (reparation; restitution of property; restitution of cultural property; historical commissions) and symbolic, such as apologies.

13

Each of these provides a form of atonement. To understand the appeal of redress, we have to go beyond legal analysis to explore the centrality of identity in redress, in particular the role of history in identity as a frame of analysis.

The force of morality in redress revolves around 1) the question of explicit <u>recognition</u> of wrongs as a precondition for redress, and 2) the relation of material redress to symbolic quest. While the form of redress varies (restitution, reparations, or retribution), for redress to play a role in conflict resolution and reconciliation it has to transcend the quest for justice and the individual guilt and responsibility, and address the group identity, paying attention to the ethics of rights and historical imagination.

Redressing the past is a developing field in politics (and scholarship) that has grown roughly in parallel to the expansion of human rights. Both began in the aftermath of World War II. Redress was most evident in the first agreement of reparation between Germany on the one side and Jewish organizations and Israel on the other. This was the first case in which a state acknowledged guilt and assumes compensation without being forced to by an external victorious military. Similar to human rights which began in earnest in the late 1940s and was overshadowed by the Cold War, only to reappear in the 1970s with the incipient growth of democratization, redress began with the German-Jewish agreement, but we associate this more with a concept that evolved in the 1990s, that is Transitional Justice. Yet, growing public interest in redress was revived, in most cases, as a matter of minimal justice and large frustration, but this was evident from the 1970s in Greece, Spain, Portugal, through the 1980s in Latin America, and finally, in Eastern Europe. By the time the South African Truth and Reconciliation Commission captured the public imagination, the concept was well entrenched within the growing group of advocates pursuing politics of redress. Redress included retributive justice (trials); restorative (restitution, compensation, apologies); and a hybrid: truth commissions which were varied among themselves worldwide. Notably, those mechanisms address mostly the immediate past and less frequently, if at all, the historical legacy. The longer historical violence, and the nature of victimization, happened through some form of engaging a historical commission or inquiry. But these left much to be desired, and rarely have the historical complexity of conflict has been adequately addressed by a historical commission.

This creates the need for civil society to engage and address historical conflicts that impact the national identity both within states and among states. It stems from the recognition that many political conflicts, internationally and domestically, are rooted in conflicts over historical narratives.

The concept of 'historical conflict' demands clarification. Many conflicts, or probably all conflicts, have a historical context. In contrast, certain conflicts are 'historical' in the sense that it is the legacy of a conflict that continues to haunt the present, the memory that shapes the identity of the protagonists and its ramification, more than a dispute as an ongoing conflict. The historical context of a conflict is distinct from a historical conflict. These are two separate categories. The historical contexts of conflicts are all around us: postcolonial conflicts in Africa, the Middle East, Russia and Georgia, and we can go on. In each case, the history of the conflict is critical to understanding, but the conflict is about the present: territory, resources, power. In contrast, a *historical conflict* is about our perspective of the past, the legacy of which has ramification at present. The legacy of the Second World War between Japan and China is a well-known example. How many died in Dresden and what is the significance of the numbers? In the conflict between Turkey and Armenia there are the historical conflicts (the question of genocide) as well as the contemporary (Azerbaijan) which is shaped by fears stemming from historical memory. In these cases, the divided memory and the lack of acknowledgment shape current relations, more than, for example, trade disputes, territorial ambitions, or electoral politics.

The historian's expertise is obviously useful for both types of conflicts. Understanding the historical *context* of a conflict may allow politicians to engage differently in efforts to resolve the disagreement. In cases of *historical conflicts*, however, the historical narrative is the very core of the conflict. In this case, constructing a narrative that bridges the differences and negotiating the polarized perspectives provides for a direct intervention at the heart of a conflict. It is a new tool of conflict resolution.

For scholars and advocates to cooperate there has to be a middle road where the constructed narrative has to address major issues of the identity of the nation, and ethnicity, while making it accessible to the public. In many cases, that will mean a simplified version of history, but one that is not on a slippery slope of propaganda. The first order is 'Not to Lie' or perpetrate myth, that is, historians should not advance presentist claims that have no historical foundations, is neither new nor controversial. I believe this should not be a contentious proposition. Accepting the 'authenticity of the past' as a requirement for historical narratives is a must not a virtue. Conversely, although being motivated by contemporary issues is frequently a worthy rationale for an inquiry, constructing a historical narrative to fit a contemporary purpose cannot be the end goal.

3. A Note about Truth

There is a great sense that once everyone recognizes THE TRUTH, the historical and the contemporary conflict will be bridged. This simplistic notion overlooks the multiplicity of truths, and the rich texture of reality. It is only through social medium that we can ac*know*ledge the truth, and that truth varies according to the mechanism and the procedure employed. This contextualism does not mean everything up for grab, and to use the ever present example of the holocaust, it does not mean the holocaust did not take place. But it does mean that when there is a controversy between two sides over what an event consisted of, such as the Armenian Genocide (and what to call it), the mechanism of the interaction between the stakeholders will be critical for any understanding of the truth for both sides.

Contemporary society revered truth like a religion, with very little investigation of its multiplicity. There are very many different kinds of truth. Even without getting into philosophical discussions about truth, relativism and realism, we can make references, which we easily recognize in our daily lives, to the provisional scope of truth. Consider, for example, the difference between judicial truth and historical truth; and the daily subjective truth in which each of us takes refuge when disagreements occur. A couple of examples will suffice. We know that testimonies in court are always challenged. Assuming that the witnesses do not perjure themselves, they ordinarily testify about truths which often and massively are invalidated by the court. The process of justice is to confront the various versions of truth. It is done with specific procedure, and often, the judicial truth depends on the procedural ruling, not on the substance at hand. When the International Court of Justice (ICJ) ruled that Serbia was not guilty of the genocide in Srebrenica, it reached a truth, which judicially was final, but even though it was the judgment of the highest court in the world, it was widely dismissed as untrue. The limited documentation in front of the Court meant that contextually, the genocide was unproven in the court. But in the public arena, the case was different. This is one major distinction between judicial as a formal truth, which is final, and historical truth which is always subject to revision. It is the latter truth, which is more critical in conflict resolution process, than is a social and political process. For the truth to carry value in conflict resolution, it has to be flexible enough to accommodate new data, and supported by a rich social context that can incorporate and interpret the new, additional data.

There have been many psychological experiments that challenge memory, both experiments that show the fragility of memory (which we are all familiar in personal life) and the constructing of non-existing experiences as a personal memory (e.g. remembering a place we never visited). Memory is very susceptible; and we should remember this when we deal with survivors testimony as the ultimate truth, which we often feel we cannot be challenged for ethical reasons. Yet, often time survivors' memory exhibit "post memory" that is the internalization of public narratives. This has been shown in cases of Holocaust testimonies where they remember things that they couldn't have known. These are the exceptions, but nonetheless, a phenomenon that is part of the truth of survivors. Or in the notorious case of Rigoberta Manchu, whose celebrated autobiography was shown to include inaccuracies. In that case, the public response has been divided, with many emphasizing the "larger" truth as one that transcended the empirical misrepresentations.

Often, we hear from Turkey regarding Armenian-Turkish relations the call for either the courts or the historians to pronounce the truth, while the Armenian position is that the truth is known and there is no need to examine it, an examination that in itself is viewed as offensive. Both positions evade the social texture of truth, and ignore the use that building such a texture is a necessary precondition to make whatever empirical truth agreed upon, also heard by the contesting stakeholders. The urge to outsource the truth, to the court, or a commission, can be useful under certain circumstances, but more helpful would be building the context to represent the narrative.

4. The goal of historical activism

Motivated by the work of human rights advocates, the question for scholars is in what ways can a civil society organization support these goals? The eventual mission I believe is to facilitate *a counter movement* to the claims by nationalists in many countries who perpetrate propaganda and historical mythologies under the guise of history aiming to inflame conflict. In times of crisis, nationalists always find an audience and supporters. In contrast, it is more difficult to hold a liberal, non-nationalist, rational position. A wider perspective of history, and of national rivalry, especially in times of conflict, has no 'traditional' or 'natural' constituency of advocates. The goal of historical activism is to facilitate a powerful counter narrative that can inform public discourse and undermine the nationalist exclusionary claims of truth well before a crisis takes hold, and in the best of cases, it is a long-term process.

The method to achieve this is to attempt and demarcate the borders of the nationalist narrative and to examine it in conjunction with those who are impacted by it, namely the "others" in the story, but who are not in a position to narrate it. Since no national narrative is told in vacuum, the goal is to bring together scholars from both/all sides of a conflict to write joint narratives that would contextualize the national history.

5. Shared narratives

The observation that historical narratives are partial should not be controversial, even if the aspiration is to transcend it. In this, they are not different from other systems of knowledge. One challenge is to reconnect between the recognition of partial truth and the public desire for more than partial truth (partial in this case should be understood both as not complete, and also as partisan).

The nature of partial truth is that it has a 'social location' and is constructed within structures such as economic, political. One way to respond to the limitation of partial truth is to expand its social location. The recognition of the social construction of truth and knowledge, historical in this case, directs our attention to what constitutes the relevant 'social' group that does the construction. In science, we know who qualifies as an authority, the scientists. There is a discipline – the history of science – that conducts an intensive exploration to locate the method of legitimization which has changed from "the genius" as an individual to "the paradigm" and in some cases to "the production of material culture". For history to contribute as a method to conflict resolution, I would like to suggest the analogous site and methodology of 'shared narrative' as a legitimizing practice.

The term 'shared narrative' is used in this context to describe a historical construction that intertwines and brings closer the perspectives of two or more national histories that are in direct conflict. The shared narrative is unlikely to be linear or mono-vocal and will most likely have distinct registers. There may be meta-agreement and a variety of interpretations about the local and the specifics, or the other way around. The aim of a shared narrative is to erase the exclusionary dichotomies along national lines, and to redirect the multiplicity of methodologies or interpretations along professional rather than identity divisions. Although there will likely remain empirical disagreements, the critical rupture will not be among the participants in the shared narrative, but between the historians who participate in a shared solidarity and the nationalist histories. For the public the conflict is very real, and the division is along two national camps. This has to be recognized as a frame, and a challenge to overcome. It is within this context that is also essential for scholars who share a commitment to the cause to participate in building a shared narrative.

Let me give an example from recent work with scholars who participated in attempts to build a shared narrative. I worked with a group of Palestinian and Israeli scholars on such joint narratives. One was a historical atlas of the 1948 war, another was on shared sacred sites, and a third one was on a history of Haifa. The atlas has gone a long way towards completion, but political deterioration in the region, and finally the Gaza war of December 2008 led to a suspension of the work. It is unclear whether it will be renewed, and whether it will be done by the same participants.

17

The project lasted a few years, and had suffered from the political tension, yet it went a long way forward, even during the second *intifada*.

The notion of challenging the national narratives can be done from various angles. Such was the participation of one of the Israeli scholars, who is politically idiosyncratic, and is viewed publicly as right winger, but does not see himself as such. His presence in a group working with Palestinians' ruffled emotions, but was agreed upon by both Palestinians and Israelis, in part not only because the expertise he brought to the team was greatly appreciated, but also because of the notion that his presence would symbolize to Israeli readers that their national concerns were included and fully represented in the emerging shared narrative. It is noteworthy that the professional standards of this scholar made him politically unpredictable; that is, although nationalist, he would support a 'Palestinian' position because he believed it to be historically true, even if it countered received Israeli narrative. Solidarity and partially in this case were both destabilized, because the professional solidarity was in tension with the national solidarity. This tension can only take place in doing, not theorizing about it.

The first task was to identify issues that are controversial, consequential, and feasible for an empirical investigation within the constraints of a limited budget. Creating an atlas presented challenges from the mundane – such as which maps exist; which will need to be created, what should be displayed; to the principled and unanticipated issue of annotating the maps. What is the narrative that is to be included? How much background? What is pertinent? How to describe and name sites and events? These and similar issues had to be worked out, some of which were divided along national lines, others were more professional dilemmas. The language problem was resolved by embracing English as a working language and committing to publish in three languages, including naming places in each language. Most of the maps from the period are British, and the needed additional maps were created by Palestinian and Israeli geographers. Several technical issues had to be resolved, including, for example, the size of a dot on a map to indicate a place. The dilemma was that too large or small dots of color represent the map and the area differently, and convey seemingly alternative realities, somewhere between the Palestinian narrative of a populated country taken over by colonialists, to the Zionist narrative of a land with no people to a people with no land. These fundamental issues had to be negotiated over the size of the dot on the map. When both sides agreed on it, they constructed a *via media* of a shared narrative.

A different issue arose over how to describe and narrate mixed cities. The existing maps do not delineate the ethnic divisions within the cities. This was one type of map that had to be drawn from historical data, which are anything but self evident. Describing the process of modernization of Palestine can go back to the early Zionist settlement in the second half of the nineteenth century, or back further to the eighteenth century and the rule of Dahir Al Omar. Choosing any one of these frames clearly has political impact.

A second Palestinian-Israeli working group was engaged in intense negotiation over which sacred sites to include in the joint narrative. One issue was how to create parity. The project had to be manageable, so not all sites could be included. But does the list have to present a similar number of sites for each group? Since there are many more Muslim and Christian sites, what constitutes parity? A straight-forward statistical representation could not work. Instead an agreement needed negotiation of what would present to the reader both a sense of shared land, and the numerical imbalance between both sides. Whether shared sites are a source of conflict or coexistence is in part a matter of representation. Too often, the nationalist narrative does not face an alternative.

The ultimate intended audience of a shared narrative is the public, which must include the scholarly community as the experts. This influences the methodology. Although the negotiations first began with the recognition by the scholars that each side was trying to persuade the other of its own position, it became clear, even if it was not always remembered or explicit, that the final texts and maps have to be acceptable – or at least defendable – to both publics. Too much imbalance would delegitimize the project. The constructing of the shared narrative has first to persuade the participants as proxies for the public.

This is one example of many ethnic and nationalist conflicts that are rooted in unresolved historical disputes and injustices. The goal of civil society ought to be to confront these distortions and myths of history by fostering joint work in order to lead to 'islands' of recognition, reconciliation and understanding of 'the other', which can provide building blocks that will contribute towards the groundwork for peace. These 'islands' are of respected scholars and civil society leaders from opposing sides of a conflict. They could work together to create and disseminate shared narratives that provide reliable facts and commentary as a basis for public debate and discussion. Through these collaborative efforts, academics and civil society organizations ought to develop civil society networks of engaged scholars.

Conclusion

Historians face the increased challenge that advocacy and redress as a human right issue continues to increase in importance. The most significant part of redress is recognition, which is within the scholarly terrain of demythologizing nationalist histories that denigrate the other and incite conflict. But reconciliation built on historical myth could be in its own way counter-productive, and may diminish the value of the enterprise if it is viewed as propaganda. This is particularly so because of the centrality of history in contemporary politics, as historians must recognize that isolation has detrimental impact and contributes to political violence in many societies. Scholars may not be able to stem the violence, but they should try. In large doses, such advocacy can be healing for societies. Too much bad and wrong history is traded by nationalists without a counter movement that can respond. Fortunately, there are many scholars who wish to participate as advocates and utilize their expertise to do so and increasing number of NGOs that take on the challenge. I believe we have responsibility to facilitate such advocacy: create the tools and build the organizational capacity. The combination of technology, new media, and human rights commitment may yet lead to a new type of advocacy – scholarship.

References

Montville J. V. The Healing Function in Political Conflict Resolution. *Conflict Resolution Theory and Practice Integration and Application.* Dennis J. D. Sandole and Hugo van der Merwe, eds. Manchester and New York: Manchester University Press, 1993. pp. 112-127.

Hans Gunnar Adén

Cultural Identities: Stumbling-Blocks on the Way to Reconciliation?

Mr. Hans Gunnar Adén is a former Ambassador of the Kingdom of Sweden in Armenia, Azerbaijan and Georgia. He has studied at Stockholm School of Economics, University of Uppsala (Slavic language, Interpreter School in Uppsala (Russian). Before being an ambassador in Armenia, Azerbaijan, Georgia (based in Stockholm), he was minister at Swedish Embassy, Kiev; Swedish Embassy, Paris; consul, Swedish Consulate General, Saint Petersburg; counselor at Swedish Embassy, Kiev; economist at Team of Economists, Kiev; economist OECD, Paris; desk officer at the Ministry for Foreign Affairs, Stockholm; economist at the Institute of East European Studies, Stockholm.

1. Coming to terms with the past

There is a German concept which is very useful, namely *Vergangenheitsbewältigung*, which means coming to terms with the past. The idea is that tragedies of history can only be prevented from happening again if they are first analyzed thoroughly. Those who forget the past are condemned to repeat it. The past must be accepted as it was and accounted for. Responsibilities for crimes must be understood and their underlying ideologies condemned. A country must have the courage to look back and come to terms with its past in order to be liberated from it and then to be able to move forward into the future.

Both Turkey and Armenia would profit from making some efforts in this respect. The atrocities committed in the Ottoman Empire during the First World War should no longer be denied, or relativized and trivialized. This is obviously an urgent task in today's Turkey. And in Armenia, like in many other former republics of the Soviet Union, the nature and the crimes of the Soviet regime have not been sufficiently analyzed and condemned. Healthy societies cannot be built on such denials.

There have, however, been some positive developments recently. In many post-Soviet countries, there has been a reluctance to come to terms with the horrors of the Soviet period. But earlier this year, after decades of official denials, Russian authorities acknowledged that Soviet troops – and not the German Nazis – were the ones who killed 22,000 Polish officers in Katyn in 1940. The need for public truth and openness about the Soviet past has been realized, instead of an uncomfortable silence or outright denial. In Armenia and Turkey also, the necessity and possibility for their societies to reconcile with painful periods of their past must be understood.

It is encouraging that this process has begun in Turkey. In his book "A Shameful Act" (Metropolitan Books, New York 2006) on the Armenian Genocide and the question of Turkish responsibility, Taner Akçam expresses himself in the following way: "all studies of large-scale atrocities teach us one core principle: to prevent the recurrence of such events, people must first consider their own responsibility, discuss it, debate it, and recognize it. In the absence of such honest consideration, there remains the high probability of such acts being repeated. … For Turkey to become a truly democratic member of the society of nations, it has to confront this 'dark chapter' of its history, this 'shameful act', as Mustafa Kemal Atatürk, founder of the republic, called the Armenian Genocide. Only full integration of Turkey's past can set the country on the path to democracy". Such insight bodes well for the future.

2. Cultural identities in the Caucasus

Armenian-Turkish relations develop in a Caucasian context. Armenia's war-like relationship with its other Turkic neighbor, Azerbaijan, is, of course, of utmost importance to the reconciliation process between Armenia and Turkey. This may not be a popular statement in Yerevan, but it is clear that the main reason why the process of rapprochement came to a halt was the solidarity between Turkey and Azerbaijan, based on a common cultural identity. The Nagorno-Karabagh issue cannot be neglected when the Turkish-Armenian rapprochement is analyzed.

In Armenia's other Caucasian neighbor, Georgia, the five-day war in August 2008 resulted in South Ossetia and Abkhazia breaking away from Tbilisi in a more definitive manner than before. Some people tend to blame Russia **only** for this development, but it is obvious that the underlying conflicts between the Georgians, on the one hand, and the Abkhaz and the Ossets, on the other, are due to clashes between different cultural identities, clashes that had been largely neglected by the Georgian government or at least badly understood and poorly handled.

Without going into details, we can thus easily see how important cultural identities are in contemporary Caucasian politics. In this era of globalization, some people in the West tend to believe that human beings are basically alike and that everyone across the earth would be happy to embrace the Western way of life with its materialism and consumerism. They overlook the importance of cultural identities. Globalization is often perceived negatively by many peoples in the world since it seems to constitute a threat to their identity. An example of this attitude is militant Islamism. And whereas the political ideologies of the 20th century have lost much of their appeal nowadays, cultural identities have come to replace them as uniting factors in many nations.

Far from condemning this phenomenon, we should be grateful that the world is not a melting-pot but a variety of different cultures that enrich mankind. The world would be so much poorer without the Armenian churches, monasteries and khachkars (stone carved crosses), without the Georgian wine, songs and dances, without the Persian and Azerbaijani carpets, without the splendors of the Ottoman culture in Istanbul and the whirling dervishes in Konya.

3. From stumbling-blocks to stepping-stones

The great danger with strong cultural identities, however, is that their importance can be exaggerated: it is all too easy to pass from being legitimately proud of one's cultural heritage to feeling superior to others because of it. And that is when cultural identities become stumbling-blocks on the way to reconciliation.

An important component of cultural identities is often religion. Who can deny that the Christian religion of the Armenian nation and Islam of the Turkish nation have played and continue to play an important role in the conflict between these two peoples? Institutionalized religions with their different rites and customs tend to become mutually excluding and hostile to each other. But that holds true only on the surface. If we imagine different religions being situated at different positions of a round wheel, at the outer circle so to speak, then there they will be quite distant and dissimilar from each other. But if religion becomes more intense and less formal, then the true believer can be said to move from the outer circle towards the middle where God is – at the same time moving closer to believers of other religions.

It is an interesting fact that great spiritual personalities of all religions, such as the mystics, express themselves in quite similar manners. The ways in which they describe their spiritual experiences are often strikingly alike, a circumstance that sometimes got them into trouble with their own religious authorities. We can think about great spiritual personalities like Master Eckhart in Christianity and Rumi in Islam.

One way of preventing cultural identities from becoming stumbling-blocks on the road to reconciliation would be to try to promote spiritual conversion as opposed to ritualized, formalistic religion. Esoteric religion can be a positive factor in bringing people from different cultures closer together, whereas exoteric religion often risks underlining differences and creating suspicion and animosity.

Another way to tackle the inherent dangers of strong cultural identities would be to promote political maturity. Cultural identities play an important role in modern nation-states; they are the very core around which such nations are built. And we remember the devastating wars in the 20th century between nations with conflicting cultural identities in Europe and elsewhere. Many countries in the world are still stuck at this stage of egocentric and ethnocentric development.

But, at the same time, we are witnessing in today's world an evolution towards a paradigm shift, from an ethnocentric worldview to a world-centric one. In the modern nation-state, care and concern extend from the individual to his group, i.e. to his country. But in the transformation of consciousness from ethnocentric to world-centric, the citizen realizes that his group is not the only group in the universe, his tribe is not the only tribe, his god is not the only god, his ideology is not the only ideology, his country is not the only country. And so we have post-modern societies building up in some parts of the world.

The best example of this paradigm shift towards a post-modern society is probably the European Union. The EU Member States have decided to give up some of their power and prerogatives as nation-states to the European Commission in Brussels because their citizens have realized that such international cooperation brings advantages to them. The result is quite impressive: less ethnocentric national pride but more peace and prosperity.

Both Turkey and Armenia are moving closer to the European Union. Turkey is negotiating membership in the EU and Armenia is collaborating closer with the EU through the Eastern Partnership. If serious efforts are made by all parties involved to pursue these processes and to implement the reforms needed, then the cultural identities of both countries will progressively stop being stumbling-blocks on the way to reconciliation. They will instead become a rich cultural heritage that the whole world can enjoy. They will become stepping-stones on the way to reconciliation.

4. The way ahead

This workshop has been organized at a very timely moment, Turkey having assumed the chairmanship of the Council of Europe earlier this month for half a year. In its priorities for these six months as leader of Europe's main organization dealing with human rights, the Turkish government states that it "attaches importance to enhanced intercultural dialogue." One of its priorities will be to address the "challenges of multicultural European societies" by creating a "Group of Eminent Persons" chaired by Mr. Joschka Fischer, the former minister of foreign affairs of Germany, a group which is supposed to define "a new concept of living together that could be proposed to the citizens of European societies". The Turkish chairmanship will organize several events of great interest in this context, including:

- a media encounter in Istanbul next week on intercultural practices;
- a seminar in Ankara in January on the "Fight against Discrimination Based on Racial, Ethnic, Religious and Other Bias";
- a conference in Istanbul in March on "The Role of Civil Society in Promoting Intercultural Dialogue."

During the next six months, the Turkish government will thus be especially sensitive to issues pertaining to intercultural dialogue. Hopefully, the reconciliation process between Armenia and Turkey will be one of them.

Harutyun Marutyan

Can Collective Memory of Genocide Lead to Reconciliation? A View from Yerevan[1]

> Mourning the past makes sense only insofar,
> as it prepares and allows us to ameliorate the future.
>
> (Barkan, Karn 2006: 25-26)

Dr. Harutyun Marutyan is a Leading Research Fellow at the Department of Contemporary Anthropological Studies in the Institute of Archaeology and Ethnography, National Academy of Sciences of Armenia, and Visiting Professor of Anthropology at Yerevan State University. Born in 1956, he was educated at Yerevan State University (History Department, M.A., 1978) and the Institute of Ethnography, Academy of Sciences of the USSR, in Moscow (Ph.D., 1984). He received his Doctor of Sciences (History) in 2007 at the Institute of Archaeology and Ethnography in Yerevan. He has been the recipient of IREX/RSEP (1998), Fulbright (2003-2004) and USHMM-CAHS (2009-2010) fellowships. His research interests include national identity transformation, Armenian collective memory, modern national movements, iconography, traditional Armenian culture, and poverty. Harutyun Marutyan is the author of three monographs: The Interior of Armenian Folk Dwellings (second half of the 19th—beginning of the 20th century (Yerevan, 1989, in Russian); The Role of Memory in the Structure of Identity: Questions of Theory (Yerevan, 2006, in Armenian), Iconography of Armenian Identity. Volume I: The Memory of Genocide and the Karabagh Movement (Yerevan, 2009, two separate volumes in Arm. and Engl.) and more than a hundred scholarly articles. He has contributed to collective monographs: Armenian Folk Arts, Culture, and Identity (Eds. L. Abrahamian, N. Sweezy, Bloomington and Indianapolis: Indiana University Press, 2001); Stories on Poverty (Ed. Hranush Kharatyan, Yerevan, 2001, in Armenian); Stories on Poverty: Book Two (Eds. Hranush Kharatyan and Harutyun Marutyan, Yerevan, 2007, in Armenian).

How does a state 'silence' history, and how does this influence the ways of recollection of the past?

As a result of massacres and genocide in the Ottoman Empire during 1894-1923, almost two million Armenians were murdered and Western Armenia was cleared of Armenians. The newly-created Armenian state was to occupy only one-tenth of its historical homeland. Along with heavy losses of human life and territory, Armenians suffered the loss of invaluable cultural assets, and were scattered throughout the world. The tragedy they lived through left a lasting imprint on the psychology of Armenians, and resulted in the formation of a new, powerful layer of collective and historical memory, one with a deep emotional quality and long-lasting effect.

After the establishment of Soviet rule in Armenia on December 2, 1920, talks about Genocide gradually died down and discussion of Turkish-Armenian antagonism was not encouraged.[2] In general, anything national began to be seen as negative and unacceptable. Nevertheless, in the revolutionary euphoria of socialism-building, the voices of "forgotten" past gradually started to be heard again. The national tragedy first appeared in Soviet Armenian literature in the form of literary descriptions of childhood reminiscences. Writers who survived

---

1   The choice of the title was conditioned not only by the content of this narration. It is an attempt to respond to an article with a similar title published a few years ago, by a participant of this conference, Professor Elazar Barkan (Barkan 2008: 389-408). The structure of my narration is conditioned by the theses proposed in the conference program. The answer to the question put forward in the title of this article will evolve in the course of the narration, through exploration, statements and highlights.

2   As early as August-September 1920, the Soviet government provided assistance in gold and armaments to the Kemalist movement gaining strength in Turkey, which was followed by an attack that caused the fall of the first Republic of Armenia (May 28, 1918–December 2, 1920). On March 16, 1921, a treaty was signed between Soviet Russia and Kemalist Turkey, of "Friendship and Fraternity." Turkey was seen as progressive and a friendly country of the USSR. In those circumstances, any anti-Turkish manifestations were perceived as anti-state activities.

the atrocities of genocide, and lost their motherland, recalled their childhood years and places dear to them, without actually speaking about the fact of genocide. Specialists described the period between 1920 and 1930s as time when memories were orientated to artistic reflection on the national tragedy and history.

After the Great Patriotic War (1941-1945),[3] there were periods when the memory of the national tragedy seemed to die down, only to be revived at an appropriate moment. It found expression in a variety of ways. Thus, the rapid expansion of the national theme in the Soviet Armenian literature of the 1960s did not start from nothing (for more details, see Khachatryan 2006). Yet it had a completely new, higher quality, due to the 'thaw' of the Khrushchev period. It found expression in a number of highly artistic works. Perhaps it was due to the internal political changes, as well as a certain liberal approach toward the issue of the Genocide, brought about by literature, that in April 1965, on the 50th anniversary of the Genocide, mass demonstrations occurred in Yerevan, something that was unheard of in the Soviet state of those days (for more details, see Harutyunyan 2005; Arakelyan 1996). These demonstrations, along with the rapid growth of interest in the theme of Genocide in arts and literature before and after, came to prove that the memory of the Genocide persisted in people's minds and hearts, despite the official policy of ignorance. In those memories, though, Armenians were seen solely as martyrs who had lost their land and were in need of compassion. Although the perception of the writers went beyond childhood reminiscences and episodes of armed struggle, and presented a wider political panorama and range of cause and consequences; nevertheless, the free circulation of the themes of the national liberation struggle, partisan heroes (*fedayee*s)[4] and independence remained under an undeclared ban from an ideological point of view (for more details, see: Eghiazaryan 1990: 36-47; cf. Kaputikyan 1997: 173).

The mainstream Genocide narrative in the literature of that period is embodied in the behest of "peaceful revenge" in Silva Kaputikyan's *Midway Contemplations*. Kaputikyan's appeal (Kaputikyan 1961: 112),[5] "You must take revenge by continuing to live," can actually be interpreted as a literary formulation of the official policy on Genocide memory (On discussion of this problem see: Ter-Minasyan 2001: 180-185).

---

3   The Great Patriotic War (June 22, 1941–May 9, 1945) refers to a part of World War II (1939-1945), or more specifically, to the war of the Soviet peoples against Fascist Germany and its European Allies. The name "Great Patriotic War" started to be used in the Soviet reality after Stalin's radio appeal to the Soviet people on July 3, 1941. Outside the Soviet Union, the formulation, the "Eastern Front" was used as an equivalent.

4   The Armenian *fedayee* movement was a form of national-liberation armed struggle by Western Armenians against Turkish tyranny. It was created in the second half of the 1880s. In its initial stage it did not pursue any precise political aims. Its objective was to defend the Armenian population against the persecutions of the Turkish oppressors, and to take revenge on the villainy and cruelty to the Western Armenian working people. From the beginning of the 1890s, the *fedayee* movement gained momentum due to the formation of Armenian national political parties and the creation of their organizations in Western Armenia. The *fedayee*s were especially active in battles for self-defense during the massacres of 1894-96. After the 1904 uprising in Sasun the *fedayee* movement declined. At the beginning of World War I, a considerable part of *fedayee*s joined the Armenian volunteer detachments, and in the days of the Genocide took part in the battles for self-defense. The people glorified the courage and self-sacrifice of the *fedayee*s, their willingness to fight in most unfavorable conditions, and wrote songs in praise of them.

5   The author practically does not dwell on the theme of massacres. The Genocide is not the object of her contemplations, but rather a starting point for them. She is more interested in the path her nation chooses to follow, in particular, as regards to the attitude to the obscure pages of its history. See: Eghiazaryan 1990: 43-44.

Not surprisingly April 24,[6] 1965, the day of nation-wide commemoration of the 50th anniversary of the Genocide, was called a "national renaissance." That day mass demonstrations of about one hundred thousand people included only a few posters calling for a fair solution to the Armenian Cause. One of the posters read: "Compensate [for] Our Lands," another, with Mount Ararat on the background, read: "Give a Just Solution to the Armenian Cause" (Armen 1991).

Thanks to the joint efforts of the Communist Party leaders and intellectuals of Armenia, resolutions of the Communist Party of the Soviet Union (CPSU) and the Armenian Communist Party's Central Committee were adopted in 1964-1965 to build a "Memorial for the Armenian martyrs fallen in World War I." Yakov Zarubian, the leader of the Communist Party of Armenia, in his letter to the Central Committee of the CPSU, brought up the anniversary of the Genocide, motivated by a universally acceptable Soviet thesis that "a similar tragedy was never to be allowed in the history of any people" (Harutyunyan 2005: 11, 30-36, 40, 48, 64). It is important to note that at the beginning of the 1960s, the construction of memorials to the victory of the Great Patriotic War, such as the "Memorial to the Heroes of Stalingrad" (1963-1967) in Volgograd, the "Monument to the Unknown Soldier" in Red Square in Moscow (1965-1967), and others, had already started in the Soviet Union. This meant that the building of a memorial to the martyrs of the Armenian genocide was part of the broader natural context of monuments of a commemorative nature (cf.: Konradova and Ryleeva 2004: 138-139).

Between 1965 and 1967, on the slope of the picturesque Tsitsernakaberd hill in Yerevan, conveniently far from the center of town, a fact not to be overlooked, the memorial complex was erected in a rather short time (Opening 1967; Harutyunyan 2006). Therefore, on April 24, 1968, the people filled not the central squares and streets of the capital, but marched in well-organized columns, toward its periphery, in order to lay flowers at the Monument to the victims of the Genocide. Thus, in succeeding years, the mass demonstrations of April 24, 1965 were to be transformed into unofficially sanctioned marches of mourners. Starting from the mid-1970s, the processions were actually led by senior officials from the government and the Communist Party leadership of Armenia (Memorial 1975: 79-80), who were the first to lay wreaths at the Monument early in the morning, thus (and with a Moment of Silence), giving official sanction to the Commemoration Day. The marches were accompanied by wreaths decorated with black ribbons with standard wording like: "To the Genocide Victims + the name of the organization", as well as by recitations: certain participants of the procession would recite verses and poems either of patriotic nature or directly related to the theme of the Genocide.

---

6   "April 24" is traditionally the Commemoration Day of the victims of the Armenian Genocide. On that day in 1915 the Turkish authorities in Constantinople, the capital of the Ottoman Empire, arrested and exiled the first groups of Armenian intellectuals. As Commemoration Day, it was first observed in 1919. More widely (at the suggestion of writer Vrtanes Papazian) it was first honored in 1920, when, by the order of Catholicos of all Armenians, a requiem mass was served in all the Armenian churches. April 24 was honored as Commemoration Day in Armenian communities of the Diaspora, while in Soviet Armenia it was first officially honored in 1965. On November 22, 1988, a law was passed by the Supreme Soviet of the Armenian SSR, declaring April 24 as Commemoration Day of the victims of the Genocide, and a non-working day.

Above, I have partly answered the question about how silence, fear and ignorance may influence a conflict resolution discourse. The memory of the Armenian Genocide in general, before the 1988 events, can be described conditionally as 'dormant', when it was mainly expressed as simple remembrance of the past, mourning or similar actions. The situation started to change right from the first weeks of Karabagh Movement (February 1988 – August 1990). In response to self-determination of Armenians in Mountainous Karabagh (February 20, 1988) there was an attack of armed mob of 8,000 on February 22 from the bordering Azerbaijani-populated town of Agdam, followed by Armenian massacres in Sumgait, a town about 25-30 kilometers far from Baku (February 27-29). Sumgait pogroms 'awakened' the dormant Armenian memory of the 1915 Genocide.

In my monograph (Marutyan 2009a), I have shown that events in Azerbaijan were unequivocally perceived as a genocide against Armenians, against part of Armenians, especially given that the violence applied almost replicated the methods used during the Genocide at the end of nineteenth and the beginning of twentieth centuries. The analysis of the available material proves that the struggle for the recognition of the 1915 Genocide, for evaluation of Sumgait massacres as an act of genocide, for the exposure of its organizers and perpetrators and the revelation of the guilty, as well as the verdicts from the trials against them, all combined to gradually lead to the political maturity of the popular masses, to transformation of the stereotypes that had been shaped in the course of centuries and decades, and that led to a processes of re-evaluation of the past and the present. From the point of view of avoiding acts of genocide in the future, there was an understanding for the need for society to hold governing mechanisms and the need for political change in general. Thus, in the years of the Karabagh Movement, the theme of genocide, transgressing the limits of pain and sorrow typical of its initial stage, drove people to activity that resulted in the formation of a new parliament, which was expected to choose the course of radical change (Marutyan 2009a: 274, 276). At the same time, the image of the victim asking for justice and sympathy gave way to that of a fighter who had realized that to achieve a nation's objectives one has to struggle.

That is, the factor of genocide had become the engine that provided the opportunity for the gradual, step-by-step change of old perceptions and stereotypes, for the transformation of an identity based on outdated values, and for the formation of a new identity. In fact, it was the genocide memory that became the means for the Karabagh Movement and, ultimately, allowed for democratic reformation. That is, the factor that is often interpreted as an obstacle to the elimination of the "bondage of the past," and hence, a hindrance to the real progress of Armenians and a "retrograde" means, became the major incentive in Armenia's reality (Marutyan 2009a: 276).

The forms of manifestation of Armenian collective and historical memory are many and diverse. Their elements and components are not set once and forever, but are rather in a process of continuous re-interpretations and re-comprehension. In a time of crisis or revolution, the processes of re-interpretation of the elements of collective and historical memory are accelerated. It is typical that in a critical situation (as were the years of the Karabagh Movement), it is precisely the collective and historical memory of past crises (the Armenian Genocide) that are drawn to the forefront and become a factor for the persistence and advancement of events. Without disputing this opinion, I still believe that this regularity may be true for any ethnic community—namely, that an adequate use of a most significant element of a people's identity in a time of crisis may become, after certain transformations, a main factor in its progress (Marutyan 2009a: 276-277).

In the 1990s to the first half of 2000s, when Armenian society was no longer in a crisis, the memory typical of a crisis was similarly no longer at the forefront. That memory, remaining a most significant manifestation of national identity, yet at the same time, having become a component of Armenia's foreign policy, was mostly transformed into a tribute of respect, a way of commemoration, and no longer has the same revolutionary, reformative capacity it had in 1988-1990 (Marutyan 2009a: 277-278). Yet the relatively 'dormant' status of this memory could 'awaken,' and be activated due to internal or external provocation, and become an active and once again, decisive factor, just as we witnessed in 2008-2009, in effect of the so-called 'football diplomacy' and the Armenian-Turkish protocols.

■

The statement as to how historical science and the studies of a memory can be included in the process of reconciliation is meant to propose practical solutions. This crucial issue is actively discussed in Western circles of historical science. Theoretical approaches, as well as a variety of practical suggestions as to the solution of the problem are being put forward. Some of them, though mostly incidentally, reflect on the link between the factor of the Armenian Genocide and the issue of Armenian-Turkish reconciliation.

As mentioned above, the "Protocol on Development of Relations between the Republic of Armenia and the Republic of Turkey" was signed in October 2009, where one of the paragraphs suggested the creation of a "sub-commission on the historical dimension to implement a dialogue with the aim to restore mutual confidence between the two nations, including an impartial scientific examination of the historical records and archive to define existing problems and formulate recommendations, in which Armenian, Turkish as well as Swiss and other international experts shall take part." Although consisting of a single sentence, the paragraph contains two theses that suggest methodologically contrary approaches, hence, allowing for contradictory comments. To be specific, the formulation "to implement a dialogue with the aim to restore mutual confidence between the two nations," supposes an approach in line with a TRC (Truth and Reconciliation Commission),[7] while the formulation "the sub-commission on the historical dimension ... including an impartial scientific examination of the historical records and archive to define existing problems and formulate recommendations, in which Armenian, Turkish as well as Swiss and other international experts shall take part," is more in line with the Historical Commission/Historical Clarification Commission.

What does this mean? The classical TRC approach supposes an *open public* discussion, often in the presence of the perpetrator and the victim (or their descendants); while the "Historical Commission/Historical Clarification Commis-

---

7   There is a significant body of literature on the TRCs and it is not our intention to reflect on the whole specter of issues related to them. Therefore, this article touches upon only a few of the characteristics of these commissions.

sion" supposes an altogether different type of action. Robert Rotberg, president of the World Peace Fund, who is a renowned expert on these issues, states that "historical clarification commissions, a variant of truth commissions, are not common. Although in theory they are constituted and operated differently from truth commissions, in practice the differences to date have been excessively subtle. Clarification commissions review all kinds of evidence – written, oral, legal, forensic (to the extent that bodies may be exhumed) – relating to specific events or a chain of occurrences in the past. On the basis of such a review, a historical clarification exercise can provide a dispassionate, or at least an agreed upon view of the past. *Historical clarification can decide whether there in fact was genocide in Turkey in 1915, and its dimensions* (emphasis is author's)" (Rotberg 2006: 38). The statement is as clear as can be, and the example refers to the issue of the Armenian Genocide.

Professor Barkan's approach to the matter is characteristic, and does not significantly differ from that of Robert Rotberg. Thus, on the one hand he recognizes the fact of the Armenian Genocide, yet on the other hand, giving in to the attitude of the Turkish prime minister, i.e. "to leave history to historians,"[8] he admits that "the Turkish declaration may well be a very good suggestion that ought to be pursued. The claim has the potential of moving the dispute into a relatively professional arena… Both sides ought to engage the historical inquiry and find external professional bodies to sponsor a professional investigation without preconditions" (Barkan 2008: 406-407). Very much the same, but with slightly different accentuation, he states at the opening of his article, "I conclude by discussing the memory of the Armenian Genocide and support a constructive engagement between Armenian and Turkish historians, preferably the formation of a formal historical commission by the two countries. Such collaboration ought to construct a memory that respects the victims, shows empathy for the suffering, rejects denial, points to the responsible individuals and government crimes, but does not indict the Turkish nation—and certainly not today's Turkish people—for the Genocide" (Barkan 2008: 389-390).

In the next few pages of his article, Robert Rotberg details the functions of the "historical clarification commissions" (Rotberg 2006: 39-40). I will only quote the passages where he speaks about the composition of such commissions, some of their functions, as well as their difference from classic TRCs. Thus, he states that "historical clarification commissions ideally comprise reputed judges, lawyers, or historians, not all of whom need be nationals, accustomed to sifting retrospective evidence, to removing barriers to truth, and to uncovering long-buried facts. These commissions may or may not proceed by taking public testimony…," "Historical clarification commissions can establish chains of culpability, offer support to or refutation of accusations about the perpetuation of atrocities, suggest plausible causality, and single out groups or individuals for criticism. Such commissions can thus provide unimpeachable grounds for apology,"[9] "Such commissions fail their mission if they offer political or prescriptive reports rather than scrupulously researched reports of times of turmoil. If their opinions are programmatic rather than abundantly factual, they cannot

---

8   The last such statement was voiced in the interview of Turkish Prime Minister Erdoğan to the "Time" daily in Istanbul, on November 9, 2010 (See "Azg" daily, November 12, 2010), http://www.azg.am/AM/2010111202, also http://www.tert.am/am/news/2010/11/12/ankara/.
9   It is known that after World War II more than twenty countries had established historical commissions to review their own countries' behavior during the Holocaust (Bindenagel 2006: 293). Following this logic, it is essential that independent commissions of historians be created in Turkey, in order to study the violence against Armenians committed in the Ottoman Empire at the beginning of the 20th century.

be relied upon to undergird a successful form of apology," "The subtle theoretical differences between an historical clarification commission and a truth commission are implicit in their titles. Historical clarifiers interrogate the ledgers and graves of the past; truth commissioners cross-examine contemporary victims and perpetrators in order to learn what really happened when individuals vanished, or when violent incidents and massacres occurred. ... Historical clarifiers can and do ask some of the same questions, but usually of documents rather than the actual victims and perpetrators. Historical clarifiers more often are attempting to assign blame to a government agency, a military group, or an insurgency unit, not to individuals. Truth commissions work more generally, with individuals. Both forms of post hoc review can provide a detailed, nearly complete, record of past or recent injustice, meticulously documented. Both methods hence can inform the basis of well-grounded apology. Depending on the quality of a commission's research and hearings, and their integrity, such reports provide a morally defensible basis for apology. The reports may also make apologies (and/or prosecutions) imperative."

Professor Rotberg notes that the societies in post-conflict situation prefer the assistance of the TRC type commissions. Since the second half of the 1970s, over thirty states have applied to such commissions (Rotberg 2006: 40). The author believes that "the paradigm for twenty-first century truth commissions (and in many ways for future historical clarification commissions as well) in method, organization, and output is the South African Truth and Reconciliation Commission (TRC), 1995-1999" (Rotberg 2006: 43. See also: Colvin 2003: 153-167; Ignatieff 1997: 169-170; Hellman 2001: 213-214; Wertsch 2002: 46-51; Sanders 2003: 77-98; Christiansë 2003: 372-395).

This commission was mandated by the country's parliament for wide-ranging activities. Previous similar commissions used to offer reports and the same was expected of this one. But the South African TRC preferred absolute transparency, fostering the dissemination of stories about apartheid victims and the facts of violence, also using television to achieve the objective. The media published stories of over 21,000 victims. This commission did not choose the option of theoretically criticizing apartheid, but rather chose the process of accumulating and presenting numerous facts about the sufferers. About 7,000 people appealed to the commission, seeking absolution for their deeds, and only 2,500 were exonerated. The author once again emphasizes that while commissions in Argentina, Chile, Guatemala (and elsewhere) were compelled to act out of the public's sight, the South African TRCs insisted on the *public's participation and the transparency of discussions* (Rotberg 2006: 43-44).

The reconciliation of the conflicting parties is a primary objective of classic TRCs, and is closely associated with apology. Nevertheless, even though the studies of truth commissions are essential for peacemaking, as well as for absolution, the activities of these commissions do not always lead to reconciliation, and in other words, reconciliation is not always their final outcome.

■

Returning to the above-mentioned paragraph of the Armenian-Turkish protocols, we would like to once again state that it reflects two methodologically contradictory approaches. It follows that the Turkish officials are not wrong in seeing the clause "the sub-commission on the historical dimension ... including an impartial scientific examination of the historical records and archive to define existing problems and formulate recommendations, in which Armenian, Turkish as well as Swiss and other international experts shall take part" as a typical function of the Historical Commissions/Historical Clarification Commissions, thus, interpreting it as the thesis "leave history to historians." This may be a correct approach in the case of such commissions having been created. As a primary objective of a "Historical Commission," they view the issue of whether or not there has been genocide of Armenians in the Ottoman Empire (exactly as Professor Rotberg interprets). Armenian political figures are justified, when in the formulation "to implement a dialogue with the aim to restore mutual confidence between the two nations," they do not see the necessity for discussions about the fact of the Genocide, but rather interpret it from the aspect of the opening of the Armenian-Turkish border, which is logical, because closed borders do nothing to achieve dialogue.

■

Studying relevant literature on the issue, one gets the impression that today's international public opinion associates the process of reconciliation both inside and outside societies with the above-mentioned Truth and Reconciliation Commissions (and similarly structured units), or with the successful functioning of Historical Commissions/Historical Clarification Commissions. Now, what is the terminology used by these commissions, and what context do they function within? In literature known to us, the terms most often used are: "acknowledgement," "apology," "restitution," (see on this issue Marutyan 2008: 135-155; Marutyan 2009b: 91-106), "reconciliation." I shall briefly dwell on these terms, based on the few works I have had access to.

In works on the issues of reconciliation it is emphasized that the role of historical science in its achievement increases by the day. Thus, Professor Barkan observes that "we used to treat history as an "objective" knowledge of past events that were largely immune from reinterpretation; history was the past, and we could do little about it. ... Increasingly, however, we recognize the growing elasticity of history and that it is anything but fixed. More recently, as history has become increasingly malleable, it has simultaneously become more central to our daily life. It informs our identity more intimately today, and being subject to interpretation, it has also become a space for contesting perspectives. ... History changes who we were, not just who we were. In this sense history has become a crucial field for political struggle" (Barkan 2000: X). In another part of this same monograph, the author observes that the novelty of the urge to amend past injustices is that it addresses history through an effort to build an interpretation of the past that both parties could share (Barkan 2000: XXII).

The study of the historical past (for an attempt at the analysis of the issue in a wider context, see Marutyan 2009a: 27-67) is an essential factor for the analysis of problematic issues both within and between societies. In both instances, the *openness and transparency of dialogues* (underlining is mine – H.M.) between the conflicting parties is viewed as essential (cf.: Barkan, Karn 2006: 8). Only in the course of such a dialogue may new knowledge of the facts of mutual history be available to both parties. New unexpected interpretations may gradually lead to a change of notions and beliefs about each other. It is characteristic, that in his speech to the Turkish parliament, US President Barack

31

Obama, while emphasizing the importance of taking into consideration the historical past for the improvement of relations between the two countries, called for its being "honest, *open* and constructive" (author's emphasis) process.[10]

As observed by Richard von Weizsäcker, the president of the Federal Republic of Germany, in his speech on the fortieth anniversary of World War II, when referring to the Holocaust, "anyone, who closes his eyes to the past, is blind to the present. Whoever refuses to remember inhumanity is prone to new risks of infection" (quotation according to Marrus 2003: 29). Referring to the past is viewed as a step essential for going forward with resolve and purpose (Barkan, Karn 2006: 26). David Crocker, professor at the University of Maryland in the US, adds yet another accent to the issue: "any society reckoning with past atrocities should aim, I believe, to include *public spaces, debate* (author's emphasis), and deliberation in its goals, institutions, and strategies" (Crocker 2003: 55).

When a dialogue on the historical past is taking place between the perpetrator and the victim (or their descendants), it usually leads to the *acknowledgement* of the wrongdoing on the part of the former. On the other hand, "acknowledgement is not the same thing as knowledge, because we may know things that we do not acknowledge" (Govier 2003: 70). Acknowledgement becomes an issue when we are aware of unfavorable facts that we do not wish to speak about or to publicly admit. The difference between knowledge and acknowledgement is solely in whether or not the fact is *voiced out or admitted* in some way. As defined by Professor Trudy Govier, "acknowledgement is knowledge accompanied by a *kind of marking or spelling out* or admitting as significantly related to oneself something that is known (author's emphasis)" (Govier 2003: 82). An unfavorable fact may be overcome through acknowledgement alone. Acknowledgement may be expressed in various ways: through criminal trials, truth commissions, public inquiries, apologies, reparations, or memorials, and this acknowledgement is of tremendous value—most obviously to victims (Govier 2003: 84), and in the case with the Armenians, also to the descendants of both victims and survivors. The author goes on to say that "when there is no acknowledgement of the wrongdoing, the initial wound develops into "the second wound of silence," because the lack of acknowledgement indicates that people condone the wrongs and do not care about the baneful results" (Govier 2003: 85). Nevertheless, Professor Barkan believes that the growing willingness to recognize past guilt may turn out to be a major innovation in future conflict resolution (Barkan 2000: 322).

Acknowledgement is succeeded by *apologies*: the decades following World War II were marked by apologies on the part of state leaders, as well as by officials of various establishments (banks, the police, professional unions, etc.) for past deeds (especially wrongdoings related to wartime activities) they had been involved in. As experts observe, "the age of apology is distinguished by its unparalleled commitment to remove the past as an obstacle to productive and peaceful intergroup relations. Although they obviously do not erase or undo what has already happened, apologies

---

10   Quote from statement of President Barack Obama's speech before the Turkish parliament: "History is often tragic, but unresolved, it can be a heavy weight. Each country must work through its past. And reckoning with the past can help us seize a better future. ... And the best way forward for the Turkish and Armenian people is a process that works through the past in a way that is honest, open and constructive." Transcript: President Barack Obama, Speech to Turkish Parliament, April 6, 2009. http://allthatnatters.com/2009/04/06/transcript-president-barack-obama-speech-to-turkish-parliament-april-6/

can *amend the past* so that it resonates differently in the present for those who feel aggrieved by it or responsible for it" (Barkan, Karn 2006: 8). Julie Fette, a professor at Rice University, notes that "scholars have suggested several reasons for the emergence of apology on a global scale at the end of the twentieth century: a new international focus on morality; a revised understanding of universal human rights, state sovereignty and international law; a willingness of state actors to show feelings of caring and regret and to view apology not as a weakness but a manifestation of strength; … as well as increased demand for recognition by past victims" (Fette 2006: 259). Through a detailed analysis of the process of apologizing of the French leaders for the wrongdoings of the Vichy regime, the author shows how the process, starting with the upper circles of the state, passes on to the civil society, and becomes a tool in the process of national recovery (Fette 2006: 259-285). Robert Rotberg, too, is positive that a national apology that flows from meaningful investigation and careful research has stronger moral and practical claims (Rotberg 2006: 36). Inside a society, apology becomes an act of *rehabilitation for the perpetrators* and their descendants rather than the victims (Barkan, Karn 2006: 17).

As Professor Bindenagel believes, "apology cannot come without understanding. Understanding history comes from knowing historical facts. Without the truth, history will remain an obstacle to the future" (Bindenagel 2006: 289). Apology, at that, can not by itself be sufficient for those who wish to do away with the past mistakes, especially in order to pave the way for democracy. "Apology is often the result, and always a part of the process of reconciliation, but in itself is no magic potion" (Barkan, Karn 2006: 9). As noted by the same authors, apology does not necessarily require forgiveness (Barkan, Karn 2006: 11). The same, in a wider context, has been emphasized by the dean of Harvard Law School, Professor Martha Minow, who stated that "apologies are most meaningful when accompanied by material reparations; and reparations are most meaningful when accompanied by acknowledgement of their inadequacy in the effort to apologize and make amends… taken together, apologies and reparations offer responses to mass atrocity that demand recognition of wrongs done without obliging survivors to forgive" (Minow 2002: 17-18, 98-99, quoted from Payaslian 2008: 423).

Reconciliation is a long process that is not terminated by the conclusion of war crime trials or truth and reconciliation commissions (Prager 2003: 14), still the process in itself may help prevent a society from lapsing back into violence as a way to resolve conflict (Crocker 2003: 54). As observed by the latter, "if reconciliation in any of its several senses is to take place, there must be some agreement about what happened and why. Former enemies are unlikely to be reconciled if what counts as lies for one side are verities for the other" (Crocker 2003: 45).

Thus, the concepts "dialogue," "acknowledgement," "redemption" and "reconciliation" imply a certain *process*. As far as I have learned from professional literature on the issue, the methodology of classic TRCs is effective for the resolution of issues within a society, while for the initiation of a peace dialogue around issues that are the result of relatively recent (rather than "olden days") interstate conflicts, preference is given to "Historical Commissions." Where the activities of the latter are closed and strictly professional, in the case of TRCs, they are *open, with the active involvement of the public at large*.

■

So then, in what context[11] can the memory of the Armenian Genocide lead to reconciliation?[12]

"Turkish-Armenian Reconciliation Commission" (TARC) activities with the involvement of experts have been recorded in the history of Armenian-Turkish relations, and took place in 2001-2004. They were carried out behind closed doors. One of the outcomes of the work of the commission (this was stated by Professor David Hovhannisyan, too, in his presentation in the conference) was the change of the former attitude of the representatives from Turkey to the assessment of violence against Armenians in the Ottoman Empire in the beginning of the 20th century. Another organization, a third party, the International Center for Transitional Justice (ICTJ), offered an expert conclusion qualifying the abovementioned events as "genocide." Have the activities of TARC promoted the process of a 'dialogue' or 'reconciliation' between the two neighboring peoples? There seems to be no evidence of any such assessment. I fully share Professor Simon Payaslian's opinion that "the formation of a truth and reconciliation commission in the Armenian-Turkish case must have *greater transparency* (author's emphasis) and must be representative of the Armenian people. The TARC experience demonstrated that that process lacked a sufficient degree of public legitimacy and, as a result, it could not function as a mediator" (Payaslian 2008: 414). Once again addressing the issue, the author emphasizes anew the importance of transparency in likely discussions around the issue: "a host of questions must be answered before any Armenian-Turkish reconciliation process can be effective. It needs to be determined whether the Armenian-Turkish reconciliation process should be confined to secret or closed door negotiations as it was with TARC, or become *more transparent, based on or operating in an environment of openness and wider participation*[13] (author's emphasis)" (Payaslian 2008: 424).

Today "Turkey itself neither acknowledges nor could conceive of apologizing for the Armenian genocide" (Rotberg 2006: 33). Quoting Germany's Chancellor Konrad Adenauer's words about the culpability of the German people, said about six decades ago, and followed by the passing of legislative acts on the payment of reparation to the Holocaust victims, Professor Michael Marrus mentions Armenians, "who still await a comparable acknowledgement from the Turkish government of its political responsibility for the genocide attacks upon them by the Turks in 1915" (Marrus 2003: 28). Speaking of persecutions of the truth that were at times accompanied by demands for unacceptable compromises, Carol Prager, professor at the University of Calgary in Canada, brings another vivid example of Turkey's behavior as a state, that still carries on in different manifestations: "an example is Turkey's recent warning to the United States that the passage of a House of Representatives' resolution blaming Turkey for genocide against the Armenians would endanger an agreement allowing the US to use a Turkish airbase in any future crisis involving Iraq" (Prager 2003: 21).

---

11   Professor Barkan also believes that the memory of the Armenian genocide could lead to reconciliation, but the context where he sees such an opportunity equates discussions of the historical heritage between Armenia and Turkey with processes of democratization. As noted above, he also believes that Armenian and Turkish historians should examine facts of the not remote past, to at least prove the actuality of episodes where there is common consent, as well as to try to elucidate the issues that cause dissent (Barkan 2008: 406-407).

12   I personally give preference to the more realistic, in my opinion, term 'dialogue,' as the notion 'reconciliation' which is to come after 'acknowledgement,' 'apology' and 'redemption,' will take decades to realize. In my opinion, the use of this term in today's reality has an implication of propagation.

13   The author very likely means the inclusion of the Armenians of the diaspora in the discussions of the issue.

This and other numerous facts come to prove that Turkish authorities are still unprepared to start a civilized dialogue. As to contacts on the level of NGOs or expert commissions, even though they may be helpful, they still cannot substitute for a dialogue between peoples which can, in theory, lead to peace only after having gone a certain distance. After all, how is it possible to acknowledge and make acceptable the public opinion of conflicting parties without reshaping animosity? Can the processes of reconciliation proceed along with democratization? It is my opinion that they can.

The abovementioned expert opinions have repeatedly stated the necessity of *openness, of transparency of dialogues, as well as of the inclusion of the public at large in the process*. So then, *what is the way for its realization*? I strongly believe that the clue to it, the keystone of its philosophy is the very first word of the title of the "Truth and Reconciliation Commissions" – "truth". But it is *the truth that the **peoples** of both parties need to have access to, not only historians and experts of closed door commissions*.

The scheme for its realization, as I see it, is as follows: a historical commission is to *only* define the range of issues of the history of Armenian-Turkish relations (first and foremost of the years of the Armenian Genocide) that are to be *presented to the Armenian and Turkish public via the most watched TV channels, by Armenian and Turkish historians, with the provision of simultaneous translation*. One thing seems to be clear: it is not likely that the historians in these debates will change their professional opinion under the weight of facts and arguments. Yet, in this case *the subject is the watching public, the actual or potential representatives of a civil society, rather than the historians*. It is these people, who will be able to hear the opposite party's views and opinions, and who will draw their own conclusions from the debates of experts. And only if these debates are expert (rather than journalistic or publicizing) and have merit, and if they are organized repeatedly over a long period, and are consistent, the Armenian and Turkish "truths" will become available to the conflicting parties, and will move from television screens into the sphere of active public discussions of a democratic nature. Moreover, along with genocide-related issues, it may be possible to discuss historical problems of the region and issues of Armenian-Turkish cultural interrelations in the course of their mutual history, which may help in getting to know each other better. This process is sure to have positive outcomes: the notions about each other of the people on both sides will certainly change, and this may just pave the way for the starting of a process of actual reconciliation.

References

Arakelyan V. (1996). April 24, 1965. *Hayk*, April 23 (in Armenian).

Armen Mkrtich (1991). Memorandum to the Central Committee of the Communist Party of Armenia. *Grakan tert*, September 6 (in Armenian).

Barkan E. (2008). Can Memory of Genocide Lead to Reconciliation? *The Armenian Genocide: Cultural and Ethical Legacies*, edited by Richard Hovannisian, pp. 389-408. New Brunswick (USA) and London (UK): Transaction Publishers.

Barkan E. (2000). *The Guilt of Nations: Restitution and Negotiating Historical Injustices.* New York and London: W.W. Norton and Company.

Barkan E., Karn A. (2006). Group Apology as an Ethical Imperative. *Taking Wrongs Seriously: Apologies and Reconciliation*, edited by Barkan E. and Karn A., pp. 3-30. Stanford, California: Stanford University Press.

Bindenagel J. D. (2006). Justice, Apology, Reconciliation, and the German Foundation: "Remembrance, Responsibility, and the Future." *Taking Wrongs Seriously: Apologies and Reconciliation*, edited by Barkan E. and Karn A., pp. 286-310. Stanford, California: Stanford University Press.

Colvin Christopher J. (2003). 'Brothers and Sisters, Do Not Be Afraid of Me': Trauma, History and the Therapeutic Imagination in the New South Africa. *Contested Pasts: The Politics of Memory*, edited by K. Hodgkin and S. Radstone, pp. 153-167. London and New York: Routledge.

Christiansë Yvette (2003). Passing Away: The Unspeakable (Losses) of Postapartheid South Africa. *Loss: The Politics of Mourning*, edited by David L. Eng and D. Kazanjian, pp. 372-395. Berkeley, Los Angeles, London: University of California Press.

Crocker David A. (2003). Reckoning with the Past Wrongs: A Normative Framework. *Dilemmas of Reconciliation: Cases and Concepts*, edited by Carol A. L. Prager and T. Govier, pp. 39-63. Waterloo, Ontario (Canada): Wilfrid Laurier University Press.

Eghiazaryan A. (1990). The Reflection of the Genocide in the Soviet Armenian Literature, *Lraber hasarakakan gitutyunneri*, no. 4, pp. 36-47 (in Armenian).

Fette Julie (2006). The Apology Moment: Vichy Memories in 1990s France. *Taking Wrongs Seriously: Apologies and Reconciliation*, edited by Barkan E. and Karn A., pp. 259-285. Stanford, California: Stanford University Press.

Trudy Govier (2003). What Is Acknowledgement and Why Is It Important? *Dilemmas of Reconciliation: Cases and Concepts*, edited by Carol A. L. Prager and Trudy Govier, pp. 65-89. Waterloo, Ontario (Canada): Wilfrid Laurier University Press.

Harutyunyan A. (2005). *Hayots tseghaspanutyan 50-amyake yev Khorhrdayin Hayastane (pastatghteri yev nyuteri zhoghovatsu)* [The 50th Anniversary of the Armenian Genocide and the Soviet Armenia (Collection of Documents and Materials)]. Yerevan: Gitutyun (in Armenian).

Harutyunyan V. (2006). How the Genocide Memorial Design Was Chosen. *Azg*, May 27 (in Armenian).

Hellman Cecil G. (2001). *Culture, Health, and Illness*. London: Arnold.

Ignatieff M. (1997). *The Warrior's Honor: Ethnic War and the Modern Conscience*. New York: Metropolitan Books.

Kaputikyan S. (1961). *Mtorumner chanaparhi kesin* [Thoughts on the Halfway]. Yerevan: Haypethrat (in Armenian).

Kaputikyan S. (1997). *Ejer pak gzrotsnerits* [Pages from Closed Drawers]. Yerevan: Apollon (in Armenian).

Khachatryan Y. (2006). Wonderful Decade. *Azg/Azg-Mshakuyt*, September 2 (in Armenian).

Konradova N. and A. Ryleeva. (2004). Heroes and Victims: Memorials of the Great Patriotic War. *Neprikosnovennyi zapas. Debaty o politike i kulture*, no. 40-41, pp. 134-148 (in Russian).

Marrus Michael R. (2003). Overview. *Dilemmas of Reconciliation: Cases and Concepts*, edited by Carol A. L. Prager and Trudy Govier, 27-36. Waterloo, Ontario (Canada): Wilfrid Laurier University Press.

Marutyan H. (2008). German Reparations to Jewry: Formation, Process and Recent Situation. *21st Century: Informational and Analytical Journal*, No. 4, pp. 135-155 (in Armenian).

Marutyan H. (2009a). *Iconography of Armenian Identity. Vol. 1. The Memory of Genocide and the Karabagh Movement.* Yerevan: Gitutyun.

Marutyan H. (2009b). German Reparations to Jewry: Formation, Process and Recent Situation. *Arevmtahayutyan pahanjatirutyan himnakhndirnere* [The Problems of Western Armenian's Claims]: Collection of Conference Papers. Editors: Shahnazaryan A., Marutyan H., compilers Arshakyan A., Vardanyan V., Yerevan, pp. 91-106 (in Armenian).

Memorial (1975). At the Memorial of the Victims to the Genocide. *Patma-banasirakan handes*, no. 2, pp. 79-80 (in Armenian).

Minow M. (2002). Breaking the Cycles of Hatred. *Breaking the Cycles of Hatred: Memory, Law, and Repair*, edited by Minow M., pp. 14-76. Princeton: Princeton University Press.

Opening (1967). The Opening of the Monument Devoted to the Memory of the Victims of the Genocide. *Sovetakan Hayastan*, November 30 (in Armenian).

Payaslian S. (2008). Anatomy of Post-Genocide Reconciliation. *The Armenian Genocide: Cultural and Ethical*

Legacies, edited by Hovannisian R., 409-428. New Brunswick (USA) and London (UK): Transaction Publishers.

Prager Carol A. L. (2003). Introduction. *Dilemmas of Reconciliation: Cases and Concepts*, edited by Carol A. L. Prager and T. Govier, pp. 1-26. Waterloo, Ontario (Canada): Wilfrid Laurier University Press.

Rotberg R. I. (2006). Apology, Truth Commissions, and Intrastate Conflict. *Taking Wrongs Seriously: Apologies and Reconciliation*, edited by Barkan E. and Karn A., pp. 33-49. Stanford, California: Stanford University Press.

Sanders M. (2003). Ambiguities of Mourning: Law, Custom, and Testimony of Women Before South Africa's Truth and Reconciliation Commission. *Loss: The Politics of Mourning*, edited by David L. Eng and D. Kazanjian, pp. 77-98. Berkeley, Los Angeles, London: University of California Press.

Ter-Minasyan A. A. (2001). S. Kaputikian's Thoughts Half-way and After. *Lraber hasarakakan gitutyunneri*, no. 1, pp. 175-185 (in Armenian).

Wertch James V. (2002). *Voices of Collective Remembering.* Cambridge; New York: Cambridge University Press.

Alexander Iskandaryan

Armenia-Turkey Reconciliation: Motives and Impediments

Mr. Alexander Iskandaryan has been the Director of Caucasus Institute (CI) since January 2005. Prior to becoming director, he headed the CI Research Unit. He teaches the Contemporary Studies and Area Studies courses. One of the founders of CI, Alexander Iskandaryan moved to Yerevan from Moscow to launch the institute in April 2002. In Moscow, he directed the Center for Caucasus Studies since 1992. He is the author of numerous academic publications in various countries and regularly gives interviews to Western, Russian and Armenian press.

Over two and a half years have passed since the start of Armenian-Turkish rapprochement. By now, International experts as well as scholars in Armenia and Turkey have analyzed Armenian-Turkish relations in every detail. In this paper I am not going to present a chronology or describe the current status in detail. Rather, I would like to focus on the levels and areas in which motives and impediments to rapprochement are now concentrated in both countries.

Let us start with motivations. Armenia clearly has several major incentives for rapprochement with Turkey. One is related to economics and communication: having two of its four borders sealed is obviously a handicap. In Armenia's case, its border with Turkey also represents its border with Europe and its potential main communication route to European markets. Routes via Georgia and Iran are insufficient to fully serve Armenia's economic ambitions. Ever since the 350-km long Turkish-Armenian border was sealed back in 1993, the only direct connection between Armenia and Turkey has been by air. An Istanbul-Yerevan passenger flight was opened in 1996 but goods from the two countries (chiefly Turkish imports into Armenia) are mostly shipped by land via Georgia. Despite the sealed land border, the trade turnover between Armenia and Turkey reaches at least 100-120 million dollars per annum[1]. According to data from the research carried out by the US Embassy in Armenia, Turkey is Armenia's seventh largest trade partner. Obviously, the indirect shipment route significantly increases transportation costs and creates unnecessary complications. For example, due to the lack of official ties between Armenia and Turkey, either Russia or Georgia is marked as the destination for Turkish goods actually intended for Armenia; alternately, businesses deals via companies registered in other countries, chiefly Switzerland, in which cases Armenia is shown as the destination, but Turkey is not marked on the goods as the place of manufacture. The need for trade and

---

1   According to estimates from Kaan Soyak, the head of the Turkish-Armenian Business Development Council (TABDC).

communication with, and via Turkey is pressing and has so far been the main driving force behind the "football diploma-cy" initiated by Armenia. Policy-makers are naturally concerned about the fact that Armenia still has two of its four land borders sealed. Ideological and historical arguments in favor of keeping the border with Turkey closed do not convince much of the establishment. Even most of Armenia's political opposition, both within and outside the parliament, was supportive of efforts toward normalization with Turkey, although very critical of the government on other counts.

In fact, right at the time of the first successes of Armenian-Turkish "football diplomacy," the Russia-Georgia war in August 2008 once again exposed the vulnerability of Armenia's trade, transit and communication links, and specifically, revealed the risks of relying on only one neighboring country for most of its trade turnover. The bombing of a bridge in Georgia during the war, for example, halted all traffic to and from Armenia for a few days, leading to panic among Armenian consumers who expected supplies to run dry in a matter of weeks. Drivers started buying and stocking up on car petrol so actively that petrol stations in Armenia were forced to ration sales.

Another major incentive, and one that is not often mentioned, but is implicitly understood by the Armenian elite, lies in the sphere of regional politics. Only Iran and Georgia offer a very limited political environment for Armenia; establish-ing ties with Turkey would, therefore, include Armenia in a much more diverse, larger and stimulating political context. This is especially pressing given the very special formats of Georgia-Russia and Iran-US relations, and confirmed by the fact that Russia and the US are the leading external players in the region and Armenia is keen on relating to both in the most positive way possible. Even as things stand now, Armenia's active engagement in the rapprochement process, with Moscow's tacit consent and the hearty approval of the US and the EU, has been beneficial for Armenia's image and weight in the region. One can even say that the initiative to normalize ties with Turkey has already to some extent en-abled Armenia to break out of the narrow limits of the regional political environment and secure an independent niche in the "Great Game" by relying on the indirect resources of the EU, the US and Russia in its negotiations with Turkey. Turkey's motives seem much less imperative, however. In terms of economics or communications, Armenia does not matter a great deal for Turkey, except perhaps for its least developed Eastern areas. Turkey's motivation in the rap-prochement is almost purely political and concerns Turkey's regional and international politics.

Where regional politics are concerned, the "zero-problems-with-neighbors" doctrine has worked better for Turkey in some areas, and worse in others. In the Caucasus, it has not worked and it is not going to work unless Turkey sorts out its relations with Armenia. You either relate to the Caucasus in all the complexity of its contradictions and ten-sions, or you do not relate to it at all. One can have brotherly relations with Azerbaijan and very nicely progressing relations with Georgia but one does not become a regional player in the Caucasus unless one is able to communicate with all the countries in the region. As far as we can see from Armenia, this is understood by the Turkish leadership. With its size and potential, Turkey is eligible to become a key regional player in the Caucasus, and its failure to do so can undermine the very basics of the zero-problems-with-neighbors doctrine, potentially even affecting Turkey's suc-cesses in other geographic areas. As Turkish expert Aybars Görgülü points out, "the lack of diplomatic ties between Turkey and Armenia jeopardizes Turkey's efforts to become a regional leader and also its attempts at mediation for the region's protracted conflicts. The Nagorno-Karabagh dispute is a good example in that sense. Turkey's involvement in this conflict as a party rather than a mediator and its unconditional support for Azerbaijan motivated by factors both strategic – oil-rich Azerbaijan's importance for Turkey – and domestic – Azerbaijan's status as a kin-state to Turkey – has limited Turkey's potential role as a mediator" (Görgülü 2009: 24).

There is another aspect to this as well. Using its new doctrine, Turkey has succeeded in improving relations with some of its neighbors – Syria, Iran and to some extent also Greece. However, three very acute issues remain unresolved: those of Cyprus and of the Kurdish and Armenian minorities in Turkey. Of these, the Cyprus problem and the Kurdish issue are the most sensitive for Turkish society. Neither of the two lends itself to any real resolution in the short-term; they will continue to hinder Turkey's domestic development and prevent it from fully implementing its foreign policy doctrine. The extreme complexity of the Kurdish problem was once again exposed when Prime Minister Erdoğan's "Kurdish initiative" was cut short, or at least strongly deterred, by a ban imposed by Turkey's Constitutional Court on the activity of the pro-Kurdish Democratic Society Party. The intricacy of the Cyprus problem is, in many ways, similar. On the one hand, those two unresolved problems make Turkey more vulnerable to external pressure over the "Armenian question." On the other hand, Turkish-Armenian normalization can potentially become the only success story in Turkish foreign policy in the last few years and, thus, serve to improve Turkey's staggering international image.

In fact, in the international dimension, Turkey-Armenia relations have become part of Turkey-Europe and Turkey-U.S. relations due to the genocide issue. With Armenian Diaspora bodies and political parties lobbying their home countries to recognize the 1915 massacres of Armenians in Ottoman Turkey as genocide, Turkey has been forced to invest considerable resources into trying to offset the activities of the Armenian Diaspora rather than focus on its own foreign policy agenda. According to Osman Bengur, a Turkish-American expert and former Congressional nominee, "By some accounts, approximately 70 percent of the Turkish Embassy's time in Washington is spent trying to persuade leading Americans to support the Turkish position on the Armenian question" (Bengur 2009: 45). While trying to prevent genocide recognition, Turkey has to face strong and well-organized Armenian-American organizations, making Ankara's task extremely difficult. The leverage of the Armenian Diaspora is not limited to lobbying; its political impact is quite significant, especially in the US, Canada, France, Lebanon and some Latin American states, because Armenians in those countries form an important segment of the society and a significant body of voters. Their influence is strongest in countries whose systems of governance allow for the strong involvement of societal groups in domestic and foreign policy decision-making – primarily in the United States and France, for the most obvious examples.

Armenia, meanwhile, is using genocide recognition claims as an unconventional weapon for exerting political pressure on Ankara (Safrastyan 2005: 3). Given Yerevan's limited leverage over Ankara, Armenia is actively using Turkish sensitivity in the genocide issue. Every time Turkey brings up the conflict over Nagorno-Karabagh as a precondition for normalizing relations with Armenia, the latter toughens its stand on genocide recognition, with the pressure exerted by the Diaspora on Western governments becoming a resource for pushing Ankara towards concessions in the reconciliation process.

According to a joint report written by Armenian, Turkish and European experts, "a growing number of Turks have realized that their country's international position on the Armenian question has only generated tension with important allies, while utterly failing to persuade them... So long as Turkey's political leaders and opinion makers continue to stoke fears of loss of territory and reparations Turkey will continue to respond defensively. By continuing to treat every mention of the 'g-word' as attack on national honor, Turkey's foreign policy has become hostage to events beyond its control, particularly when dealing with the Caucasus" (Noah's Dove Returns 2009: 22).

As things stand now, Turkey's relations with Armenia have become part of its relations with the West. External players, especially the US, are in many cases both the subject and the object of the "Armenian factor" in policies with regard to Turkey. The European Union uses the issue of genocide recognition to pressure Turkey into carrying out democratic reform; although it is not directly concerned with rendering justice to survivors or heeding the interests of Armenia, the EU has, in a way, become part of the lobbying game. While Armenia and the Armenian Diaspora employ their advocacy resources in the United States and Western Europe in order to exert pressure on Turkey, Washington and Brussels use the issue of the 1915 Genocide and the need to open Armenian-Turkish borders as a means for criticizing and containing Ankara, including where Turkey's potential accession to the EU is concerned. As of now, Armenia-Turkey normalization is unlikely to disappear from the negotiating table between Turkey and the EU, or from its relations with the US, giving Turkey a strong incentive to address the issue.

Summing this part up, we can say that while Armenia's incentives for rapprochement are very concrete and practical, but also rather pressing, Turkey's potential gains from it lie on a different level: they are about Turkey's international image and its success as a regional power. In a way, it can be argued that Armenia's motivation is tactical, whereas Turkey's motivation is more of a strategic nature.

I am using the present tense although I'm well aware that the normalization process has been stagnating throughout 2010. The two nations obviously launched it largely unaware of the degree of its complexity. In fact, the reconciliation process had stalled many times even during its almost two-year-long active phase. It was amidst widespread public protests in Turkey, Armenia and throughout the Armenian Diaspora communities that the foreign ministers of Armenia, Turkey and Switzerland pre-signed the texts of two "protocols" on the establishment of diplomatic ties and the opening of mutual borders in August 2009. The October 2009 signing of the protocols in Zurich had been a display of considerable political will by the Turkish and Armenian governments, yet the actual signing ceremony remained uncertain until the very last moment – the issue was not with the protocols themselves but with the speeches officials were intending to make after the signing. The signing ceremony was delayed by several hours and it was only through the personal mediation of the US Secretary of State that the sides finally agreed to sign the protocols without making any speeches.

Once signed, the protocols could only come into legal force following their ratification by both countries' parliaments. It was at this stage that impediments to reconciliation became insurmountable. The ratifications never happened; the protocols were never submitted to the parliaments at all, with Armenia insisting that Turkey make the first move, and Turkey procrastinating. By spring 2010, the process came to a standstill, leaving a bitter aftertaste and a new extent of polarization inside both societies concerning the future of the two nations' relationship.

However, the results are not all negative. The path that Armenia and Turkey passed until they signed the protocols, and the protocols themselves, represent a completely new level in the relations between the two countries, and whether or not the stagnation persists for a long time, they have laid a foundation on which Turkey and Armenia can theoretically continue to build a future.

Potential impediments to normalization were quite obvious for both countries from the very start, and nothing radically different emerged during the two years between the first moves of football diplomacy and until the freezing of the rapprochement project. What made the process especially difficult, and what I consider to be the main reason why it stalled, is that those impediments, which were much more of an external nature at the time the process was launched, gradually became important issues — and bargaining chips — in the domestic politics of both countries. In fact, while the incentives, especially in Turkey's case, lay in the field of foreign politics, the main impediments arose in the domestic realm.

From the very start, it was clear that Azerbaijan would be radically opposed to any kind of thaw in Armenia-Turkey relations. It was solidarity with Azerbaijan that originally made Turkey seal its borders with Armenia back in 1993 at the peak of the war in Nagorno-Karabagh; until that point, Turkish-Armenian interaction had been going rather smoothly, if not very actively; Turkey was even one of the first countries to recognize Armenia's independence in 1991. However, by the time the conflict over Nagorno-Karabagh expanded into a large-scale war, stifling Armenia's economy by means of a double land blockade — on the side of Turkey as well as Azerbaijan — became one of the cornerstones of Azerbaijan's strategy. Leaving landlocked Armenia with just two open borders — one with Georgia in the midst of its 1990s civil war, and the other with Iran, with communication and trade constraints ensuing from its "axis of evil" status — was expected to impede Armenia's economic development and, thus, force it to make unilateral concessions on Nagorno-Karabagh. However, the plan failed to prove its efficiency over the years: although Armenia barely survived its mid-1990s economic crisis triggered by the disintegration of the USSR and enhanced by the war and the blockades, by the beginning of the third millennium, its economy was on a rise. Indeed, for several years up to the start of the global economic recession in 2008, Armenia even boasted several years of double-digit economic growth.

Nevertheless, Baku continued to bargain on the blockade as a means of settling the territorial conflict. Although it was quite clear that the sealing of Turkey's border with Armenia had not worked the way Azerbaijan had hoped, the very probability that the border may be unsealed was certain to cause resentment in Azerbaijan and impair its relations with Turkey. This was indeed what happened. Starting in late April 2009, Azerbaijan did not just sharply criticize Turkey's policy with regard to Armenia, but even made a few threatening gestures against Turkey, such as banning broadcasts in Turkish by its TV stations, threatening to stop selling gas to Turkey and expressing its readiness to discuss the option to sell all its gas to Russia. Azerbaijani President Ilham Aliyev's visit to Moscow and his meeting with Russian President Dmitry Medvedev in mid-April 2009 were vivid illustrations of Baku's stance. However, bullying with the "Russian factor" failed to induce Turkey to review its policy with regard to Armenia; nor did Moscow agree to alter its approach to the conflict over Nagorno-Karabagh in exchange for Azerbaijani gas. A series of crises in Turkish-Azerbaijani relations ensued, the worst in post-Soviet history. Even subsequent friendly gestures exchanged by Baku and Ankara failed to obliterate the negative aftertaste in bilateral relations and societal perceptions.

The crisis in Ankara-Baku relations did not just extend to the governments; the reaction of Azerbaijani society to Turkey's "treachery" was in fact more acute than that of the establishment. According to Turkish expert Bülent Aras, "the attempts for normalization with Armenia triggered a nationalist Azeri response and this response found support in Turkey in a form of allegation that the Turkish government is selling out Azerbaijan" (Aras 2009: 15). The issue caused wide domestic repercussions in Turkey amongst actors and groups with strong feelings for Azerbaijan, and became part of domestic political discourses and political games. Part of Turkey's establishment began insisting that the settlement of the conflict over Nagorno-Karabagh, on terms which would be favorable from Azerbaijan's perspective, should be made a precondition to normalization with Armenia. Turkey's government tried to handle its domestic problems by regularly making public speeches to the effect that rapprochement with Armenia will be to some degree dependent on the settlement of the conflict over Nagorno-Karabagh to Azerbaijan's best advantage. Meanwhile, the very notion of Armenia-Turkey "football diplomacy" was based on the vision of normalization without preconditions, and would not have started at all had the precondition been on the negotiations table. Any link between Nagorno-Karabagh and Armenia-Turkey rapprochement was unacceptable for Armenia and was certain to ground the reconciliation initiative. Turkey's leadership could not have been ignorant of the rather trivial fact that it is impossible to gratify both Armenia and Azerbaijan as long as whatever is acceptable for one is – by definition – unacceptable for the other, and consequently, each step towards normalization with Armenia cannot fail to trigger a new crisis in its relations with Azerbaijan. The very fact that Turkey became involved in the rapprochement project at all seemed to indicate that it no longer wished to be involved in the zero-sum game between Armenia and Azerbaijan and remain Azerbaijan's hostage in the region, giving up all prospects to ever becoming an independent regional player.

Whatever its original intentions may have been, under growing domestic pressure, Turkey's political establishment began a precarious balancing game, simultaneously going forward with unconditional normalization with Armenia on a diplomatic level and tying the normalization to Azerbaijan's interests on the level of public discourses. Some pretty strong statements tying Armenia-Turkey normalization to that conflict were thus made by Turkey's Prime Minister Erdoğan during his visit to Azerbaijan in May 2009; however, the protocols were pre-signed several months later and signed by October, and no mention of any preconditions to their implementation or ratification was made in the text. There was reportedly the intention to make one in a speech following the signing ceremony, to which Armenian officials reacted by a threat to make a speech mentioning the Armenian Genocide; eventually, international mediators talked the signatories out of making any speeches at all. Yet directly after the signing of the protocols, Turkey's top public officials announced that Turkish parliament would not ratify the Protocols unless the settlement of the Karabagh issue moved forward. Armenian President Serzh Sargsyan reacted by saying in a December 2009 speech that should Turkey fail to ratify the protocols "in a reasonable amount of time" and continue procrastinating, Armenia would revoke its signature under the protocols. Although Armenia did not fulfill this threat, and even went ahead with having the protocols reviewed by its Constitutional Court in early 2010, there has been no progress in the reconciliation after that point.

Something of a similar nature, if of a lesser scope, has happened in Armenia, where hostility to rapprochement was originally concentrated in the Diaspora, the majority of which resented the idea of Armenia establishing ties with Turkey until the latter recognizes the genocide. It is important to bear in mind that Armenian Diaspora communities outside the former USSR, primarily those in Western countries, Lebanon and Syria, were formed as a result of the massacres and deportations perpetrated by Turkey in the early 20th century. These communities consist of direct descendants of genocide survivors, so that the memory of the genocide is central to their identity. As assimilation trends prevail in many Armenian Diaspora communities, with Armenian language, culture and religion losing their importance, the memory of the Armenian Genocide remains the one pillar of diaspora identity, making third- and even fourth-generation descendants of genocide survivors extremely distrustful of Turkey.

The Armenian Diaspora has significant impact on the political life of modern Armenia. Given its structure and *modus operandi*, the Diaspora has ways of influencing the political, social and economic life of Armenia varying from political advocacy in countries with Armenian communities to money transfers, or remittances, from ordinary citizens and donations from large-scale benefactors that reach billions of US dollars and constitute a significant part of the budgets of both Armenia and Nagorno-Karabagh. In the early 1990s, political parties which had existed in the Diaspora for over a century came to Armenia and became active there. These parties, of which the Armenian Revolutionary Federation (ARF), or Dashnaktsutyun, is the most powerful, maintain ties with the Diaspora and have access to financial and political support and human resources from Armenian communities worldwide.

In contrast to the resentment of the Diaspora, domestic Armenian elites were almost unanimously in favor of rapprochement with Turkey. As time went by, the issue also became part of domestic politics; the Dashnaktsutyun party even withdrew from the ruling coalition in protest over the Armenia-Turkey roadmap agreed to in April 2009. One can argue that the Dashnaktsutyun has stronger ties to the Diaspora than any other party in the Armenian landscape, but the political moves did not end there. Attitudes to rapprochement with Turkey have become a "shibboleth" in Armenian politics, causing tensions and regroupings. The resulting discourse has stimulated the rise and appeal of nationalist groups, until then very marginal in Armenian society. A growing number of hardliners insist that recognition of the genocide by Turkey should be a precondition for normalization.

Following this logic, in which incentives are chiefly external but obstacles are domestic, it would be unrealistic to expect any changes in Armenia-Turkey relations until the parliamentary election in Turkey due in June 2011. A lot will depend on how the election goes, how many seats the ruling Justice and Development Party (AKP) secures and whether it enters into a coalition with the opposition Republican People's Party of Turkey (CHP). In fact, the way things look from Armenia, the results of the upcoming election will largely determine the fate of the rapprochement initiative in the short term. This does not imply that the renewal of reconciliation efforts is certain or even probable; however, but it may still be possible. Should rapprochement be resumed, its course is not obvious: it might continue to rely on the ratification of the protocols, or it may take a detour of some kind, such as the de-facto opening of borders or the establishment of some alternative formats for diplomatic interaction.

References

Bülent A. (2009). Davutoğlu Era in Turkish Foreign Policy. SETA Policy Brief, No 32.

Görgülü A. (2009). Towards a Turkish-Armenian Rapprochement? Insight Turkey, Vol. 11, No 2.

Görgülü A., A. Iskandaryan and S. Minasyan (2010). Turkey-Armenia Dialogue Series: Assessing the Rapprochement Process. TESEV-Caucasus Institute Joint Report. Istanbul. http://www.caucasusinstitute.org/upload/files/Turkey-Armenia.pdf

Görgülü A., S. Gundogar, A.Iskandaryan and S. Minasyan (2009). Turkey-Armenia Dialogue Series: Breaking the Vicious Circle. TESEV-Caucasus Institute Joint Report. Istanbul http://www.caucasusinstitute.org/upload/files/CI-TESEV-2010.pdf

Iskandaryan A. (2009). Armenian-Turkish Rapprochement: Timing Matters. Insight Turkey, vol. 11, No. 3.

Iskandaryan A. and S. Minasyan (2010). Pragmatic Policies vs. Historical Constraints: Analyzing Armenia-Turkey Relations. Caucasus Institute Research Papers, No. 1. Yerevan: Caucasus Institute.

Noah's Dove Returns. Armenia, Turkey and the Debate on Genocide (2009). European Stability Initiative (ESI) Report www.esiweb.org/index.php?lang=en&id=156&document_ID=108

Osman B. (2009). Turkey's Image and the Armenian Question. Turkish Policy Quarterly, Vol. 8, No. 1.

Safrastyan R. (2005). The Recognition of the Genocide in Armenia's Foreign Policy: Multi-Level Analysis. 21st Century Journal, no 1, Yerevan: Noravank Foundation.

David Hovhannisyan

Process of Normalization of Armenian-Turkish Relations:
The Official and Societal Dimensions

Dr. David Hovhannisyan is currently heading the Center of Civilization and Cultural Studies at the Yerevan State University. At the same time he is advisor to the rector of the Yerevan State Linguistic University and Professor at the YSU Department of Oriental Studies. He is Ambassador Extraordinary and Plenipotentiary of the Republic of Armenia. He held the position of the Ambassador at large at the Ministry of Foreign Affairs and has been the first Ambassador of the Republic of Armenia to Syrian Arab Republic. He has authored various monographs and articles on Islamic Studies, Medieval Arab Literature, Qura'nic Studies, International Relations, etc. Dr. Hovhannisyan is member of different local and international organizations amongst others Transcend, Armenian-Turkish Reconciliation Commission (TARC), South Caucasus Institute of Regional Security, "Arabic Studies" journal editorial board.

The Armenian-Turkish official relationship has up to now remained in much dispute. What is the reason for Turkey's unchanged negative position on the matter of the establishment of relations with Armenia?

It seems that the first Armenian president's policy on the matter of Armenian genocide recognition by Turkey was discreet enough and provided the authorities of our neighboring country with the opportunity, by showing political "pragmatism," to establish diplomatic relations with the newly independent state of Armenia, to open the border, and to create active trade and economic contacts, thus, strengthening its presence in our country with all the consequences emanating from it: the political impact, cultural and civilizational penetration, etc.

The second president of Armenia, adopting a tough policy on the genocide issue and making the international recognition of the latter one of the crucial and most urgent matters of Armenian foreign policy, simultaneously took an unprecedented step: in an exclusive interview with prominent Turkish journalist Mehmet Ali Birand, he stated that regarding Turkey, Armenia does not raise any territorial or other claims stemming from the genocide or its consequences. It was a statement after which, actually, all the anxieties of the Turkish political and strategic establishment should have been dissipated in connection with the possible infringement of the Armenians upon their territorial entity.

The protocols signed but not ratified during Serzh Sargsyan's presidency have been much spoken and written about, so there is no need to recall that process. However, it does make sense to re-examine the causes of the failure of this process.

For Turkey, normalization of its relations with Armenia is conditioned with the settlement of Armenian- Azerbaijani relations. And this is in case when Turkey has frequent relations with a number of countries with which it has numerous controversial issues, including that of a territorial nature (for instance, with Greece, Syria, Iran, etc.). The only possible logical inference is that "Turkey doesn't consider Armenia as a state with which, inter alia, it can normalize and improve relations step by step, build a joint security system, collaborate on the border zone, unanimously participate in settlement of regional issues and so on."

According to the Turkish criteria, Armenia does not correspond to standards of "normal" country. The issue of the normalization of relations with Armenia can come to a halt only after the end of some events as a result of which there will occur certain changes which will make our country correspond to these standards. What events are we speaking about and what changes should take place?

■

In April 1992, at the first summit of Turkic-speaking states held in Uzbekistan, the president of Turkey, Turgut Özal, stated in his speech that the 21st century will be the "century of Turks" if mistakes are not made. In the 1990s, one could often come across similar statements.

The next Turkish President Süleyman Demirel's statement is distinctive as well: being a Turk, it is impossible to renounce Pan-Turkism, but not passing by the limits of realism. "If in the future the Turkish-speaking countries get united and create Commonwealth nobody will be against it but today it remains unrealistic," he said. Similar announcements testify to some Neo-Pan-Turkism trend of the leading political circles in Turkey no matter how deep it underlies the political lexicon of western sonorousness.

Such formulations in the 1990s triggered a positive reaction in the West. Much of the Western political leadership extensively advertised the image of Turkey as a secular Muslim state built on a system of progressive, democratic values the political and social system of which should set a good example for newly independent Muslim states. The Prime Minister of Great Britain, Margaret Thatcher, attached an importance to the role of Turkey in one more sense. In a speech in 1993, she depicted Turkey as a fortress holding out against revolutionary Arab nationalism and aggressive Muslim radicalism.

The western similar "Post-Cold War" approaches coincided with the policy Turkey carried out and favored that allowed it, entering into competition with Russia, to reorient the former Soviet Turkic-speaking states which would one day contribute to the "formation of unity of Turkish-speaking states" as well as the fulfillment of Neo-Pan-Turkism aims.

Once again, the only thing that hampered the achievement of these aims – the important component of which should become the ground connection as well with the Northern Caucasus that was part of the Russian Federation and with the Turkic-speaking republics in the Volga Basin – was Armenia. This connection was necessary for the promotion of the disintegration processes rather active within a weakened Russia after the breakup of the Soviet Union and for providing an effective competition with Russia. Already in 1997, the Turkish Ministry of Foreign Affairs' Department

Head of Central Asia, the Caucasus, the Slavic countries and Mongolia, Halil Akıncı stated that "the radical changes that occurred on the political stage not only pushed Turkey forward to leading strategic positions at the epicenter of Eurasia but also sketched a new and progressive role for it in this extensive geographical area. At the present Turkey should focus its attention on simultaneously several directions-starting from the European integration and the new architecture of the latter's safety to zone formation of the states of Turkish origin in Caucasus and Central Asia."

Throughout the 1990s, in addition to the statements of political leaders and diplomats expressing themselves on such a position of Turkey, we can also add the active operations of Ankara in all Turkish-inhabited conflict zones starting from Bosnia and Kosovo to the Northern Caucasian Republics.

The Armenian presence prevented them from carrying out this project-the establishment of the ground connection. At the same time, Turkey fully realized that on the eve of the 21st century, "the Armenian question" was impossible to settle the way the Young Turks tried to settle at the beginning of the 20th century. It would be possible to settle the question not by annihilating Armenia as a whole, but that part of its territory that would provide with the long-wished-for ground corridor joining it with the territory of Azerbaijan or Turkey. For all this, the Turkish leading political circles, first of all, should have been engaged in the Karabagh conflict which would have given them a chance to achieve their aim and moreover, relations with Armenia should not be normalized for the long-range purpose of maintaining high-level tension between the two sides and providing the political justification for anti-Armenian operations of any type. Only after the fulfillment of all this, would it be possible to regulate relations with the remaining part of Armenia, which would have already become "uninteresting" and would have lost its geopolitical role.

It is quite comprehensible that the above-stated, not being based on necessary supplementary data and documents, can be observed only as a hypothesis. However, we should take into account that in such cases, we rarely come across such facts that are unequivocally reliable and acceptable for all sides. I think, nevertheless, that the imagination submitted for logical analysis is getting along pretty well as to motives of policy implemented by the Turkish authorities and ideological basis.

■

However the events developed differently. The victory of the Armenian army in the Karabakh war and the allocation of the Russian military base on our territory-the general geopolitical developments made unrealistic the Neo-Pan-Turkism aims so longed for in the 1990s.

A situation emerged in which, firstly, for the fulfillment of US aims, some importance was attached to the basic issue of the normalization of Armenian-Turkish relations, the result of which would be the acquisition of a political homogeneity of the Southern Caucasian countries (if the hazards of Turkey vanish, we no longer need the presence of the Russian military base in our territory, besides, if the Turkish policy on the Karabagh conflict is more balanced, the probability of settling it peacefully will drastically increase).

Secondly, after the September 11th, the US gained an immediate military presence in the Central Asian states, which means that the Americans evaluating Turkish policy toward Central Asia, not being West-Central but being Turkish-Central, determined to implement their policy in this area.

Finally, Russia overcame the deep crisis by making its policy more distinct from that of the US and the European Union, and obtained a free hand of action in the Northern Caucasus, particularly in Chechnya, which allowed Moscow to exclude the possibility of foreign influence in this part of the Russian Federation.

After the Justice and Development Party (AKP) came to power, Ankara's policy adopted an essentially new coloring. On the one hand, one of the initial aims of the new foreign policy was expressed with the slogan "zero problems with neighbors," but on the other hand, Turkish leaders made fiery statements about the "revival of the Ottoman spirit." Taking into account the fact that similar statements were made by the high-ranking leaders of the religious party in power, such as Prime Minister Erdoğan and Foreign Minister Ahmet Davutoğlu, for example, one must infer that they testify to the presence of similar aims in their party program provisions or fundamental tenets which means that, firstly, the Republic of Turkey is no longer Kemalist and is not led by the constitution authored by Ataturk, and secondly, all of the statements of the present authorities on the fact that Ankara keeps implementing the Turkish traditional policy in order to become a member of the EU are open to question.

The above-mentioned circumstances shaped a new context for the Armenian-Turkish relations.

Getting involved in "football" diplomacy, Ankara maintains the very line carried out by Turkish diplomacy before the Justice and Development Party (AKP) came to power- an imitation of negotiations and, in addition, to other playing cards, the policy to turn the issue of the normalization of the Armenian-Turkish relations into an object of bargaining in negotiations with the US, EU, Azerbaijan, and the Russian Federation. Maneuvering all the time, entering into various, diverse negotiation processes, offering its services and acting as a go-between in some conflicts, such as in cases of the Arabs and the Israelis, the US and Iran, Azerbaijan and Armenia, etc, Ankara is keen on acquiring as many levers as possible which, as some Turkish observers and diplomats evaluate, should allow it to curtly increase its influence in some regions. In this connection as well, as to relations with Armenia, the Gül-Erdoğan policy is rather noteworthy.

Throughout the first decade of the 2000s, before the beginning of negotiations that finished with the signing of the Armenian-Turkish protocols in Zurich, keeping on with Armenian-Turkish official periodical meetings, Turkey was implementing the policy of Armenia's ground blockade; its official position on the Nagorno-Karabagh conflict and the recognition of the Armenian Genocide have not been reconsidered. On the contrary, Turkish officials of different ranks at times re-established the loyalty of their authorities to already shaped viewpoints on these issues. At the same time, throughout these years, contacts between the representatives of the two societies at different levels have become rather frequent.

From this point of view, it happened because it was the first serious undertaking: the activity of the Armenian-Turkish reconciliation committee was rather interesting, the formation of which was not unanimously accepted in Armenia and Turkey. Taking into account the binding political statements of Turkey's official authorities, by the immediate initiative of the US State Department, the negotiation technology of the so-called "second track" was put into service, the implication of which, is that some authoritative representatives of social and political circles of the conflicting states organize non-binding, but principled discussions during which they make an attempt to find ways for the settlement or normalization of the most urgent radical issues. The negotiations carried within the framework of the "second track" have been crowned with success in various world conflicts resolution.

The Armenian-Turkish reconciliation committee was created within the framework of this technology logic. It is clear that the circle of the questions on which the committee members focused their attention after long discussions, were connected with the genocide, embracing the present-day political importance of this issue. It was also important that the discussions could be kept away from primitive repudiation. The argument touched upon mainly the following issues: whether the real rapprochement is possible without Turkey's recognition of the genocide and to what extent this recognition is possible in the nearest future. The Turkish members of the committee noted that the genocide issue is alien to the wider social class of Turkey and the Turks are unaware of their history up to the establishment of the Turkish Republic and that in the political and psychological context, this question for the Turkish state and society either should not be discussed at all, or that it should be discussed, but not in the nearest future.

From the point of view of the Armenian committee members, the real reconciliation between the two societies, and the two nations, is impossible without the recognition of the genocide, however, it cannot hamper the normalization process of relations between two neighboring countries, the establishment of diplomatic relations, the opening of frontiers and the elimination of the blockade, the legalization of the already existing trade and economic relations and their development. Turkey has, let us say, at acceptable level, to some extent civilized relations with Greece, Syria and some other countries with which there also exist various problems both coming from history and generating from the present-day geopolitical situation, therefore, nothing hinders them in establishing similar relations with Armenia, indeed, if there are no other non-proclaimed aims.

It is obvious that along with these issues, other numerous questions as well were discussed, for instance, the easing of the established order of requiring Armenian citizens to obtain entry visas to Turkey, the restoration of historical monuments of Ani and Akhtamar and their restitution under the patronage of the Armenian Patriarchate, not hampering Armenian citizens of different countries to visit different places of the Western Armenia, etc.

As a result of the activity of the ATRC, at the committee's request the "analyses" made by an outstanding international organization, the "International Center for Transitional Justice," was published and which referred to legal interpretation of the genocide. According to the published analyses, the features of the events that took place at the beginning of the 20th century correspond to the standards presupposed by the UN convention on the genocide prevention and punishment: thus, these events are qualified as genocide.

Of utmost importance, according to us, is the following event: for the first time the Armenian and Turkish political figures, high-ranking diplomats and prominent intellectuals unanimously applied to a third party in order to obtain an evaluation of the radical basic issue separating the societies of the two countries and this very third side unconditionally confirmed that what happened from the legal point of view was genocide. The evidence, being very important itself, makes room for more important inferences.

First, it is evident that if not for US participation, the Turkish side would not have given its consent for the creation of such a committee. Moreover, it would be impossible as well to jointly apply to the "International Center for Transitional Justice" with a request to examine the question. No less important is that the committee's activity, breaking numerous taboos and stereotypes, served as a sort of "provocation" in the societies of the two countries for open discussions connected with the genocide. The matter, indeed, concerns, first of all, the Turkish society, as for the first time after a long silence, the events at the beginning of the 20th century captured public attention.

The contacts and discussions in various formats of public and national diplomacies became more frequent. Numerous joint cultural auctions were organized: concerts, exhibitions, film exchanges, participation of artists representing both countries in various international festivals taking place in Armenia and Turkey. The reciprocal visits of journalists became more frequent, as a result of which numerous articles were published.

The goal of all this was that the two neighboring nations, between which the genocide, perpetuated during the period of the Ottoman Empire decline, had driven a wedge and who for decades had been estranged (for various reasons) from their own history, could, as far as possible, become aware of each other and imagine what is going on in Armenian and Turkish societies. No less important is that due to these developments, they started using the term "genocide" and the Armenians were given a chance to visit the places with toponyms of sacred honor and meaning for them.

As a result of the above-mentioned procedures, it was once more confirmed that the Armenian and Turkish nations were on their way to real reconciliation, facing solely one fundamental issue- the recognition of the genocide. Unlike the authorities, which take into consideration numerous other political factors-right or wrong, the nations have realized that there is no alternative to reconciliation and the genocide should be recognized, however, the mythological perception of the world and the myth-policy on this matter are contradictory as well.

The genocide issue is the most essential one for both sides to establish their identity. The more for us and especially for our Diaspora it is connected with mythologies of a "lost paradise" and "promised land" (indeed, without the component of "the people selected by God"), with the restoration of divine justice and rediscovering "homeland," the more for the present-day Turkish society, it is connected with the Ottoman Empire as a sidereal hour of the Turkish nation, the rise of exclusive civilization, unfair infringements upon the Islam flare.

The period of the Armenian Genocide which is perceived as "Mets Eghern" coincides with the period of the fall of the

Ottoman Empire /mythologeme "fall of the glorious kingdom"/ which the Turks due to Atatürk, perceived as the end of the old history. The basic issue of the identity establishment creates extra complications in specification and regulation process of the Armenian-Turkish relations.

Armenia and the Armenians continue to perceive Turkey as a source of immediate harm and danger; they think that Turkey is not sincere and candid in manifestation of its goodwill. The reason is in search and found in the genocide recognition/non-recognition issue as the historical memory dictates to struggle for such solutions the implementation of which will let us exclude recurrence of a catastrophe, exclude the genocide. Here is the distinctive feature prevailing in the approaches of the Armenian Diaspora and Armenia to genocide.

The mythological component for the Diaspora is the most essential factor of identity establishment and nation preservation in condition of estrangement. "Ergir" (homeland, country) as a root and a fact of suffering and unfair loss and returning to "Ergir" as a "lost paradise" are pivotal concepts for the national identity preservation out of the native land.

Genocide recognition for Armenia, above all, is connected with the state security issue solutions as it means recognition of the committed sin, that is- expiation. Expiation means awareness of the committed sin which is already a pledge or a guarantee of the fact that similar tragedies will never reoccur, and it lies deep in the consciousness of representatives of many Armenians, Greeks, Arabs, Kurds and other nations that Turkey has lost genocidal nature and the Turkish society has shaped and developed into a mature civil society the actions and reactions of which are foreseeable.

From the point of view of Armenian-Turkish relations, genocide recognition will mean drawing near the value system based on a similar evaluation of the past which will serve as a basis for creating common future in the same region. The formation of the Caucasian, or to put it more extensively, the Black Sea-Caspian security system is considerably connected with the solution of this fundamental question. And such a sub-regional security system is vital from the point of view of global security. The project implementation of the US and European Union in the "Greater Middle East" requires the formation of a stable system in this part of the world and if it is created, the intersection point of the two "mega-regions" will become not the zone of spread of commotion and antagonism, but a barrier to commotion and conflicts.

To what extent it will be possible to implement the formation of the Caucasian security system, whether it will be possible to find ways for the resolution of the Karabagh conflict today depends only on the solution method of Armenian-Turkish relations. The opening of frontiers, being a positive phenomenon itself, can be observed in reality only as a concession under US pressure, but not a manifestation of goodwill and, moreover, a first attempt to improve relations with Armenia and the Armenians.

Yeghishe Kirakosyan

Armenian-Turkish Reconciliation: the Reality and Possibilities
A Legal Perspective

"Who after all is today speaking of the destruction of the Armenians?"

Adolf Hitler[1]

Dr. Yeghishe Kirakosyan is a Ph.D. in Public International Law from the Yerevan State University, Yerevan, Armenia. From November 2009 to May 2010, Dr. Kirakosyan was a research assistant at the Georgetown University Law Center, Washington, D.C., United States, where he completed a Master of Laws in International Legal Studies (LL.M., with Distinction). Some of his recent publications include: "The formation and determination of the existence of a rule under customary international law – the International Court of Justice and the ad hoc Tribunals compared," in *The Diversification and Fragmentation of International Criminal Law*, (T.M.C Asser Press, Cambridge University Press: 2010/2011), (in progress) (in English); "Custom in the System of Sources of International Law," in *Contemporary Problems of Jurisprudence*, Yerevan, 2007, pp.194-219 (in Russian); "General International Law and Customary International Law," Moscow State University Bulletin, Law, #3, 2006 (in Russian).

1. Introduction

The purpose of the paper is to discuss the model of a mechanism suitable for achieving Armenian-Turkish reconciliation from the legal perspective. The protocols signed in October 2009 offered little faith for the success of the possible reconciliation between Armenia and Turkey. Although the process was largely fostered by major political powers, namely the United States and Russia, nevertheless, for a short period of time it created the semblance of positive developments in a very complex political region. The two protocols were signed between the two states on 10 October 2009 in Zurich: a Protocol on the Establishment of Diplomatic Relations between the Republic of Armenia and the Republic of Turkey and a Protocol on Development of Relations between the Republic of Armenia and the Republic of Turkey. The instruments are the result of several years of talks between the two governments, ongoing since 1992. Armenian and Turkish borders have been closed since 1993. Negotiations over the protocol on diplomatic relations was almost completed in 1993, with the remaining issue to be agreed the recognition of existing borders, when the discussions were overtaken by the events in the Nagorno-Karabakh war in April 1993. Following that, Turkey ceased negotiations and halted the ongoing transit of wheat into Armenia (Libaridian 2004: 269-270).

The controversies between the two countries are deeply tied to history and have far-reaching roots and are not just a matter of politics, but rather, stem from the ethnic identities of each nation coupled with historical experience. In the present contribution, we will attempt to introduce a feasible content for the reconciliation structure enshrined in the protocols of 2009.

---

1   7 Documents on British Foreign Policy 1919-1939, at 258 (E.L. Woodward & Rohan Butler eds., 3d ser. 1954) (1939) cited in Dadrian, 1998: 538 & Cassese, 1998: 2.

The present contribution will focus on the legal aspects of Armenian-Turkish reconciliation, attempting to analyze the challenges that latter faces, as well as emphasizing the necessary steps needed to be taken for ensuring the start of the process.

2. Background: the Origins and the Underpinnings of Historical Injustice

During World War I, the Ottoman Empire carried out one of the largest genocides in the world's history, slaughtering a large portion of its minority Armenian population (Dadrian 1989: 223). The maiming, torture, starvation, disease, abduction, rape, mental and physical abuse, and mass execution of Armenians took place in Ottoman Empire in the end of the 19th and in the beginning of 20th centuries (Bloxham 2005).

The first wave of Armenian massacres in the Ottoman Empire took place in 1894-96, which represented a specific small-war action undertaken in peacetime to exterminate at least a portion of the empire's Armenian subjects (Reid 1992: 37). The 1890s massacres were a prequel and, arguably, a staging ground for the full-scale genocide of 1915 (Levene 2005). According to most historical documentation and evidence, almost 1.5 million Armenians were killed from 1915-1923. A large portion of Armenians fled the Ottoman Empire and sought refuge throughout the world forming the Armenian Diaspora.

Interestingly, the Ottoman Empire acknowledged some atrocities, and made basic efforts at holding domestic tribunals, some of which secured convictions against the offenders (Dadrian 1989: 509-10; 551-53). However, the consecutive Turkish government under President Atatürk, who had been a one-time target for prosecution, the government rescinded its official recognition of the genocide (Balakian 2003: 373 cited in Kielsgard 2008: 36). Since then, the Turkish state continues to deny the fact of Armenian Genocide, which is one of the core reasons for the continuous victimization of Armenians. The latter makes the need for reconciliation especially crucial. As correctly noted regarding Holocaust claims, "human beings are routinely assaulted by history and the living memory of past wrongs, misdeeds and injustices…. Germany's military defeat and the revelation of the crimes of the Holocaust touched off a flood of demands for the punishment of wrongdoers, material restitution, truth-telling, and various types of conditional reconciliation." (McAdams 2009: 291). Unfortunately, relevant political conditions have never been in favor of the Armenians and so for many decades, the Armenians suffered the unconditional denial from the Turkish part of the atrocities committed at the beginning of the 20th century. The Allies (Great Britain, France and Russia) issued a joint declaration on May 24, 1915 condemning "the connivance and often assistance of Ottoman authorities" in the massacres (Dadrian 1998: 57 in UWLA L.Rev). After World War I, in January 1919, the Preliminary Peace Congress in Paris established the Commission on Responsibilities and Sanctions. A proposal was made during work of the Commission to adopt a new category of war crimes meant to cover the massacres of the Armenians, declaring that "technically, these acts did not come within the provisions of the panel code, [but they constituted grave offences against] the law of humanity" (Dadrian 1998: 59 in UWLA L. Rev.). The final report of the Commission included, but did not sharply highlight, the crimes which Turkey was accused of having perpetrated against her Armenian citizens (Dadrian 1998: 59).

Further, the idea of holding the perpetrators responsible was embodied in the Treaty of Sevres, signed in August 10, 1920:

[T]he Turkish Government recognizes the right of the Allied Powers to bring before military tribunals persons accused of having committed acts in violation of the laws and customs of war. Such persons shall, if found guilty, be sentenced to punishments laid down by law. This provision will apply notwithstanding any proceedings or prosecution before a tribunal in Turkey or in the territory of her allies (The Treaties 1924: 787, 862).

The Treaty of Serves was a very progressive one, besides the mentioned clause, as it was also stipulated in Article 230, the idea of establishing a tribunal for the prosecution of crimes committed by the Turkish authorities. According to the article, "the Turkish Government undertakes to hand over to the Allied Powers the persons whose surrender may be required by the latter as being responsible for the massacres committed during the continuance of the state of war on territory which formed part of the Turkish Empire on August 1, 1914."

The Allied Powers reserved the right to designate the tribunal, which shall try the persons, so accused, and the Turkish Government undertakes to recognize such tribunal (The Treaties 1924: 863). Unfortunately, the Sevres Treaty did not enter into force (Schabas, 2009: 26). The failure of the mechanism foreseen in the Sevres Treaty and further political developments backed the denialist policy of Turkey throughout the subsequent decades.

Recent developments indicate more of an understanding of the issue of reconciliation on both sides, however. In October 2009, the Republics of Armenian and Turkey signed two documents aimed at the normalization of mutual relations. Talks with Turkey on the issue have started in the beginning of 1990s, right after the establishment of the Republic of Armenia. As mentioned above, the protocols are aimed at establishing diplomatic relations between the two countries and the development of relations. The relevance of the protocols forms the point of view of the present study that is particularly linked with the provision establishing a sub-commission covering historical dimension. For the first time in history, the two nations are willing to speak about their common history.

However, reconciliation cannot be achieved that easy. It can merely be considered only as the first step of a long road, which the two countries have chosen. The history and precedent of restorative justice indicates how difficult reconciliation can be achieved.

Obviously, in both countries, or to put it correctly, in both societies, there is a portion of nihilism towards each other, which is a quite natural result of the national identities formed separately of each other, visualizing the other as an enemy nation.[2] Thus, in these realities we have to construe a viable mechanism to pave the way for reconciliation.

---

2   The notion of conflicting national identities is elaborated in more detail in Libaridian 2004: 2.

Below, we will make an effort to comprehend the feasible reconciliatory mechanisms for Armenian-Turkish controversy and to stress the challenges of the process.

3. Is Reconciliation Possible Within the Framework of the Protocols? Understanding the Challenges. What Do We Miss?

The provision enshrined in the protocol states:
"The sub-commission on the historical dimension will implement a dialogue with the aim of:
1.   Restore **mutual confidence** *between two nations;*
2.   *Impartial scientific examination of the* **historical records and archives** *in order to*
○   *Define existing problems, and*
○   *Formulate recommendations"* (Protocol on Development 2010).

First and foremost, considering the very large gap in time and the absence of victims, clearly, there can be no just reconciliation without a consensus on truth (Payaslian 2008: 411). In this particular instance, the term "victims" is utilized *stricto sensu* in the legal (formal) perspective, i.e. the eye-witnesses and survivors of massacres. However, for the purposed of this paper, it is important to note that the term "victim" should be understood as a much wider term, including not only the survivors and eye-witnesses, but also their descendants.

For construing a more comprehensive structure of the mandate of the sub-commission (hereinafter – Commission), it will be useful to refer to relevant historical examples of similar situations. The closest ones to the Armenian-Turkish contradiction are the German-Israeli and French-German reconciliation cases. The core issue is that in both relations, a focus was placed on the understanding and learning of history (Gardner Feldman 1999: 340). Accordingly, the starting point in Armenian-Turkish relations lies in a common understanding of the history. For this purpose, the Commission should have an initial focus on historical research and providing a foundation for a mutually positive perception. However, it is important to stress and understand one crucial issue: we are not dealing with a mere academic disagreement between scholars of different persuasions or schools (Libaridian 2005). The problem is rooted in the identity of each nation, hence, mere historical research or scholarly dialogue will not help to foster reconciliation. Hence, the work of the Commission should be backed by the continuous work of the other sub-commissions in different fields, i.e. legal, environmental etc., as prescribed by the protocol.

The second paragraph of the second point calls on the parties to "...implement a dialogue on the historical dimension with the aim to restore mutual confidence between the two nations, including an impartial scientific examination of the historical records and archives to define existing problems and formulate recommendations." The wording does not seem to support the reconciliation argument that we are trying to make. The protocols are strictly focused on the examination of historical records and formulating recommendations based on them. It is understandable, that Turkey would not have signed any wording that even implicitly admitted any acknowledgement. At the same time, the language is very adaptable and can be interpreted to include the proposed notion of reconciliation. For example, the provision asserts that the aim of the process is to "restore the mutual confidence between the two nations," which allows the interpretation of the provisions of the protocol in a much wider sense, through engaging the tools of interpretation enshrined in Articles 30 and 31 of the Vienna Convention on the Law of the Treaties. In this particular instance, we are resorting to a contextual interpretation, as well as understanding the treaty provisions in the light of its object and purpose. However, as subsequent developments indicated, the wording enshrined in the protocols is not favorable for commencing the reconciliatory process.

The core problem of the entire process is the different perceptions of the objectives of the instruments by each party. The latter was evidenced by the decision of the Constitutional Court of Armenia on the matter of constitutionality of the protocols and the hostile attitude of Turkish authorities toward that decision, which clearly demonstrated the deep dichotomy in understanding the essence of the protocols. The Court found that the protocols were consistent with the provisions of the Armenian Constitution. However, the Court also stressed the following:

> [T]he RA Constitutional Court also finds that the provisions of the Protocols on Development of Relations between the Republic of Armenia and the Republic of Turkey cannot be interpreted or applied in the legislative process and application practice of the Republic of Armenia as well as in the interstate relations in a way that would contradict the provisions of the Preamble to the RA Constitution and the requirements of Paragraph 11 of the Declaration of Independence of Armenia (Protocol on Development 2009).

Paragraph 11 of the Declaration of Independence of the Republic of Armenia, to which the Court refers, states that "the Republic of Armenia stands in support of the task of achieving international recognition of the 1915 Genocide in Ottoman Turkey and Western Armenia" (The Declaration of Independence 1990).

Beyond any doubt, the legal position of the Constitutional Court can impact the bilateral relations of Armenia and Turkey, when it will be expressed in an appropriate international legal manner, e.g. reservation, interpretive declaration or agreement with the other party in any other mutually acceptable form. The idea behind this point is that the Armenian Government, or at least the Constitutional Court, is very certain in that the acknowledgement of the fact of genocide is very crucial and, moreover, is enshrined in the founding document of the Republic of Armenia.

The Turkish Ministry of Foreign Affairs immediately after the decision was adopted, issued an official statement:

> [T]he decision undermines the very reason for negotiating these Protocols as well as their fundamental objective. This approach cannot be accepted on our part. Turkey, in line with its accustomed allegiance to its international commitments, maintains its adherence to the primary provisions of these protocols. We expect the same allegiance from the Armenian government (Turkey says 2010).

This mutual battle in the foreign political arena indicates that the reconciliation in a selected framework is facing a deadlock. The most reasonable explanation for such a complication is the absence of the political will. Or, otherwise, the parties have different perceptions and understanding of the protocols, especially the one concerned with the creation of the Intergovernmental Commission.

Before signing the protocols, the countries did not have bilateral relations. Borders were closed since 1993 (Naegele *Caucasus*). During the Soviet period it was even forbidden to talk about the Armenian Genocide within the country (Naegele *Caucasus*). Maybe the protocols were an extremely radical turn in the Armenian-Turkish stalemate?

Furthermore, the cumulative victimization of Armenians continued for more than a century, starting from the Hamidian massacres in the 19th century (Hovannisian 1997: xii cited in Kielsgard 2008: 36). The outcome of the victimization process is the perception of Turks as an inimical people. Therefore, if we try to frame the term "dialogue" in the image drawn above, it will mean that both parties have to make a step forward in order to start the dialogue. For Armenians, that will be changing its attitude towards Turkey and Turkish people,[3] and for Turkey, admitting the fact of Armenian Genocide or not labeling it as the massacres committed by the government of Young Turks.

This explains how far apart the two societies (Armenian and Turkish) are in terms of perception and understanding the same issues.

The other major issue which needs to be taken into account is no preconditions, especially as the fact that the Turkish government now links the ratification of the protocols with the resolution of Nagorno-Karabakh conflict (Tocci et al. 2007: 27). During a recent official visit to the US, Turkish Prime Minister Erdoğan emphasized in his press conference that Azerbaijan-Armenia relations (or the Karabakh conflict) are connected to the normalization process of Turkish-Armenian relations. The Turkish Prime Minister has also repeated this view in other places and during other state visits (President Obama and the Protocol 2010). Speculation over the issue of reconciliation closes the doors for any further steps in the process.

The important thing in such cases is that each of the parties should hold a real intent for reconciliation.[4] Avoiding fruitless discussions on political will, let us assume, for the purposes of this paper, that both parties have a commitment to reconcile, and to return to the shaping of the mandate of the commission. It is agreed that it will be crucial for the Commission to clarify what happened, i.e. to establish a common truth and history about the past.

---

3   A very good point made in Shamsey 2002: 368.

4   This might mean that in order to have an effective reconciliation structure there needs to be a third party intervention. For example international organization, like UN, OSCE, Council of Europe, EU in cooperation with key NGOs in the field of Human Rights, such as the Human Rights Watch or Amnesty International, could do a better job. A similar model is suggested in Payaslian 2008: 417-420.

However, it should be emphasized that reconciliation is a mutual process, which requires cooperation and mutual understanding. The mandate, scope, funding, power and other necessary issues are not regulated properly in the text of the protocols; the latter only provides the basis for such regulation. Hence, the parties will need an instrument, for example an addendum to the main treaty, which will define all of the mentioned issues.

4. Armenian-Turkish Controversy. Restorative and Retributive Approaches?

At first sight, this unique controversy might not well fit in the framework of the logic of restorative justice. As conflict situations and problems can be of a various nature, each one of them requires an individual approach in tackling the issues raised by that specific conflict. The cases of restorative justice show the fallacy of "truth or justice" dichotomy (Lutz 2006: 327). This clearly states that the notion 'restorative justice' is, and should be, a flexible concept, to include the rich variety of situations and to serve its purpose. One of the fundamental concepts of restorative justice is the "acknowledgement and acceptance of fault for the wrong committed by the offender with recognition of the harm caused (with apology, if not coerced)" (Menkel-Meadow 2007: 10.4). From the restorative perspective, retributive punishment is seen as insufficient for reestablishing a peaceful social coexistence, in contrast restorative paradigm is only concerned with the future, and is not concentrated on the guilt of the offender. Restorative justice is more oriented at making the offender conscious of the harm caused, admitting responsibility and trying to repair this harm (Uprimny & Saffon: 1-2). This is crucial for the Armenian-Turkish reconciliation process, as in this case, we need a very balanced approach in order to achieve actual reconciliation.

John Shamsey emphasizes that in the case of the Armenian Genocide, establishing a Truth and Reconciliation Commission (TRC) may be the best avenue available, because of several reasons: no amnesty issue, no sense of guilty individuals escaping punishment, and others (Shamsey 2002: 379). As the Armenian-Turkish controversy requires a historical approach, the traditional notion and understanding of a TRC should be adapted respectively.

As the history of the Armenian Genocide illustrates, when there is no justice in response to the extermination of a people, the result is that victims are led to take the law into their own hands, both to exact retribution and to draw attention to the denial of the historical fact (Cassese 1998: 1). This indicates the importance of healing past wounds for mutual relations.[5]

To fill this gap and to pave the way for actual reconciliation, it is more appropriate to apply, firstly, retributive justice, as described by renowned scholar on the issue of Armenian Genocide Vahakn N. Dadrian, (Dadrian 1998: in Yale J.I.L.) and which should include the legal qualification of the heinous crimes committed, with relevant legal consequences. The notion of restorative justice is more applicable to different fact patterns than the one in our case (Menkel-Meadow 2007: 161-187).

---

5   Though, Cassese brings the example to argue in favor of international criminal justice vs. forgiving. However, the example can at the same time be utilized to prove the need for reconciliation, moreover, if we consider the features of the Armenian-Turkish affair.

The factor that makes this situation unique is, first of all, the gap in time between the human rights violations and the attempt to reconciliation. There are no perpetrators, hence, no issue of individual criminal responsibility. Considering that this is more or less evident, the focus of the sub-commission established by the protocols should be more focused on reconciliation based on comprehensive historical research.

Although there are no perpetrators in the present instance, however, the aim of retribution can be accomplished through the legal qualification of the conduct committed by the Ottoman Empire. Even if no direct or actual retribution is possible, the moral one is fundamental for starting the reconciliation process in this particular case.

Therefore, in this specific instance, we have the elements of different types of justice – historical, restorative and retributive, which makes this case a unique one.

Thus, to make the overall aim of reconciliation feasible, we have to deviate slightly from the wording incorporated in the protocols. Departing slightly from the wording of the protocols, the overall aim of the mechanisms foreseen should be:

1) making the perpetrator, in this particular case Turkey, conscious of the heinous crimes committed against the Armenians, which will take the form of acknowledgment;

2) helping the Armenians to overcome the victimization; and,

3) paving the way for further reconciliatory processes between the two nations. The indicated objectives can be achieved through a careful implementation of a thorough mechanism of reconciliation, which still needs to be developed.

5. Prospectus and Challenges; Necessary Preconditions for Ensuring Reconciliation

Furthermore, acknowledgement should be the starting point on the way of reconciliation and should take the form of a legal qualification.

The core problem for Armenians is the fact of continued denial, which entails victimization of a whole nation (Kielsgard 2008: 36). However, the healing of past victimization is crucial for successful reconciliation (Staub 2006: 873). A valuable observation made by an Armenian ethnographer states that:

[W]hen it comes to improving or "healing" relations, as is shown by the experience of former Yugoslavia, Rwanda, as well as Chile and Argentina, the past continues to torment because it is *not* past. For the simple reason that as long as justice is not administered, historic realities have not been condemned as crimes, and the guilty have not been held responsible, those facts will continue to be rooted in the collective memory of their historic past as well as of the present (Marutyan 2010: 44).

The collective historical memory shapes the national identity (Marutyan 2007: 24), thus, making the status of a victim a part of the Armenian identity. Acknowledging the fact of atrocities committed is the initial and most crucial step to be taken in the reconciliation process. Without this step, the entire logic of reconciliation will be devastated and jeopardized.

As a good example, which is more or less close to Armenian-Turkish issue, is the fact of acknowledgement by Poland. For a long time, the role of non-German populations as collaborators and perpetrators of the Holocaust has always been part of the Jewish narrative, and was, and to a degree, continues to be denied in Eastern Europe. In Poland, a major shift took place as a result of the publication of the book *Neighbor* by Jan Gross (2000), which dealt with the massacre of the Jews in Jedwabne. It has led to extensive public discussion, formal investigations and commissions, presidential apologies, further ongoing investigations of the extent of similar events. Fortuitously, Poland had established the Institute of National Remembrance for the purposes of investigating Nazi and Communist crimes (Barkan 2008: 393). This example indicates the importance of the recognition and the acknowledgement of the crime by the perpetrator.

Another example comes from German colonial history. From 1904 to 1908, the colonial German military in the South-West Africa, or present day Namibia, exterminated about 65,000 of approximately 80,000 members of the Herero ethnic group. German settlers wanted Herero land, and the Herero resisted giving it up. In January 1904, the Herero rebelled. The German commander, Lothar Von Trotha, reacted by issuing explicit orders to exterminate all Herero men, women, and children (Howard-Hassman & Lombardo 2008: 100). Modern Germany has recognized that its predecessor state committed this genocide. In August 2004 German Minister for Economic Cooperation and Development Heidemarie Wieczorek-Zeul attended a commemoration of the genocide's hundredth anniversary, where she apologized on behalf of all Germans (Sher 2005: 181 200 cited in Howard-Hassman & Lombardo 2008: 100).

The core dichotomy in the terms that the two nations face is the problem of labeling the perpetrated acts. Armenians forge the policy of worldwide recognition of the Armenian Genocide, while Turkey will barely ever admit to such a labeling. Therefore, it is not that simple for Armenians, especially the Diaspora, to give up the policy of labeling the heinous crimes committed by Young Turks regime as genocide. In this particular case, the labeling the acts as genocide is necessary for emphasizing the fact that Young Turks had the "*...intent to destroy, in whole or in part"* (Convention on the Prevention 1951) the Armenians as a group.

The issue of labeling is especially a sensitive one among Diaspora Armenians. The Diaspora has been and continues lobbying for the recognition of Armenian Genocide in many countries. This means that the further steps which are going to be taken by the Republic of Armenia will greatly be influenced by the Diaspora, simply because the psychology of victim has been a powerful factor for safeguarding and preserving the national identity in a foreign society and country (Libaridian 2004: 5-6).

At the outset of Armenian massacres, international law was rather uncodified and underdeveloped. Especially in the human rights area, which was strengthened by treaty regimes incorporating rudimentary principles of human rights, but with an ineffective extradition regime, resulted in a preliminary grounding in domestic criminal jurisdiction regarding territoriality principles (Brierly 1963: 402-3). Several ministers of the Young Turk regime were found guilty by a court martial in Turkey of 'the organization and execution of crime of massacre' against Armenian people (Dadrian 1989: 307). The term 'genocide' was later introduced by Raphael Lemkin, having in mind the annihilation of Armenians (Schabas 2009: 29-30). The efforts of Lemkin paved the way for the adoption of the Genocide Convention in 1948.

It is important to stress that a number of legal treatises qualify the massacres of Armenians committed as genocide. After the adoption of the Genocide Convention, the United States government told the International Court of Justice that 'the Turkish massacres of Armenians' were one of the 'outstanding examples of the crime of genocide' (Written Statement 1951).

In a comprehensive opinion on the legal issues of Armenian Genocide, Geoffrey Robertson QC expresses the following view with regard to labeling the acts perpetrated before the adoption of the Genocide Convention as "genocide:"

> [I] do not consider that the Genocide Convention is retroactive and I do not accept the view of those legal scholars who believe that the treaty was declaratory of pre-existing international law and thus argue that it can be applied retrospectively ... But plainly the term "genocide" may be applied to massacres before the passage of the Convention: those who drafted and debated it spoke repeatedly of other historical events as "genocide" even though they had occurred centuries before (the decimation of the Spartans and the destruction of the citizens of Carthage provide early examples)... (Robertson 2009: 14).

Let us briefly reflect on the experience with the Holocaust. The main issue, for which the Nuremberg trials have been criticized, was the fact that the perpetrators were prosecuted under the material rules created after the commission of the crimes. United States Supreme Court Justice William O. Douglas indicated:

> [N]o matter how finely the lawyers analyzed it, the crime for which the Nazis were tried had never been formalized as a crime with the definiteness requires by our legal standards, nor outlawed with a death penalty by the international community. By our standards that crime arose under an ex post facto law. Goering *et al.* deserved severe punishment. But their guilt did not justify us in substituting power for principle (Kennedy 1964: 190 cited in Goldstone & Smith 2009: 54).

In such circumstances, a balance should be found between the legal formalism and liberal legal approaches. Understandably, the heinous nature of the atrocities committed by Nazi Germany justifies the approach. The International Criminal Tribunal for Rwanda in *Prosecutor v. Kambanda* noted, "...the crimes prosecuted by the Nuremberg Tribunal, namely the holocaust of the Jews or the "Final Solution", were very much constitutive of genocide, but they could not be defined as such because the crime of genocide was not defined until later" (Prosecutor v. Jean Kambanda 1998: 14). In his opening speech, Justice Robert H. Jackson emphasized:

[T]he privilege of opening the first trial in history for crimes against the peace of the world imposes grave responsibility. The wrongs which we seek to condemn and punish, have been so calculated, so malignant and so devastating, that civilization cannot tolerate their being ignored, because it cannot survive their being repeated (International Military Tribunal 1946).

The speech gives the impression of the time and the gravity of the situation, which requires not being limited by the formalistic restraints of law. However, the major difference between the Nuremberg Trial and the situation at hand is that we did not have such favorable political atmosphere, which was crucial for the success of the trial.

Summing up the mentioned, one should be convinced that labeling the massacres of Armenians in Ottoman Empire as genocide reasonably fits into the logic and practice of contemporary international law. Moreover, for the purposes of the present study, it is important to view the issues from a wider angle, setting aside more narrow and formalistic legal approaches.

In a study conducted by the request of the European Parliament, it was emphasized that the historical research should avoid a narrow focus on the genocide question. Turks and Armenians share five centuries of common history, which the nationalist narratives constructed in the 20th century have almost entirely erased from the memory on both sides of border (Tocci et al., 2007: 27). It is hard to agree with the assertion, as there is no point in understanding the common history if the initial step, i.e. the acknowledgement of the wrong committed has not taken place.

"The moral, political, and legal consequences that follow from withholding or applying the genocide label vary with the circumstance, and … can truncate options for dealing with the situation," (Kelly, 2007-2008: 148) and at this very instance, we are still talking of a moral retribution, as for the legal consequences a separate procedure that will be needed. On October 10, 2007, the U.S. House of Representatives Foreign Affairs Committee adopted a resolution, which labeled the atrocities genocide. The Turkish ambassador to the U.S. reacted to the decision by stating that being labeled as precursors to Hitler "is a very injurious move to the psyche of the Turkish people" (Unearthing the Past 2007: 150).

Nevertheless, it is undisputable that Turkey has to acknowledge this and adopt the labeling, and that this is the least that Turkey can do for the process to begin. We will not even consider other legal consequences that may follow from that kind of recognition, as it will not fit into the framework of this study. The issues of legal consequences should be subject to a separate procedure that can be established simultaneously with other reconciliatory institutions.

As noted by a Canadian international lawyer, "nothing emboldens a criminal so much as the knowledge he can get away with a crime. That was the message the failure to prosecute for the Armenian massacre gave to the Nazis. We ignore the lesson of the Holocaust at our peril" (Matas 1989-1990: 104 cited in Dadrian 1998: 532, in Yale J.I.L.). The citation above indicates and emphasizes the importance of not only the acknowledgement of the conduct, but also the necessity of a proper legal qualification with relevant legal consequences.

In conclusion, it should be emphasized that a need for a legal-historical appraisal of the atrocities committed in the Ottoman Empire is an indispensable precondition for moving forward towards the process of reconciliation. This is a necessary retributive step that Turkey should take in order to open the way for an atmosphere of mutual understanding.

6. Concluding Remarks

Thus, it is essential to bear in mind that the mechanism can only work if both parties have the overall political will. Recent political developments between the two countries have now created a deadlock. Moreover, the protocols, if they would have been successful, could only represent the will of both parties to start the process. The road for construing a viable mechanism of reconciliation requires an extreme commitment and patience. One should bear in mind that the process has priorities that have to be observed for being able to move forward. First of all, the acknowledgement by the current government of the Republic of Turkey of the heinous crimes committed by its predecessor government and the legal qualification of those atrocities as 'genocide' are of utmost importance for commencing the process and paving the way for the operation of the mechanisms, which, though superficially, are prescribed by the protocols.

One of the core problems of Armenian and Turkish societies has been appropriately described by a renowned Armenian historian, Michigan University Professor Gerard J. Libaridian, in stating that: "… not only were the Turkish and Armenian Diaspora totally alienated from each other, but also the logic of the position of each evolved almost independently from each other, neither having to account for the failures or successes of their policies against the other's means and resources" (Libaridian 2005: 3). The idea that the author tries to stress in his work is that the two nations, which co-existed side by side without any interaction, even the scholars of both nations were not meant to promote understand of each other's position, but to state positions and satisfy their own audience (Libaridian 2005: 3). Unfortunately, the political atmosphere is far from being favorable for commencing the process described in the present paper. Currently, the issue of the protocols and further Armenian-Turkish reconciliation has turned into a political tool for Turkey to exert pressure on Armenia regarding the Nagorno-Karabakh conflict. Obviously, Turkey has barely any political or economic interest in starting the reconciliation process with Armenia. Surely, the reconciliation is much more beneficial for Armenia, both economically and politically, and thus, it is Armenia that should trigger the process using available political and diplomatic tools. In such circumstances, the full membership of Turkey in the EU may shift the attitude towards the Armenian question within Turkish governmental structures. To put is more precisely, Armenia will only gain if Turkey becomes an EU member state, in many respects. Accordingly, the reasonable path for triggering Armenian-Turkish relations is the European integration of Turkey.

References

Barkan E. (2008). Can Memory of Genocide Lead to Reconciliation? *The Armenian Genocide: Cultural and Ethical Legacies*, edited by Richard Hovannisian. New Brunswick (USA) and London (UK): Transaction Publishers.

Brierly J. L. (1963). *The Law of Nations.* Oxford: Clarendon Press.

Bloxham D. (2005). *The Great Game of Genocide: Imperialism, Nationalism and the destruction of the Ottoman Armenians.* Oxford: Oxford University Press.

Cassese A. (1998). Reflections on International Criminal Justice. *Modern Law Review*, vol. 61, 1 (January 1998). http://www.jstor.org/pss/1097333

Convention on the Prevention and Punishment of the Crime of Genocide. (1951). 78 U.N.T.S. 277. http://www1.umn.edu/humanrts/instree/x1cppcg.htm

Dadrian V. N. (1989). Genocide as a Problem of National and International Law: the World War I Armenian Case and It's Contemporary Legal Ramifications. *Yale Journal of International Law* 14, 2: 221-334.

Dadrian V. N. (1998). The Armenian Genocide and the Legal and Political Issues in the Failure to Prevent or to Punish the Crime. *University of West Los Angeles Law Review* 29: 43-78.

Dadrian V. N. (1998). The Historical and Legal Interconnections between the Armenian Genocide and the Jewish Holocaust: From Impunity to Retributive Justice. *Yale Journal of International Law* 23, 2: 503-559.

Gardner Feldman L. (1999). The Principle and Practice of 'reconciliation' in German Foreign Policy: Relations with France, Israel, Poland and the Czech Republic. *International Affairs*, vol. 75, Issue 2: 333-356.

Goldstone R. J. and Smith A. M. (2009). *International Judicial Institutions: The Architecture of International Justice at Home and Abroad.* London; New York: Routledge.

Hovannisian R. G. (1997). Introduction. *The Armenian People from Ancient to Modern Times*, vol. I, edited by Richard G. Hovannisian. NY: St. Martin's Press, pp. VII-XI.

Rhoda E. Howard-Hassmann & Lombardo A.P. (2008). *Reparations to Africa.* Philadelphia, PA: University of Pennsylvania Press.

International Military Tribunal. (1946). The Trial of German Major War Criminals by the International Military Tribunal Sitting at Nuremberg Germany (Commencing 20th November, 1945) 3 (1946) Mr. Justice Robert H. Jackson.

Kennedy J. F. (1964). *Profiles in Courage.* New York: Harper and Row.

Kelly M. J. (2007-2008). "Genocide" – The Power of a Label. Case of Western Reserve Journal of International Law, 40, pp. 147-162.

Kielsgard M. D. (2008). Restorative Justice for the Armenians, Resolved: It's the Least We Can Do. *Connecticut Journal of International Law*, Vol. 24, No. 1.

Levene M. (2005). *The Rise of the West and the Coming of Genocide.* London; New York: I.B. Tauris.

Libaridian G. J. (2004). *Modern Armenia: people, nation, state.* New Brunswick, N.J.: Transaction Publishers.

Libaridian G. J. (2005). The Past as a Prison, The Past as a different future, *Turkish Policy Quarterly*, vol. 4, No. 4, http://www.esiweb.org/pdf/esi_turkey_tpq_id_45.pdf

Lutz E. (2006). *Transitional Justice: Lessons Learned and the Road Ahead. Transitional Justice in the Twenty-First Century: beyond Truth versus Justice,* edited by Naomi Roth-Arriaza, Javier Mariezcurrena. Cambridge, UK; New York: Cambridge University Press.

Marutyan H. (2010). *Iconography of Armenian Identity, Volume I: Memory of the Genocide and Kharabakh Movement.* Yerevan: "Gitutyun" Publishing House.

Marutyan H. (2007). Collective and Historical Memory in the Dialogue of Cultures, *21st Century,* № 2 http://www.noravank.am/file/article/312_en.pdf

Matas D. (1989-90). Prosecuting Crimes Against Humanity: The Lessons of World War I, *13 Fordham International Law Journal*, 86.

McAdams J. A. (2009). The Issue that Won't Go Away. *Historical Justice in International Perspective. How Societies Are Trying to Right the Wrongs of the Past*, edited by Manfred Berg, Bernd Schaefer. Washington, D.C.: German Historical Institute; Cambridge; New York: Cambridge University Press.

Menkel-Meadow C. (2007). Restorative Justice: What Is It and Does It Work? *Annual Review of Law and Social Science.* 3:10.1–10.27. http://arjournals.annualreviews.org/doi/pdf/10.1146/annurev.lawsocsci.2.081805.110005

Naegele J. Caucasus: Burden of History Blocks Turkish-Armenian Border, Radio Free Europe Radio Liberty-Online, http://www.rferl.org/nca/features/1998/07/F.RU.980728135300.html (last accessed 7 February 2010)

Payaslian S. (2008). Anatomy of Post-Genocide Reconciliation. *The Armenian Genocide: Cultural and Ethical*

Legacies, edited by Richard Hovannisian. New Brunswick, N.J.: Transaction Publishers.

Protocol on Development of Relations between the Republic of Armenia and the Republic of Turkey (2009). http://www.armeniaforeignministry.com/pr_09/20091013_protocol1.pdf

President Obama and the Protocols. (2010). *History of Truth.com.* http://www.historyoftruth.com/authors/president-obama-and-the-protocols-5222.html

Prosecutor versus Jean Kambanda. (1998). Case. No. International Criminal Tribunal for Rwanda, 97-23-S, Judgment.

Reid J. J. (1992). Total War, the Annihilation Ethic, and the Armenian Genocide, 1870-1918. *The Armenian Genocide. History, Politics, Ethics*, edited by Richard G. Hovhannisian. New York: St. Martin's Press.

Robertson Geoffrey QC. (2009). Was there an Armenian Genocide? Opinion, 9 October http://groong.usc.edu/Geoffrey-**Robertson**-QC-**Genocide**.pdf

Schabas W. A. (2009). *Genocide in International Law.* Cambridge University Press.

Shamsey J. (2002). 80 Years Too Late: the International Criminal Court and the 20th Century First Genocide. *Journal of Transnational Law and Policy*, 11.

Sher G. (2005). Transgenerational Compensation, *Philosophy and Public Affairs*, volume 33, Issue 2, pp. 181–200.

Staub E. (2006). Reconciliation after Genocide, Mass Killings, or Intractable Conflict: Understanding the Roots of Violence, Psychological Recovery, and Steps toward a General Theory. Political Psychology, Vol. 27, No. 6, pp. 867-894.

The Treaties of Peace 1919-1923. (1924). Vol. II. New York: Carnegie endowment for international peace.

The Declaration of Independence of the Republic of Armenia (1990), 23 August, the English translation is available on the web-site of the Ministry of Foreign Affairs of Armenia http://www.armeniaforeignministry.com/htms/doi.html

Turkey says Armenian top court's ruling on protocols not acceptable. (2010). *Today's Zaman Istanbul*, 20 January, http://www.todayszaman.com/tz-web/news-199092-turkey-says-armenian-top-courts-ruling-on-protocols-not-acceptable.html

Tocci N. (coordinating editor and author), B. Gültekin-Punsmann, L. Simão, N. Tavitian. (2007). The Closed Armenia-Turkey Border: Economic and Social Effects, Including Those on the People; and Implications for the Overall Situation in the Region, *European Parliament's Committee on Foreign Affairs (European Parliament)* http://www.europarl.europa.eu/activities/committees/studies/download.do?file=18288

Uprimny R. and Saffon M. P. Transitional Justice, Restorative Justice and Reconciliation. Some Insights from the Colombian Case, *'Coming to Terms' with Reconciliation – Working Paper Library* http://global.wisc.edu/reconciliation/library/papers_open/saffon.pdf

Unearthing the Past, Endangering the Future. (2007). *Economist*. Oct. 20.

Written Statement of the United States of America. (1951). *Reservations to the Convention on the Prevention of Genocide (Advisory Opinion) and Punishment of the Crime of Genocide*, Pleadings, Oral Arguments, Documents.

Diba Nigar Göksel

Reconciliation Initiatives: Emerging Patterns in Turkey

Ms. Diba Nigar Göksel joined the European Stability Initiative (ESI) in 2004 where she is Senior Analyst and Caucasus Coordinator. Since 2003 she is also Editor-in-Chief of Turkish Policy Quarterly (TPQ). Diba Nigar Göksel writes regularly for the "On Turkey" series of the German Marshall Fund and she is a frequent contributor to Armenian, Azerbaijani and Turkish publications on issues concerning the Caucasus and Turkish foreign policy. For the past three years Nigar has been leading ESI's research in Armenia and Azerbaijan , and has travelled extensively in both countries, with a view to analyzing socioeconomic and institutional trends. She has also closely followed the social and political dynamics in Turkey towards these two countries.

In the last ten years, steps aimed at reconciliation between Turkey and Armenia have exponentially increased. Armenians and Turks have been meeting each other regularly and visiting each other's country more and more frequently every year. Over the course of the 2000s the Turkish drive for reconciliation with Armenians has been a result of the interplay, or synergy, of three main components: general democratization, driven by an intellectual elite and aided by Turkey's EU accession process; bilateral civil society projects – funded almost entirely by Western sources; and diplomatic initiatives between the two countries.

Donor-funded reconciliation projects between non-governmental organizations (NGOs) have fostered more informed media coverage about "the other," forged links between businessmen, youth, artists, and academics, and helped to create a community of stakeholders in the reconciliation process. However, a significant gap exists between those involved in bilateral initiatives and the wider public at large. This reality also has policy implications, by limiting the maneuvering space of decision makers, and shaping political expedience patterns. This paper seeks to provide a perspective from the Turkish side about both what has been achieved and the weak links of the civilian component of Turkish-Armenian rapprochement over the past decade.

1. Democratization in Turkey and the beginnings of a new debate
Over the past decade, strides in Turkey's democratization have empowered critical thinking within segments of society, increased the freedom to explore and express new opinions on history, and have helped to connect with Armenian counterparts. In turn, more and more Turkish historians and writers have challenged the official "1915 narrative".

In 2000, Professor Halil Berktay of Sabancı University gave a full-page interview to the daily newspaper "Radikal," placing responsibility for the death of

600,000 Armenians on the top echelon of the Turkish nationalist movement leading the Ottoman government at the time ("Young Turks") (Duzel 2000). This interview was emblemic of a new development in Turkey – a debate of the Armenian question: wheras previously challenging historical taboos on this issue had previously been limited to relatively more marginal circles of society (i.e. reaching and influencing a narrow audience) (Noah's Dove Returns 2009) it was now on the verge of becoming mainstream.

Since the turn of the century, Turkish books uncovering different facets of the Armenian question, such as Fethiye Cetin's *Anneannem* (My Grandmother) in 2004, Elif Şafak's *The Bastard of Istanbul* in 2009, for some examples, were not only published, but became bestsellers. The 2005 publication, *90. Yılında Ermeni Trajedisi – 1915'te Ne Oldu* (The Armenian Tragedy in its 90th year – What happened in 1915?), edited by *Hürriyet* columnist Sefa Kaplan, provided a wide range of views on the issue. Ece Temelkuran's *Ağrı'nın Derinliği* (The Depth of Ararat) in 2008 was another example of the diversification and mainstreaming of Turks challenging taboos on this topic.

In September 2005, a conference on the fate of Ottoman Armenians was held at Bilgi University, entitled "Ottoman Armenians during the Decline of the Empire: Issues of Scientific Responsibility and Democracy." Many panelists referred to the 1915 tragedy as a "genocide" and "the world kept turning," to borrow a phrase from the headlines of the daily "Radikal" newspaper at the time (Radikal, 25 September 2005).[1]

Another groundbreaking event was the apology campaign of December 2008, in which a number of signatures were collected protesting against the "insensitivity showed to and the denial of the Great Catastrophe that the Ottoman Armenians were subjected to in 1915" (Academics' Armenia apology to test taboos 2011).

The widening of debate was aided by certain policy improvements as well. On 30 April 2008, amendments to Article 301 of the Turkish Criminal Code were adopted by the Turkish parliament.[2] Although there is still leeway for judges to prosecute statements "that offend the Turkish nation," the amendments expanded the scope of the freedom of expression, reducing the maximum sentence and requiring the minister of justice's consent for the launching of a criminal case regarding the charge of insulting the nation." The leader of the ultra-nationalist Grand Union of Jurists Association, Kemal Kerinçsiz, who had been in the forefront of initiating court cases against such prominent names as authors Elif Şafak, Orhan Pamuk, and others, was imprisoned in January 2008 as part of an investigation against a secret ultra-nationalist network within Turkey.

Another positive policy-related development was a change to the Foundation Law, lifting some obstacles particularly relevant for the property rights of Armenian minority-owned (as well as other) foundations – and opening the way for

---

1   For additional views on this event from the same newspaper: www.radikal.com.tr/haber.php?haberno=165025
2   Novelist Orhan Pamuk and "Agos" newspaper editor Hrant Dink have also been prosecuted under Article 301.

the restoration of unused Armenian churches in Anatolia.

The relative mainstreaming of a more open debate about Turkey's joint history with Armenians has not only pushed Ankara to adjust policies and practices,[3] but has also added nuance to the perception of a monolithic Turkish nation among Armenians. The outpouring of sadness and solidarity among Turks following the murder of Turkish-Armenian journalist Hrant Dink in January 2007, for example, stimulated the breaking of traditional stereotypes among Armenians.

Armenian television coverage at the time broadcast footage from the mourning during the funeral procession, and the subsequent debate reflected in the written media was emblematic of both changing and unchanging perceptions – and evidence of a new, more pluralist discourse within Armenia regarding Turkey and Turks.

While the nationalist Armenian Revolutionary Federation (ARF) youth group held a protest with banners alleging that "The genocide is continuing" and "Turkey, your hands are bloody!", the daily newspaper affiliated with the ARF, "Yerkir," explained that "European civil society should be alert and conclude from this murder that there was never and there is no democracy and freedom of speech in Turkey" (Yerkir, 22 January 2007).

Levon Melik-Shahnazaryan, an Armenian political scientist, noting that while some were claiming Turkey was becoming more democratic and tolerant, argued that it was only "window dressing," contending that "today we see the same phenomenon which was in the past: flowers and banner for the outside world and internal readiness to kill in reality. A nation's mentality is quite conservative, and does not change with time" (PanARMENIAN.Net , 27 January 2007).

Others argued in a different vein, however. For example, "Haykakan Zhamanak" newspaper columnist Anna Hakobyan, known for her critical views on Turkey, wrote:

"The scene on TV was really impressive. The waves of hundreds of thousands of people accompanying Hrant Dink's coffin were impressive; the applause that was audible from time to time was impressive; "We are all Armenians, we are all Hrant Dink", "Stop Article 301", "Shoulder to shoulder against fascism" posters and similar sounding calls were impressive" (Hakobyan 2007).

2. The evolving scene of NGO projects

Throughout the course of the 1990s, there was relatively little contact between Turkish and Armenian NGOs, and press coverage during that period reflected little information and much emotion in covering issues relating to Armenia.. There were various reasons for this situation.

First, the two countries were separated by the USSR border since the 1920s – and much of the coverage of Armenians

---

3   Including the replacement of the hardline president of the Turkish Historical Society in August 2008.

and the Armenian issue was negatively affected by the terrorism conducted against Turkish diplomats by the Armenian Secret Army for the Liberation of Armenia (ASALA) throughout the 1970s and 1980s. Atrocities committed during the Nagorno Karabagh war also inflamed Turkish public opinion.[4] Armenian pursuit of genocide recognition in parliaments around the world was perceived as an act of hostility against Turkey. Using the Anti-Terror Law as well as the Turkish Penal Code, court cases were repeatedly launched against intellectuals challenging Turkish state policies and rhetoric. Legislation, under which Turkish NGO's functioned, was also restrictive. In short, the climate in the 1990s was largely negative in Turkey, and not conducive to the already weak civil society organizations to make overtures to Armenian counterparts (of which there were, of course, few at the time).

In the 1990s, the bulk of bilateral civil society engagement involved Turkish and Armenian academics meeting in various European cities to present historical analyses and discussion.[5] Most Armenian participants were from among the Armenian diaspora, while Turkish participants were usually left-leaning liberals who found themselves at odds with the Turkish state on numerous human rights issues since the 1970s and 80s. Reactions to such gatherings and the publications produced in their aftermath were highly negative in the Turkish press, and occasionally penalized by the state in the form of the banning of books and the initiation of court cases.

By 2000, an era more conducive to Turkish and Armenian NGO collaboration had dawned. The Karabagh-related anger within Turkey lost some of its vigor, NGOs were stronger, Turkey had been admitted as a candidate for EU membership, Ankara was reaching out to neighbors with which its relations had been problematic – such as Syria, Greece and Russia – and the country was undergoing a dramatic course of legislative reform.

Bilateral NGO projects began on a more systematic basis in 2001 with financing from the US State Department, managed by the American University's Center for Global Peace in Washington, DC. The first wave of approximately 13 projects lasted until early 2005. Of these, the one with the highest profile was the Turkish Armenian Reconciliation Commission (TARC).

At the time of the start of these projects, the issue was novel not only for the NGOs who got involved, but for the public and media representatives in both countries as well. Negative reactions from nationalist groups and parties of both countries erupted, but with lessening fervor and impact as the interaction become more common.

An evaluation of the strengths and weaknesses of the projects managed under the supervision of the American University's Center for Global Peace was prepared with the support of the Eurasia Partnership Foundation (EPF) in 2006, released in the form of a book by the Yerevan-based International Center for Human Development (ICHD) (Track 2

---

4   Depicted in detail from the press coverage presented in Hurç 2008.
5   Exceptions include the advocacy of an open border by the Turkish Armenian Business Development Council (TABDC) since 1997 and such personal initiatives as the trip to Armenia by Gurbuz Capan, then Esenyurt mayor. Details see in Mkrtchyan 2011.

Diplomacy 2006). The book pointed out that many of the projects seemed to have had little impact beyond increasing familiarity between a narrow circle of people from both countries towards "the other," fond memories of socialization, and providing temporary livelihood to the NGOs involved. In 2005, David Phillips – who was the facilitator of TARC and was also leading the planning phase of the bilateral NGO projects – also authored a book, primarily relating the experiences of TARC entitled, *Unsilencing the Past: Track Two Diplomacy and Turkish-Armenian Reconciliation* (Phillips 2009).

From 2006-7 onwards, a new phase can be identified in Turkish-Armenian reconciliation efforts among civil society. A diverse group of donors with experience working in the Caucasus region started to support Turkish-Armenian rapprochement projects. The range of actors from both Armenia and Turkey involved in the bilateral work expanded. The increased traffic and coverage "normalized" interaction between musicians, businessmen, youth, think tanks, media, and opinion makers. This process was aided by high-level contacts between the Turkish and Armenian authorities, which "legitimized" the notion of interaction between the two peoples. In this sense, the visit of President Abdullah Gül to Yerevan for the World Cup qualifying football match in September 2008 was most noteworthy. The changing paradigms in Turkey's domestic scene, described in the previous section of this article, also positively effected bilateral NGO collaboration.

Funding from the US Agency for International Development (USAID), dispersed through the implementation of the Eurasia Partnership Foundation (which has an office in Armenia, although not in Turkey), provided grants for Turkish-Armenian reconciliation projects since 2006. Grants from, among others, the Swiss, German, British, Norwegian, and British diplomatic corps, German foundations (such as the Friedrich Naumann and Friedrich Ebert Stiftungs), and the Open Society Institute (OSI) have helped to diversify sources of funding and widen the scope of stakeholders.[6]

Although NGO activities are still on the rise in terms of frequency and the range of actors involved, a plateau may be discerned in terms of the relative added value (the marginal returns) of projects. A circle of activists and intellectuals on both sides are accustomed to traveling to the other country and working with colleagues from the other country, as well as having enjoyable times together. The newspapers and TVs cover a wider range of views. There is already a 'normalcy' in meeting and hearing each other. But what next? On the questions that the bilateral stalemate boils down to, and in terms of expectations and priorities of the two societies, is there, or should there necessarily be, fundamental change to celebrate yet?

3. The impact of civil society initiatives on Turkish policymaking

Despite the boom in bilateral NGO collaboration and changes in the debates reflected in the media, progress on the

---

6   A manual of bilateral projects and actors in this field can be accessed at: www.esiweb.org/index.php?lang=en&id=477

diplomatic front has stalled, for now. And while initiatives by liberal historians and intellectuals in Turkey have certainly expanded the space for debate and broken down taboos in Turkey, questions abound about the pace and process of this reality transforming official narratives and/or views of the wider public. These disjoints have raised questions about the impact and value of the civilian reconciliation efforts.

Official normalization of relations

From the Turkish perspective, there are roughly three obstacles to Turkey-Armenia official reconciliation: disagreement on how to discuss and come to terms with history, territorial demands voiced by some Armenian circles, combined with the lack of formal recognition of the joint border by Armenia, and finally, the lack of progress in the resolution of the Karabagh conflict. Detailed accounts of these three problems have been related by representatives of both sides over the years, thus this article will not attempt to elaborate. Suffice to say that to the extent that there is unwillingness and/or concern in Turkey about moving forward in normalizing relations with Armenia, it is these three issues that are commonly evoked. It is also these three issues that the two bilateral protocols (which were signed but not ratified) meant to address (Göksel May 2010). Therefore, one way to assess the impact of NGO projects and civilian initiatives on the policies of Ankara is to gauge how much these projects affect the political calculus of Ankara.

To affect the political calculus in Ankara the single most determinant variable is Turkish public opinion. And to design NGO projects that would have an impact on the Turkish society at large, an important starting point would be to have a comprehensive public opinion poll geared at understanding what the fears and concerns among different constituencies in Turkey are regarding reconciliation with Armenia. For example, is there concern about the implications of the word 'genocide' among Turks living in provinces where Armenians used to also live because of concerns of territorial implications? Do acts of the organized Armenian diaspora that are perceived to be hostile negatively affect the image of Armenians among the Turkish society? Do Turks whose ancestors were ethnically cleansed from neighboring regions (such as the Balkans and the Caucasus) have more or less empathy when it comes to the plight of Armenians in Anatolia? How important is it for ordinary Turks for the plight of Azerbaijanis who were purged from their homes around Karabagh to be remedied? Without knowing the answer of such questions, it is difficult to design outreach for overcoming obstacles within the Turkish society to reconciliation. Designing NGO projects with a view to fostering reconciliation is like a shot in the dark in the absence of a comprehensive opinion poll geared at learning what the main considerations of different constituencies in Turkey are on this topic.

Although there is interplay among them, reconciliation of the two nations and normalization of state relations (i.e. establishment of diplomatic relations and opening of the border) can be taken up as two separate tracks. Each of the two tracks is driven by separate dynamics, though they impact each other along the way. While normalization of the state relations will boil down to the relatively straightforward act of establishing diplomatic relations and opening the border (which Turkey currently hinges on progress in the resolution of the Karabagh conflict), reconciliation between the peoples is a long term complex process that can proceed regardless of the developments in the diplomatic scene.

Reconciliation of the people

Reconciliation means different things for different people in the context of Turkey-Armenia relations. For many, it boils down to more Turks knowing about the plight of Armenians in Anatolia under the Young Turk government of the Ottoman Empire. This form of reconciliation is ongoing, mostly as a factor of Turkey's democratization, expanded freedom of speech, and the spread of information and ideas. In many ways dialogue with Armenians aids in developing understanding within Turkey of the two nations' joint history. Oral history work is perhaps the most effective in this sense, as it puts forth the human dimension in a debate that is too often focused on cold arguments about numbers of victims or reasoning of policies.

In discussing history, the starting point of the two sides is often so disparate though that encounters can be tense and uncomfortable for both sides. To avoid negative exchanges, dialogue is too often limited to counterparts who already think alike. This can be counterproductive in the setting of realistic expectations on both sides.

In Turkey, generating interest in reconciliation – beyond a relatively small circle of activists and intellectuals – has proven challenging. Various reasons for this can be listed as follows:

■ Reconciliation with Armenia, be it diplomatic normalization or unsettled history, is but one of many problems Turkey faces, and not the most pressing one. (For example solutions to the Kurdish problem or the Cyprus deadlock would have more immediate and far-reaching effects on Turkey's domestic and international politics). Therefore interest in Armenia-Turkey reconciliation efforts is less in Turkey compared to in Armenia, and the coverage in national media is more sporadic.

■ NGO projects have arguably not been designed with a focus on effecting Turkish public opinion. In almost all donor-supported projects the main partner (writing and implementing the proposals) is Yerevan-based NGOs, while selection and oversight is carried out by the respective donors' Yerevan or Tbilisi offices. This may contribute to a weaker factoring in of realities in Turkey. In addition, the lack of comprehensive public opinion surveys in Turkey to illuminate the nature of the Armenia-related perceptions hinders a more information-based design of efforts. Furthermore, the size of population of Turkey makes it harder for any civil society initiative to reach a critical mass. And finally, the Turkish partners in bilateral projects are not always sufficiently 'in touch' with the larger public.

■ The necessity to use English as a joint language in most projects limits the grassroots dimension of the dialogue. Use of Turkish and more outreach on TV – through which it is possible to reach a much wider segment of society, can help build a stronger understanding in Turkey of the Armenian perspectives.

■ The Turkish government representatives' positions throughout 2010 have been shaped largely by the consideration of nationalist votes. This stems from the nature of the political constellation in Turkey: there is strong competition for the relatively large nationalist vote, yet little competition for the vote of the liberal, progressive segments of society. [7] Therefore, rather than providing leadership and trying to sway public opinion, the govern-

---

7   This reality might be changing now with the new leader of the main opposition party, CHP.

ment 'follows' public opinion on this issue (this is also related to the above point, that other problems on Turkey's agenda consume the political capital of the Turkish government).

Sustaining interest in reconciliation and momentum among mainstream Turkish civil society representatives and intellectuals is important in the near future – to influence a wider segment of the Turkish society, and to provide the Turkish government with incentive to proceed in challenging age-old official narratives. And there are steps that can be taken from Ankara that can in turn stimulate critical thinking – such as fostering the objective study of history, shedding the defensive approach to Armenian cultural heritage in Anatolia, and lifting impediments to 'insulting the Turkish nation' or 'countering the Turkish national interests'.

The protocols proved not to be a magic wand that could merge or make invisible the mutually exclusive demands and sensitivities of the two societies. It is more likely that reconciliation will be a gradual process – driven by democratization in Turkey and Armenia, the incremental building of trust, the slow process of learning more about history with all its complexities, development of tolerance and even respect of differences. History textbooks and teaching will also be important to this end. These social processes, by calling into question identity constructions and challenging official narratives, can also open the way for reconciliation between Armenians and Azerbaijanis. Though bound to be aggravatingly slow, such a dialectic process may indeed be the most solid scenario.

References

Academics' Armenia apology to test taboos (2011). Hurriet Daily News, February 26, 2011, http://www.hurriyet.com.tr/english/domestic/10566612.asp

Düzel N. (2009). Ermenileri özel örgüt öldürdü (A special organization killed the Armenians), *Radikal*, 9 October 2000, http://www.radikal.com.tr/2000/10/09/insan/erm.shtml

Göksel N. (2009). Turkey and Armenia: Adjusting Expectations, *GMF On Turkey Series*, May 2009, http://209.200.80.89//doc/Nigar_Turkey_Analysis_0509_final.pdf

Göksel N. (October 2010). Turks and Armenian Walking the Reconciliation Tightrope, *GMF On Turkey Series*, October 2010, www.gmfus.org/galleries/ct_publication_attachments/Goksel_Churches_Oct10_final.pdf;jsessionid=asgIyl WvUFgcK3SMMU

Göksel D. N. (May 2010). *The Rubik's Cube of Turkey-Armenia Relations*, May 2010, www.ucm.es/info/unisci/revistas/UNISCI%20DP%2023%20-%20NUMERO%20ENTERO.pdf

Hakobyan A. (2007). Everything is heading to reconciliation, *Haykakan Zhamanak*, January 24.

Hurç Y. (2008) *The Karabagh Policy of Turkey*. MA thesis Department of History Institute of Social Science University of Kahramanmaraş Sütçü İmam.

Knaus G. and P. Zalewski. (2009). *Red Herrings in the Turkish Armenian debate*, June 2009, www.esiweb.org/rumeliobserver/2009/06/20/red-herrings-in-turkish-armenian-debate/

Mkrtchyan T. (2011). The Role of NGOs in Turkey-Armenia Rapprochement. *Non-Traditional Security Threats and Regional Cooperation in the Southern Caucasus.* Ed. by Mustafa Aydın, NATO Science for Peace and Security Series - E: Human and Societal Dynamics, Volume 77.

Noah's Dove Returns. Armenia, Turkey and the Debate on Genocide (2009). European Stability Initiative (ESI) Report www.esiweb.org

PanARMENIAN.Net (27 January 2007). XXI Century Nothing Changed in Turkey, www.panarmenian.net/eng/world/news/20791/

Phillips David L. (2005). *Unsilencing the Past: Track Two Diplomacy and Turkish-Armenian Reconciliation.* Berghahn Books: New York.

Radikal, 25 September 2005, www.radikal.com.tr/haber.php?haberno=165051

Track 2 Diplomacy, Armenian-Turkish Track 2 projects: Assessment of Best Practices, ICHD, Yerevan, 2006. www.ichd.org/files/pdf/T2D_Book.pdf

Turkey-Armenia Manual. (August 2010). www.esiweb.org (supported by the Eurasia Partnership Foundation and USAID).

Yerkir Newspaper. 22 January 2007, yerkir.am/archive/

Hasan Samani

Association for Historical Dialogue and Research (AHDR) And Reconciliation through History in Cyprus

Dr. Hasan Samani works as an Assistant Prof. at History Teaching Department, Near East University, Nicosia, Cyprus. He holds a Ph.D in History from the Hacettepe University (Ankara-Turkey). Hasan Samani is also an active member of the Association for Historical Dialogue and Research (AHDR).

Before starting my presentation, which is going to focus on the reconciliation process in Cyprus and particularly the role and significance of the Association for Historical Dialogue and Research (AHDR) within this process, I would like to thank everyone who has worked to organize and finance this conference. In order to be able to understand the political climate and motivations that have encouraged the Greek and Turkish Cypriots to initiate various attempts for the reconciliation of the two communities, and to give meaning to these attempts, we should first examine a very brief background of the "Cyprus Problem" and the recent political developments related to the attempts to solve the problem in Cyprus, and the reconciliation process through history itself.

1. The Cyprus Problem and Recent Political Developments

As is well known, Cyprus is an island identified with more than anything but the unsolved 'Cyprus Problem.' No need to go into details, as the roots of this problem date back to the 1950s when the British, who ruled Cyprus since 1878, decided to de-colonize the island after World War II. Then who would govern the Island? From the Greek, Greek Cypriot and Greek nationalist point of view, the 'natural' answer and solution to this question was ENOSIS, the unification of Cyprus with mainland Greece. On the contrary, as a reaction to the Greek nationalism, the Turkish Cypriots, a new component in the society of Cyprus since the conquest of the island by the Ottomans in 1571, developed their own national program, which basically was based on being against ENOSIS and espousing TAKSIM, that is the partition of island between Greece and Turkey. The establishment of EOKA (1955) and TMT (1958), the Greek Cypriot and Turkish Cypriot underground militia organizations, were nothing but preparations for an armed ethnic war to reach the national goals.

Yet, Cyprus has not been (and still is not) a scene where only the internal politics and dynamics played their role. The external powers, namely Britain, the

US, Turkey and Greece, the members of NATO also, sought to maintain cooperation and agreed on a political solution: *the Republic of Cyprus*, as a bi-communal common state for the Greek and Turkish Cypriots. Later developments indicated that this political project, which was based constitutionally on the principle of political equality in the representation of two communities created by the London and Zurich Agreements (February 1959), was far from satisfying the two nationalist programs on the island, particularly that of the Greek Cypriot leadership.

As a matter of fact, the establishment of Republic of Cyprus as a bi-communal state in 1960, unfortunately did not become a final solution to the issue. Just three years later, in December 1963, inter-ethnic fighting broke out between the two communities. The short-term political result of this conflict was the withdrawal/expulsion of the Turkish Cypriot members from the House of Representatives, and three ministers from the government, and turning the Republic of Cyprus into a Greek Cypriot State in practice. In 1964, the UN Security Council declared the Republic of Cyprus government now composed of only the Greek Cypriot representatives, to be the legal authority in Island. Meanwhile, periodically, armed conflict between the two nationalist militia organizations supported by their 'motherlands,' continued until 1967. In the 1963-1967 period Turkish Cypriots suffered much more than the Greek Cypriots. In addition to the causalities, about 20 percent of their population was displaced. In 1968, the communal leaders met for the first time (in Beirut) to negotiate a political solution to the Cyprus problem. This was the first of the many fruitless negotiations lasting through the present.

In the period of 1967-1974, the conditions on the island became, relatively normalized. Turkey's airstrike to stop the Greek military attack in 1967 was effective on this. Turkey's unbending attitude made the Greek Cypriot national leader archbishop Makarios, the first president of the Republic of Cyprus, revise his ENOSIS policy, at least for the time being, and to follow a policy based on the maintenance of an independent Republic of Cyprus. However, this and other factors led to the deterioration of the relations between Makarios and Greece. On July 15 1974, a military junta that had been in power since April 1967 in Greece, in cooperation with EOKA-B (the ultra rightist and radical section of Eoka), organized a coup and overthrew Makarios to bring about *Enosis.*

The Greek military coup in Cyprus, not surprisingly, provoked Turkey, who could not accept this *'fait accompli'* and five days later, on July 20 1974, Turkish troops organized a military operation in Cyprus. The result of the war between the two guarantor states of the Republic of Cyprus, had become the invasion of Northern Cyprus by Turkey and the division of the island into two parts: the Northern Part, where a separate and "independent" Turkish state (the Turkish Republic of Northern Cyprus-TRNC) was established in 1983 (but denounced by the United Nations and recognized by only Turkey), and the Southern Part, controlled by the Republic of Cyprus, the internationally recognized legal authority on the island. According to an agreement on the exchange of populations just after the war in 1975, under the supervision of the UN, the Greek Cypriots (numbering about 200,000) living in the north, and Turkish Cypriots (numbering about 45,000) living in the south, were relocated to the 'other side.' Thus, the *Green Line* not only separated Cyprus into two parts, but the two communities who had lived together since the late 16th century were also divided.

Mutual killings, missing persons and internal and external migration were the results of the 1963-1974 inter-ethnic conflict. No doubt, these happenings deepened the hate and enmity between the two communities and contributed much to the mental division between the Turkish and Greek Cypriots. For nearly thirty years, the two communities, save for some exceptions, had no contact and lived in "their own part." On the other hand, Turkey, since 1975, has been implementing a 'Turkifying' policy in the north. In this context, many Turkish people from Turkey had been settled in North Cyprus and were allocated Greek Cypriot properties. This not only has become another dynamic that complicates matters related to the Cyprus problem, but is also a dynamic that is perceived by most of the Turkish Cypriots as a threat to their cultural and political identity.

2. The Annan Plan Period (2000-2004): A Turning Point?

The intercommunal talks that started in 1968 continued both during 1968-1974 and through the post-1974 periods. Despite the Denktash-Makarios (1977) and Denktash-Kiprianos (1979) agreements, by which a bi-communal and bi-zonal federative structure was agreed to, none of the several plans and proposals prepared for a comprehensive political solution to the Cyprus problem was accepted by the actors involved. When we come to the 2000s, the political climate created by the internal and external factors revived the hopes for solution among certain sections in Cyprus, particularly within the Turkish Cypriot Community.

From 2000 on, when the negotiations between the two communal leaders, Denktash and Clerides, under the supervision of UN General Secretary Kofi Annan began once more, civil society in North Cyprus started to brisk. The economic crisis, especially the collapse of many private banks caused a negative reaction among the Turkish Cypriots against the regime in the north. The leading trade unions and civil society activists openly expressed their discontent against the Denktash regime, Turkish Government (Turkey) and strongly demanded the solving of the Cyprus problem and the re-unification of the island. "Ankara we do not want your money or support, nor advice of your bureaucrats. Peace and Solution" had become the popular slogans against the so-called "status quo" government in the north. The associations and syndicates – the two Teachers' Unions (KTÖS and KTOEÖS) were the leaders – under the umbrella of *This Country is Our Platform,* successfully mobilized the masses and organized demonstrations in favor of the *Annan Plan* when its first version was published in 2002. Meanwhile, in April 2003, the border in Nicosia, which had been closed and separated the two communities for more than thirty years, was reopened. This development did not end the Cyprus problem, but it was important in that after thirty years, the Cypriots regained their freedom to travel in their own country.

In the Annan period, Cyprus witnessed another unique development regarding the attempts for a political solution to the Cyprus problem. For the first time, a comprehensive plan (the Annan Plan) for solution to the Cyprus problem was submitted for the approval of two communities. In 2004, a referendum was hold in both the north and south. The Turkish Cypriots' 65 percent YES vote for the Annan Plan was not sufficient against the Greek Cypriots' 76 percent NO vote, however. Despite the fact that the Annan process did not bring a political solution to the Cyprus Problem, it did help the Greek and Turkish Cypriot communities to open new channels for communication and to initiate the process of building peace culture through reconciliation.

3. Reconciliation Through Historical Education on an Divided Island

The first step for reconciliation through history, not surprisingly, came from the official Turkish Cypriot authorities in the north. Although the Cyprus problem remained unsolved, the dynamics that the Annan Plan brought strengthened the left-wing political parties who were identified with 'peace, solution and unification.' For the first time in history of Northern Cyprus politics, a left-wing party (the Republican Turkish Party-CTP) won the elections in 2003 and 2005. Immediately after the formation of the new government led by CTP leader Mehmet Ali Talat, who later became president, the process for revising the history textbooks taught in secondary schools began. The commissions, composed of academic historians and history teachers, within a short period, re-wrote history textbooks that eliminated the ultra-nationalistic and ethnocentric approaches, narratives and explanations that demonized the 'other' (Greek Cypriots and Greek) and victimized 'us' (Turkish Cypriots and Turks). The use of visual sources and caricatures was the other positive aspect of the new textbooks.[1] As a matter of fact, the requirement for the revision/rewriting of the history textbooks had already been emphasized by the teachers' unions, academic circles and had always been a part of CTP and other left-wing parties' programs. Presently, the new textbooks are not "new" anymore. The UBP (National Unity Party) – right-wing and nationalist – who strongly opposed Annan Plan and CTP's policies on history textbooks during the revision process won the 2009 general elections and formed the new government. This time, the UBP government replaced CTP history textbooks with the new ones which represented Turkish Cypriot history by stressing ethnocentric and nationalistic narratives and explanations. Unlike the CTP, history textbooks in which Cypriotness was strongly presented as a main instrument of the Turkish Cypriot identity, UBP history textbooks emphasize the strong cultural and historical connection between the Turkish Cypriots and Turkey, 'Motherland.' In short, UBP textbooks reflect the party's political view on the Cyprus problem, based on separatist nationalistic ideology and the national goal of the recognition of the TRNC by the Greek Cypriots and the international community, that is the recognition of TAKSİM or partition of the island. The legitimization of the national goal and justice of the Turkish Cypriot side in the 'national cause' is the main ideological framework that shapes the UBP textbooks.[2]

What is the situation in South (the Republic of Cyprus)? Despite the developments mentioned above in the northern part of Cyprus related to the revision of the history textbooks, the Greek Cypriot authorities have not taken any step to revise the history textbooks taught in their schools. Now we know that very recently, the Greek Cypriot authorities brought up education reform including the issue of the history textbooks. We do not know whether this process will result in any real reform covering the revision of the outdated history textbooks taught in Greek Cypriot schools, which are formulated and designed in a way that the history of Cyprus is presented as an extension of the history of Greece. The Greek Cypriot

---

1   For details see Textual 2002.
2   For a comparison of CTP and UBP history textbooks see Education 2010.

history textbooks, except the CTP textbooks, are similar to those of the Turkish Cypriot ones in that they are full of ethnocentric and nationalistic narratives that defend and emphasize the "historically Greek character of Cyprus," and either excludes or trivializes the Turkish Cypriots. The formulation of presentation of Greek Cypriot history textbooks is based on the legitimization of the Greek Cypriot or Greek national goal. As Papadakkis states, "in all the Greek Cypriot textbooks, "Cypriot Hellenism" is the central actor of history from beginning to end" (Papadakkis 2008).

4. The Role and Importance of the AHDR as an Non-Governmental Organization in the Reconciliation Process
From the general picture of Cyprus I have tried to draw, one can extract some remarks;
1. As long as the Cyprus problem remains unresolved, the pedagogical ameliorations on history teaching and learning in the schools of Northern Cyprus will depend on which political party comes to power;
2. The Republic of Cyprus, despite its accession to the European Union, has not been eager to revise or rewrite the history textbooks. However, one can say as a member of EU, an organization where one of the principles of educational policy is teaching cultural diversity and accepting and respecting the "other," the Greek Cypriot authorities will no longer be able to maintain their position on the history textbooks which are not compatible with the general principles of the European Union.

Under these circumstances, the Association for Historical Dialogue and Research (AHDR) assumed a multifunctional duty that would contribute to and help the reconciliation process through history between the Greek and Turkish Cypriot communities.

AHDR, a multi-communal, nonprofit and non-governmental organization in Cyprus, was established on 21 April 2003, on the eve of the opening of the border in Nicosia. The membership of the AHDR Board reflects one of its main principles; *diversity and cooperation* and comprises Turkish Cypriot and Greek Cypriot educators and academic historians. By this aspect, the association is a good example of how productive collaboration, creative ideas, volunteering and respect can blossom across the divide.

AHDR members are also from various ethnic, linguistic, and professional backgrounds working at various educational levels in Cyprus and abroad.

AHDR's mission is to defend and promote productive dialogue and research on issues regarding history, history teaching and learning in order to strengthen peace, stability, democracy and critical thinking. By these goals, AHDR aims to contribute to the reconciliation process, which in the long-term will contribute to the establishment of peace culture on the island.

In order to maintain its mission, AHDR cooperates with many institutions and NGOs at local, regional, European and international levels. The association is also a partner of
▪ the **Council of Europe** in Cyprus;
▪ **Ferrara Municipality** (project 'Dialogues of Peace in Cyprus' in Cyprus carried out by the Municipality and

the Province of Ferrara, Italy, in close cooperation with Italian civil society organizations);

▮ 'American History in America: A Cooperative Faculty Development Program' administered by the **Cyprus Fulbright Commission, in cooperation** with the Association for Historical Dialogue and Research **and Kenyon College** and by the people of the United States of America, through the United States Embassy and the Office of Educational and Cultural Affairs of the US Department of State with the cooperation of Kenyon College in Gambier, Ohio, USA;

▮ **POST-Research Institute** for the organization of workshops on history education Island-wide;

▮ The **Center for Democracy and Reconciliation in Southeast Europe (CDRSEE)** for the presentation of the Joint History Project phase on the island (translation of educational material into Turkish, workshops, dissemination of material and reviews);

▮ **EUROCLIO, the European Association of History Educators;**

▮ The Teacher Trade Unions of Cyprus across the divide: K.T.Ö.S, K.T.O.E.Ö.S-HISTORY RESEARCH CENTRE, POED, OELMEK, OLTEK, SEFK-OELMEK and co-organizer of the series of seminars and workshops leading to the implementation of many events.

AHDR is also a supporter of

▮ the Conference on '**Exploring Europe and Ourselves: Geographies and Identities at Work**' Coordinated by: Department of Education Sciences, European University-Cyprus in collaboration with: POST-Research Institute and funded by the UNDP-ACT;

▮ the Conference on '**Exploring Europe and Ourselves: Geographies and Identities at Work**' Coordinated by: Department of Education Sciences, European University-Cyprus in collaboration with: POST-Research Institute and funded by the UNDP-ACT.

5. The Supporters and co-organizers of AHDR educational events are

▮   Council of Europe;
▮   EUROCLIO;
▮   TEACHER TRADE UNIONS across the existing divide: KTÖS, KTÖEOS, OELMEK, OLTEK, POED;
▮   United Nations Development Programme-ACT;
▮   Other local, European and international organizations.

6. The main activities of AHDR include

1. Teacher training programs
Considering the importance of the teachers' role in teaching history and reconciliation process AHDR gives weight to teacher training programs. AHDR has organized many conferences and workshops where the teachers had the opportunity to improve their teaching talents and to discuss the concepts like Critical Thinking, Historical Thinking, Historical Understanding, Historical Empathy, Multi-perspectivity in teaching and learning history, sensitive and emotional issues in teaching history.

2. Research programs
An oral history research on the former mixed villages has been completed. It is going to be published in near future.

3. Development of supplementary educational material and ideas
Under the MIDE (Multi-perspectivity in Intercultural Education Project), one of the focuses of the ongoing work is the preparation of supplementary History Materials under the headings: Ottoman Period, Artifacts, Missing People, Mixed Villages and Home for Cooperation. For the first time Greek and Turkish Cypriot Academic Historians and Educators are working on common supplementary materials for the teachers and students across the divide.

A FINAL NOTE: HOME FOR COOPERATION or
CHANGING the FUNCTION OF BUFFER ZONE

To me, the most exciting project that AHDR is conducting is the establishment of a HOME FOR COOPERATION (H4C) in the UN controlled Buffer Zone, Nicosia, the capital of Cyprus.

Why Do We Need a Home for Cooperation in the Dead Zone?
BECAUSE,
  ▮   it will help to give the 'dead zone' a new function and role, and transform it from a symbol of segregation to a **symbol of cooperation**;
  ▮   it will ensure we conserve our shared cultural heritage and allow local people to develop their **knowledge** through a program of **education** and training, **research** and **dialogue**, and by promoting **critical thinking in order to become active and democratic** citizens of the world;
  ▮   We need to create the opportunity for multi-communal activities by securing a physical space for Cooperation;
  ▮   Public opinion in Cyprus needs, without delay, examples of **successful cooperation** based on **mutual respect**;

AHDR's H4C project proposal was
  ▮   approved under the EEA (European Economic Area) Financial Mechanisms by the donors Norway, Iceland and Liechtenstein that will contribute most of the overall costs. A building belonged to an Armenian of Cyprus, AVO MANGOIAN was bought and put under construction. So an Armenian House will make the dead zone identical not with separation and division, but a home for cooperation;
  ▮   is also supported by individuals, organizations, local authorities in Cyprus and abroad, embassies and UNFICYP;
  ▮   has also received significant donations by Switzerland and Sweden and by friends and members of the Association for Historical Dialogue and Research, historical and intellectual societies and organizations, academics and civil society in Cyprus, Germany, Denmark, Netherlands, United Kingdom, United States of America.

HOME FOR COOPERATION TARGET GROUPS ARE

- People of Cyprus across the divide;
- Local, European and international NGOs: interested in architecture, archaeology, history, museum and heritage studies, education, cultural studies;
- Teacher Trade Unions;
- Architects;
- Town planners;
- Historians and Archaeologists;
- Researchers;
- Academics, Educators;
- Children;
- Tourists and visitors;
- UNFICYP personnel;
- Technical Committees.

And as a last word, I wish the reconciliation process between the Turkish Cypriot and Greek Cypriot communities, in which AHDR has an important place, becomes a successful model for the Turkish and Armenian civil societies who aim to foster Turkish-Armenian reconciliation.

Thank you very much-Çok Teşekkürler-Efgaristo Bolli.

References

Education (2010). *Barış İçin Eğitim III Kıbrıs Tarihi Ders Kitaplarının Metinsel ve Görsel Analizi. Eski ve Yeni Kıbrıs Tarihi Kitaplarının Kıyaslamalı Analizi (Education For Peace III textual and visual analysis of the History of Cyprus textbooks. Comparative analysis of old and new history of Cyprus textbooks*, POST Research İnstitute, Nicosia, 2010.

Papadakkis Y. (2008). History Education in Divided Cyprus: A comparison of Greek Cypriot and Turkish Cypriot Schoolbooks. *"History of Cyprus" Report*, PRIO Cyprus Centre.

Textual (2002). Textual and Visual Analysis of the Lower Secondary School History Textbooks. *Comparative Analysis of the Old and the New History Textbooks.* POST RESEARCH INSTITUTE, 2002.

Evren Ergeç

Creating Global Understanding on Peace among Young People through Youth Work

Mr. Evren Ergeç is a youth worker. He was born in Istanbul in 1975. While he was a graduate student at the Galatasaray University at his last year of the International Relations Department, he started working on the NGO field as a "Project Coordinator" of a community outreach project for assisting the people's living at the prefabricated houses in Düzce in 2001, two years after the Marmara Earthquake. After the graduation, he continued working on the NGO Field. Since 2003 he has been working in Toplum Gönüllüleri Vakfı (TOG- Community Volunteers Foundation- respectively as "Field Coordinator", "Head of Field Department" and "Head of International Relations Department". As a youth worker he believes that the increase of the involvement of young people at the international, global projects that are also implemented by the participation of young people will show the senseless of the borders – constructed, imagined – while overcoming the prejudices and the stereotypes amongst young people. As an idealist, he works to make real the "global citizenship" as he believes the mottos like "above all nations is humanity".

The world political system is still based on nation-state relations. However, the emergence and the development of new actors such as nongovernmental organizations (NGOs) inescapably abrade the world political system itself. Not only new actors, but the technology and new social media tools foster change and somehow rescue the "citizens of the nations" and free them from their constructed identities such as nationalities through the indoctrination of the education and such constructed belongings.

We live in the times that the humans, the individuals, now have more opportunities for becoming independent and interdependent for the world. Human beings now have more opportunity to have interdependent and reciprocal relations on the global level. But what is global understanding in terms of commonality and interconnection? The commonality is the human responsibility, human conscience that we, as humans, have common interests. The global understanding is the one's contribution of the fact that there are no strangers any more in a globalized world or we, as the strangers of the world, live in the same and similar neighborhood.

The reality of living in the "same and similar neighborhood" as world citizens can be fostered among young people as well by the youth civil society organizations (CSOs) through international exchange projects. Toplum Gönüllüleri Vakfı (TOG – Community Volunteers Foundation) as a youth CSO promotes respect for differences and social peace by empowering, connecting and mobilizing youth in self-created projects. Youth mobility is important to increase the awareness, self-confidence, independence and personal development of young people. TOG worked with the NGOs from Armenia to foster dialogue among young people living in Armenia and Turkey. The common youth mobility projects realized in 2008 and 2009, in cooperation with two NGOs from Armenia, are two concrete examples of the creation of the global understanding among young people. The international youth work that TOG tries to create is based on mutual understanding of the young people coming from different constructed identities of different countries showing that the strangeness is the richness of human dignity. Stimulating young people to get out of their daily environment in global self-created projects broadens their horizons, breaks down stereotypes and increases respect for differences. This mobility also motivates youth to engage in intercultural dialogue and inspires them to take initiative in their local environments.

1. TOG as a Youth NGO

TOG, one of the Turkey's largest youth non-governmental organizations with over 20,000 project volunteers every year, works to motivate young people between the ages of 17 and 25 to implement their own projects under the umbrella of youth organizations that are founded by young people mostly in the universities of Turkey as student clubs. TOG was founded in December 2002 with the vision of realization of social peace, solidarity and change through participation and leadership of young people. The mission of TOG is to transform the energy of young people toward social benefits by encouraging young people for developing and realizing various projects of their own and to contribute to the formation of a youth with social awareness and self-esteem and to enhance democratic participation for young people with young people.

Some 18 percent of Turkey's population is composed of young people between the ages of 15-24, corresponding to approximately 12.5 million people. These figures prove the great youth potential Turkey has as a developing country. TOG has started its journey by valuing this potential for creating a civic milieu for young people to solve their problems through volunteerism, to shape their own future and to learn life lessons through experimentation. Since 2002, TOG works to provide support to young people in the cities of Turkey in order to raise their voices and empower them. It supports the projects of young people, organizes peer-to-peer trainings, makes it possible for young people to realize their own social responsibility projects according to the local needs at summer camps, and provides youth with an opportunity for mobilization both within and outside the country. Since its formation in December 2002, young people implement social service, social awareness and social advocacy projects. All these projects are mainly planned and implemented by young people. TOG supports these projects; partly funds the projects or helps to raise fund for them; communicates with public and press, and empowers young people with trainings, traineeships, grants, and mentorship. TOG not only fosters volunteerism among young people, but also pursues other priorities as well, including:

▮ Respect for diversity: Respect for differences during all activities (cultural diversity). No segregation based on religious, ideological, political views or ethnicity;

▮ Transparency and Accountability;

▮ Youth participation, visibility of young people;

▮ Teamwork;

▮ Social Entrepreneurship;

▮ Peer-to-peer training, aiming to increase both the level and quality of non-formal education, promotion of life-long learning.

TOG provides an alternative social environment for young people, and supports personal development of young people. Through the approach of lifelong learning, it allows young people to express themselves out of the school environment and to gain their own life experience. The objectives of TOG can be summarized as: the personal development of young people, influencing decision-makers and change in the society.

Personal Development of Young People
▪ Values: active citizenship, respect for differences;
▪ Skills: entrepreneurship, self-confidence, team work.

Influencing the decision makers
▪ Developing the rights and freedom of young people.

Change in the society
▪ Changing the attitudes and actions that constrain personal development of young people.

For reaching these objectives, TOG uses and develops tools such as volunteering, trainings, youth mobility and advocacy.

Volunteering
▪ Social Responsibility Projects of TOG Youth Organizations: For the purpose of the empowerment and coordination of the TOG youth organizations, TOG runs a number of Coordination Centers located in different major cities of Turkey. Their aim is to stay in close contact with the youth organizations and to provide them with facilities to hold regular training sessions and seminars.

Trainings
▪ Non-formal trainings of young people to young people: TOG organizes trainings for their volunteers to provide them with the adequate knowledge and skills to conduct their projects. Trainings are based on non-formal techniques and peer education.

Peer Education: Trainings inside the organization are mainly based on peer-to-peer trainings which fill the gap between the trainers and the participants and also provide an incentive for multiplying information gained in the trainings. It basically reflects the idea of "training a group of young volunteers" who can conduct trainings all around the country. These young trainers can travel from one club or organization to another and conduct trainings which results in a serious impact of trainings on a large number of participants. Also, another advantage of this method is the creation a strong platform that young people can share their ideas and experiences freely which leads to a big motivation in-between the young volunteers. Also carrying out the information between youngsters is another powerful consequence of this method.

1) Experiential Learning: Experiential Learning is mainly the base methodology of the trainings inside the organization. This method mainly allows the youngsters to experience the power of learning by doing. This gives the youngsters a chance to experience a specific issue. Experiencing can lead a youngster to think and analyze on the issue and create a sustainable research philosophy. This methodology not only gives an experience but also a way of thinking.

2) Non-formal training: Community Volunteers Trainings consists of non-formal training methods which can be easily adopted into a peer training. Comparing the formal training, non-formal trainings methods are mostly participant-oriented. Under the guidance of a trainer, young volunteers can express themselves in different ways by using brain-storming, role plays, drama and theater techniques, small group and plenary discussions, simulation games etc. Very briefly a non-formal training method is likely having an informal technique but includes formal training information.

Youth Mobility

▪ Summer Projects, TOG Youth Council, International Youth Mobility Projects: Being basically an umbrella organi-zation for the different TOG youth organizations, the major part of TOG's work is to regularly bring the participants of these different groups together in trainings, projects and meetings to promote an active dialogue between them.

Advocacy

▪ Research, Counseling/Lobby (Youth Law, Council of Europe), Monitoring (institutions serving the young people): TOG does political lobbying work for the rights of young people, for example by sending letters of comment to central education institutions like the High Commission on Universities concerning specific decisions taken by them.

4) Youth Work

TOG does "youth work" with, for and by young people. Youth work seeks the real participation, liberation and empow-erment of young people. The definition of youth work is developed by Peter Lauritzen, the former head of the Youth Department and Deputy Director at the Council of Europe's Directorate of Youth and Sport: 'The main objective of youth work is to provide opportunities for young people to shape their own futures. Youth work is a summary expres-sion for activities with and for young people of a social, cultural, educational or political nature. Increasingly, youth work activities also include sports and services for young people. Youth work belongs to the domain of 'out-of-school' education, most commonly referred to as either non-formal or informal learning. The general aims of youth work are the integration and inclusion of young people in society. It may also aim towards the personal and social emancipation of young people from dependency and exploitation. Youth Work belongs both to the social welfare and to the educa-tional systems. In some countries it is regulated by law and administered by state civil servants, in particular at local level. However, there exists an important relation between these professional and voluntary workers which is at times antagonistic, and at others, cooperative. The definition of youth work is diverse. While it is recognized, promoted and financed by public authorities in many European countries, it has only a marginal status in others where it remains of an entirely voluntary nature. What is considered in one country to be the work of traditional 'youth workers' – be it professionals or volunteers – may be carried out by consultants in another, or by neighborhoods and families in yet another country or, indeed, not at all in many places. Today, the difficulty within state systems to adequately ensure global access to education and the labor market means that youth work increasingly deals with unemployment, educational failure, marginalization and social exclusion. Increasingly, youth work overlaps with the area of social services previously undertaken by the welfare state. It, therefore, includes work on aspects such as education, employment, assistance and guidance, housing, mobility, criminal justice and health, as well as the more traditional areas of participation, youth politics, cultural activities, scouting, leisure and sports. Youth work often seeks to reach out to particular groups of young people such as disadvantaged youth in socially deprived neighborhoods, or immigrant youth including refugees and asylum seekers. Youth work may at times be organized around a particular religious tradition (Lauritzen 2008: 369)."

In the resolution on a renewed framework for European co-operation in the youth field[1] (November 2009), youth work has also been defined in such a way: "youth work is a broad term covering a large scope of activities of a social, cultural, educational or political nature both by, with and for young people. Increasingly, such activities also include sport and services for young people. Youth work belongs to the area of 'out-of-school' education, as well as specific leisure time activities managed by professional or voluntary youth workers and youth leaders and is based on non-formal learning processes and on voluntary participation." But as the subjects of the youth work, how we define young people? Who are they?

There are two general approaches that define, construct young people. The instrumentalizing approach constructs the "wrong perception" for young people. This approach takes young people as agents of problem. They may be trouble-making, unruly and dangerous. For this approach, the youth is a transition from childhood to adulthood, to maturity therefore youth as a position of deficiency is considered to be as not-yet adult. They are always been taken as the future leaders of some ways. For that approach, the young people are the aims of political futurism and there is not "present" for them but the future – as they will become adults – is always the reality for them. This approach is very common when it comes to the understanding of young people and when it comes to define them in the society. On the other hand, the youth work cannot accept this approach that is why it nurtures the participative approach that takes the young people as *agents of change.*" They are autonomous, independent active citizens. Only young people can determine their own needs, defend the rights that pertain to these needs, and organize to expand the sphere of rights available to them. TOG's youth work is constructing this participative approach and trusts the young people, listen and learn from them and creates areas for them to express themselves so that they, themselves, can shape their own future. It is certain that the young people do live at that moment. The volunteerism as a way of participation gives them an area of being. When it comes to the international youth mobility, the voluntary participation of the young people at the projects based on non-formal learning processes brings them the opportunity of knowing the others different from them coming from different countries.

---

1   http://youth-partnership-eu.coe.int/youth-partnership/documents/EKCYP/Youth_Policy/docs/YP_strategies/Policy/doc1648_en.pdf

International youth mobilization is a unique tool for promotion of the global understanding amongst young people providing opportunities to young people from different countries, ethnic backgrounds and cultures to meet and to reflect on the experiences gained in the intercultural dimension and to widen their cultural knowledge and enhance their personal skills (i.e. interaction, communication, and understanding).

Concrete International Youth Mobilization Projects: Changing the Lives of Young People living in Armenia and Turkey – Peace Building Projects

At the level of societies, it is too common that there is a process or processes of dehumanization. In every society, one may need an evil, an enemy to create his or her identity. The national identity construction always tends to create enemy and enemies from the other constructed nationalities as the human history; the past is full of pain, wars, memories etc. The past does not want to let go and let free of the individuals from constructed belongings. The peace process and mutual understanding amongst individuals are negatively affected by this dehumanization process. Every nation tries to create a cave that excludes and demonizes the ones that they name as the enemies, as the "others." These caves can only be broken down by creating areas of dialogue through international youth mobility with concrete learning projects. TOG succeeded to realize two international youth mobilization projects with two NGOs from Armenia in 2008 and 2009 to break down the hatreds and the prejudices of young people living in two countries.

2008 - TOG&AYWA

An International TOG ATAK (a social sensitivity happening that gathers young people from different ethnicities, from different backgrounds, life styles etc. for the promotion of tolerance and dialogue of TOG) in Kars was held by partnership of Kars TOG Youth Organization and Armenian Young Women Association.[2] The project was carried out from May 16- to 19. Fifty young people from Turkey and twenty young people from Armenia participated in the project. Participants renovated a primary school in Arpaçay, Kars and organized workshops on intercultural dialogue.

2009 TOG & FTR

TOG was the partner of "Bridge of Benevolence – Tolerance through Cultural and Educational Dialogue" project with Future is Yours[3] (FTR) – from Armenia. To develop mutual understanding and dialogue amongst young people in two countries, 14 young people from Turkey and 16 young people from Armenia participated in two exchange projects in Istanbul and Yerevan. The project was sponsored by US Embassy in Armenia, OSCE Office in Yerevan and Black Sea Trust for Regional Cooperation. The project was implemented in three stages: 1) formation of groups and preparation of mutual visits of the participants 2) field visits to Yerevan and Istanbul 3) evaluation of the project and publication

---

2   http://www.aywa.am/
3   http://www.ftr.am/news.php

of the summarizing guide-book. An essay competition on the topic "How to create a bridge of benevolence" was announced to form the group of the project participants from the two countries. Training courses on principles of democracy, tolerance, history of cultures of Armenia and Turkey and their interrelation were organized for the selected participants. From July 27 to August 2, 2009, visits of young people from Turkey to Yerevan and of young people from Armenia to Istanbul took place. Trainings, discussions, events, meetings were organized during the visits. In addition, the groups visited historical and cultural sites and museums which gave an opportunity to promote intercultural dialogue amongst group members. As a result, leaning on mutual respect and listening to one another's opinions, concerns, discovering the best manifestations and showing deep sense of responsibility, young people of the two countries succeeded in creating a real bridge of tolerance and benevolence. Young people of Armenia and Turkey expressed their opinions and impressions of the project in their discoveries and evaluations, which assert the truthfulness of the project's fundamental ideas.

These international youth mobilization projects changed the lives of young people. This is very clear from their evaluations after the projects. Here are some examples of participants' evaluation after the project was implemented:

"My thoughts changed because Armenian youngsters are very friendly and kind. So I believe that we could solve the misunderstanding between these two countries. If the borders open I will make foreign trade with my friend." "After the exchange, now, I've changed my mind about the relations between the two neighbor countries. Before I couldn't imagine that one day I could have any relations with Turks, but now I have a lot of good Turkish friends." "The most interesting thing I've seen was the museum we visited in Armenia. I got impressed and got really sad for the tragedy between the two nations." "I've changed my mind about Turkish people. I didn't know that they were soooooooooooooooooooooooo hospitable...!!!!!!" "The most impressive time I remember when we were at the church. I had joined a lot of ceremonies but I hadn't seen one like this in my life. After this ceremony while we were dancing, an old man asked some question about us and he learnt we are from Turkey. What did he say to us? He told us peace is here, so nice to see Turkish guys. And he told us let's go on, your excitement mustn't finish for peace... I can't forget these sentences...... We have so similar cultures. Just before I came to Armenia I knew that our songs are so similar but I saw that our meals, our people, our costumes are so similar. We lived together somewhere in Anatolia. We shared a lot of things. There is nothing standing in our way to do these things again. I don't understand why we waited until now without doing anything." "The most impressive time I remember was outside of the monument of genocide, in front of (on the other side of) Ararat Mountain, the sorrow of the dead and questioning myself about the responsibility of all these... At the end, nothing would bring them back, and the hard feeling was "to be", "to exist" as a human being with all the death caused by mankind. That was a shame even the mighty Ararat couldn't have handled. Apart from that, the day before last day, while having dinner at Galata Bridge, whole members of the group were crying, even the tough ones wept and no, that was not because of the too much chlorinated water at the pool, it was the realization of the end that was coming..." "This can be a very long list. Apart from the things I've said up to now, I learned that Armenians also say "Can" to express their love. I learned my name's Armenian meaning and its implications and importance (pomegranate). I knew we had Sarı Gelin as a common song, now I know more shared songs. I learned some Armenian words and was told that I pronounce them well. I've learned about myself, my new friends (both Turkish and Armenian) ... And as long as we are in touch, this learning process will go on." "After the exchange, now, I've changed my mind about all things that I thought about Turkey and Turkish people before. I had wrong ideas before." "After the exchange, now, I've changed my mind about people of Istanbul. They came happy when they knew that we are from Armenia, I didn't see any negative-minded people in Istanbul."[4]

The increase in the international youth mobility projects between the two neighboring countries will definitely foster dialogue and mutual understanding of young people and will create an area of speaking, understanding and sharing. The youth workers, youth leaders and youth trainers of the two countries must think on developing these kinds of exchange projects for reconciliation. The reconciliation starts with friendship. Friendship between young people of the two countries can only be established with these projects. Knowing the others, the ones that are different from me, from us and learning to love them, to live with them, the only way for the perpetual peace and for the full integration with a borderless region can only be realized with these small steps of international youth mobility projects and the youth work is at the core of this new understanding through creating new values.

References

Peter Lauritzen (2008). *Eggs in A Pan – Speeches, Writings and Reflections.* Strasbourg: Council of Europe Publishing.

---

4   To read the booklet of the project you can look to the web page at http://www.osce.org/files/documents/6/0/40034.pdf

Garegin Chugaszyan

Old Conflicts and New Media: The Role of New Media in Reconciliation

Mr. Garegin Chugaszyan's career path has moved across different institutions, different sectors and different nations. He has experience covering governmental, business, civil society and academic sectors. Currently he is a member of the Bureau of the Steering Committee on the Media and New Communication Services (CDMC) of Council of Europe, member of the High-level Panel of Advisers of the UN Global Alliance for Information and Communication Technologies and Development (GAID) and a member of Armenia's Presidential IT Development Support Council under the Prime Minister's chairmanship. He is co-founder and executive director of ITF (Information Technologies Foundation), Yerevan. Among projects fulfilled by ITF it is worth mentioning organization of the Global e-Content Summit and the Pan European Forum on Human Rights in the Information Society in October, 2006 in Yerevan, Armenia, as well as three All-Armenian e-Content contests (2005-2008). Chugaszyan has been active in the sphere of multimedia production for the last 15 years, managing outstanding projects including the first Web casting of World Chess Olympiad in 1996 and World Summit Award winning titles in 2005. Chugaszyan is also co-founder and the President of Information Technologies Education JSC, Yerevan. In 1999-2001 he was a member of the Open Society Institute (OSI) Information Sub-board (Budapest, Hungary) making strategic decisions for information and communication programs (Internet, libraries, electronic publishing) for OSI network in about 30 countries. In 1997, as the Director of the Department of Information and Publishing for the Armenian Government, Chugaszyan successfully initiated introduction of the first Armenian Satellite TV channel.

In recent years, the explosive growth of new media has given unprecedented access to information and transfrontier events with immediate communication. The power of global digital communications largely benefits human rights, although not all people benefit to the same extent, and there is a strong argument that the "digital divide" further marginalizes the poorest.

Despite the recent prominence of "Facebook revolutions" and the like in public debate, we know very little about whether and how new media affect the complex process of conflict management and transformation. Journalistic accounts are inevitably based on anecdotes rather than rigorously designed research.

Ordinary people in different conflicting nations have more direct access to more people than at any time in the past – this creates new opportunities but also new challenges for conflict resolution as those people need to be aware of how they can be manipulated, and on the impact their online activities can have on exacerbating or calming the conflict.

In this article, we present a small case study that demonstrates good practice. The article concludes by posing some issues for further research and action to facilitate the new media being used more widely for Armenian-Turkish civil society dialogue.

1. Interactive Multimedia DVD-ROM "Komitas. Life and Works"

In September 2009, my company started to work on a new interactive multimedia project entitled, "Komitas. Life and Works". Komitas or Soghomon Gevorki Soghomonyan, by Western Armenian transliteration also Gomidas, was an Armenian priest, composer, choir leader, singer, music ethnologist, music pedagogue and musicologist. He is widely recognized as the founder of modern Armenian classical music.

95

From 1910, he lived and worked in Constantinople (the name for Istanbul at that time) where he established a 300-member choir Gusan. On April 24, 1915 he was arrested and the next day, together with 217 other Armenian notables, was deported to northern-central Anatolia, a distance of some 300 miles.

Komitas was dispatched back to the capital alongside eight other Armenians who were deported. But he suffered a mental breakdown after witnessing the 1915 Armenian Genocide and is ranked among the most prominent of the Armenian martyrs of genocide.

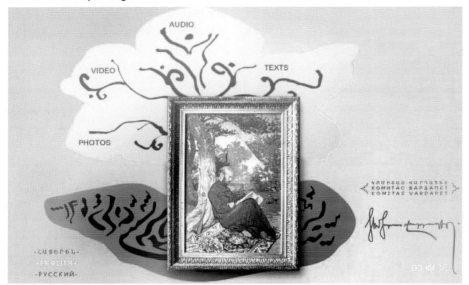

The interface of the interactive multimedia DVD-ROM "Komitas. Life and Works"

While working on this new media project, I realized that music is one of the rare tools for overcoming communication barriers between ordinary Armenians, Turks and Kurds. People have a deep affinity for music; it reaches beyond words, to their hearts and souls, thus, creating a basis for true dialogue. I also understood the power of new media in establishing that kind of communication channel.

My first glimpse of understanding that truth came to me when I realized that I needed photographs of Kütahya, the city in Ottoman Empire where Komitas was born on September 26, 1869. The city at that time had a thriving Armenian community, with churches, schools and rich cultural life.

I did my research and found some old photographs of Kütahya. But we were lacking both contemporary and historic photographs of Armenian district. Along with my colleague Tiran Lokmagiazian, who had physically visited the city, we investigated Google Earth and located the Armenian district and determined the possible location of Komitas' family house there.

Kütahya on Google Maps

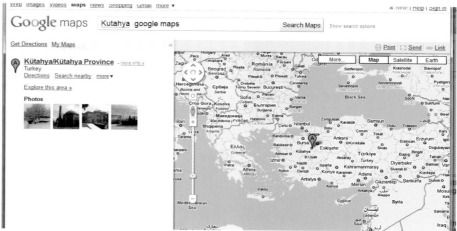

Armenian district in Kütahya

At that time, I also visited a Facebook page devoted to Komitas Vardapet (www.facebook.com/ara.shirinyan?ref=ts#!/Komitas). And all of a sudden I noticed a posting from a person unknown to me – Aziz Tuday: "Komitas is great...I am from the same city, where he was born..." The posting was dated Aug 7, 2010, 1:22 am.

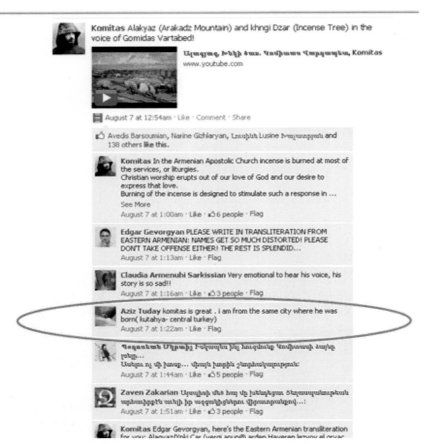

The posting dated Aug 7, 2010, 1:22 am.

At 1:34 am, I wrote a message to Aziz …" Hi Aziz, I am glad to hear that you like Komitas' music. I am sending you satellite image of Kutahia with an indication of the place, where Komitas was born. Could you, please, send some photos of that street and buildings there? Or, maybe people still remember where was his family living… regards Garegin Chugaszyan"

At 1:39 am, I received a reply: "I know actually where his house is. I live in the UK. There is an Armenian church there and many old houses behind the church. As far as I know, Armenian people in Kutahya had to leave around 1950s. All of them moved to Istanbul. Thanks…"

We continued our dialogue until 3:00 am and I obtained a number of links with photographs, which I needed so much. Those sites once again revealed to me the true borderless nature of cyberspace. I found myself inside an Alevi forum in the Turkish language about Armenian settlements in Ottoman Empire, but it took me just seconds to get enough

Our exchange of messages dated Aug 7, 2010, 1:34 am to 3:00 am.

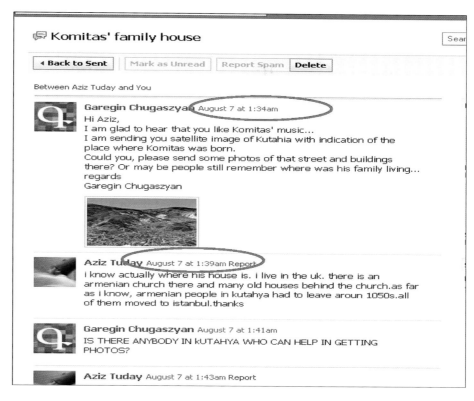

from a Google translation into English to understand the meaning. This forum alone had 113,000 views and more than 200 postings. Here I managed to find old photographs of the Armenian district of Kütahya, which I later included in the DVD-ROM.

Alevi forum on "Units of Armenian Settlement in Anatolia," in Turkish. http://www.alevilerbirligi.com/showthread.php?t=6349

Alevi forum on "Units of Armenian Settlement in Anatolia," through Google translation into English

Alevi forum on "Units of Armenian Settlement in Anatolia," through Google translation into English. Kütahya Armenian Church photographs

Tracing the links provided by Aziz, I finally also found the modern photographs of Armenian district and houses belonging to Armenians before 1915 on a Facebook page, "Bir zamanlar Anadolu'da Ermeniler." This page had around 4,000 friends and thousands of photographs about Armenian cultural heritage being added almost daily. Thus, started my journey into Turkish social media devoted to Armenian heritage which is continuing until now...

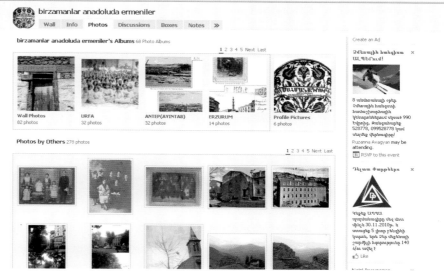

Facebook page "Bir zamanlar Anadolu'da Ermeniler" http://www.facebook.com/profile.php?id=655158510#!/pages/birzamanlar-anadoluda-ermeniler/297491638134

Kutahya Armenian District Facebook page "Birzamanlar anadoluda ermeniler"

But that heritage was mostly about Armenian architectural monuments and artifacts.

While gathering musical material for the Komitas multimedia project, I noticed that the earliest study of Kurdish music was initiated by Komitas Vartapet in 1904, in "Quelques spécimens des mélodies kurdes," in Recueil d'Emine, Moscow 1904, and re-edited in Yerevan in 1959. The first academic center for Kurdish music was also founded in Yerevan, where the Kurdish *dengbêj* style of music was studied.

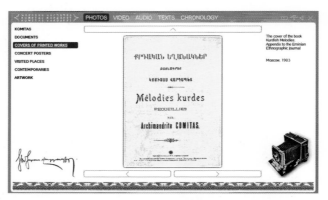

The cover of the book of Vartapet Komitas, "Quelques spécimens des mélodies kurdes," in Recueil d'Emine, Moscow 1904, and included in interactive multimedia DVD-ROM "Komitas. The Life and Works"

Interestingly enough, right at that time, I was informed that a group of Kurdish Zaza musicians headed by Mikail Aslan had been in Yerevan for a joint project connected with Komitas' disciple Mihran Toumajan, who had collected Armenian folk songs from Dersim. I searched the Internet and found a marvelous Kurdish artist who had a huge popularity driven by a hundred thousand page views on Youtube.

Mikail Aslan and Petag Project: "No voice echoing in the universe is lost."

Youtube page of Mikail Aslan's "Petag" album, http://www.youtube.com/watch?v=iHAWXuOEHCg

A writer, composer and popular Kurdish performer, Mikail Aslan, who is producing albums in his native language, Zaza, released his new album Petag in 2010. The artist has some Armenian songs from Dersim region in his new album.

This is what he says about Armenians and Armenian songs:

"Even during my childhood, there were certain villages whose names I used to repeat over and over in my mind. "Norşin," "Hopik," "Axweşî," "Sorpiyan"... Even though Zaza was my mother tongue, I somehow couldn't manage to find a meaning for these words. Then I'd ask my mother, and she'd quickly brush them off, saying "my son, those names are left from the Armenians.""

"The Armenians who gave our villages their names no longer existed; it was as if the earth had opened up and swallowed them. Where could these people have gone, who left us our villages' names, their dilapidated churches and their gravestones? Sometimes, the stones left from their ruined churches would turn up in the walls of our old-style houses. Did these stones have no tongue; was there nobody who understood their language?

Was there anyone to understand their language? No voice echoing in the universe is lost, it is always recorded somewhere. With this hope and this quest, I was visiting my dear friend Hosvep Hayreni in 2005. ... When I read some passages from the book entitled Hampartsum Kasparyan "Çımışgadzak yev ir Küğeri (Çemişgezek and villages), I suddenly thought of this sentence: "Dersim and Armenian folk songs".""

"The esteemed musicologist Mihran Toumajan, a disciple of Komitas, noted folk songs preserved by the Bagikyan and Celalyan families who found refuge in the United States before and after the genocide of 1915. I consulted this book. ... From this source and through the sharing of personal archive of my very dear friend Ilda Simonian, we found nearly 100 works specific to the region of Dersim and its surroundings. After working for nearly four years, we have decided to release these songs by producing an album. Among the 100 songs that we could gather, we chose twelve. We recorded these songs with our esteemed friend and musician Cebrail Kalin. My friend Levent Güneş joined us later. Thanks to his contributions and research in the archives of the Armenian Folk Music, this album has begun to find its identity."

See:
http://seyidersimi.kazeo.com/-rojname-journal/Mikail-Aslan-et-les-chants-populaires-armeniens-de-Dersim-interview,a1911825.html

Thus, we included a whole TV film about Mikail Aslan in our Komitas multimedia DVD.

1. Komitas (Gomidas) Platform

Then came the time for my next discovery. In November 2010, at the Surp Yerortutyum Armenian Church, a concert was organized and broadcasted live online at www.gomidasplatform.org/live. The choir performed Vartapet's polyphonic "Badarak" (Divine Liturgy), which the maestro composed for the Armenian Apostolic Church. The music was

Komitas Vardapet with his former students. From left to right: Hayk Semerjian, Mihran Tumajian, Vardan Sargsian, Artashes Abajian, Vagharshak Srvandztian, Barsegh Kanachian, Constantinople, 1914

Photograph of Komitas Vardapet with Mihran Toumajan. And other disciples. Constantinople, 1914. Included in interactive multimedia DVD-ROM "Komitas. The Life and Works."

Kusan (Gusan) 2010 Choir

performed in Turkey for the first time in fifty years by the Kusan (Gusan) 2010 Choir, the descendent of the original Kusan Choir that Vartapet formed himself over a century ago.

Apparently, Turkish and Armenian youth in Istanbul began working for more understanding between the communities at the beginning of 2010 when they organized a platform to commemorate Komitas Vartapet in Turkey with music and hymns. On the 140th anniversary of his birth, Komitas had been honored not only in the diaspora and Armenia, but eventually also in Turkey. Thanks to the group's work, a number of events and concerts were organized throughout the year to commemorate the great ethnomusicologist.

The commemoratory "Gomidas Liturgical Music" concerts, which were made possible by a grant from the Istanbul 2010 European Capital of Culture Agency, were held in November 2010 at the Surp Yerortutyum Armenian Church and at Istanbul Kültür University.

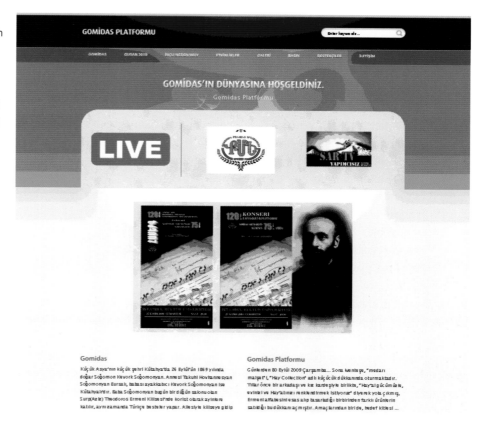

Another concert was held in collaboration with Anadolu Kültür, the Istanbul Foundation for Culture and Arts and Kalan Music and featured American Armenian Sahan Arzruni, as well as the Istanbul State Opera and Ballet's Armenian soloists Sevan Şencan, Kevork Tavityan and Ari Edirne. The Boğaziçi Gösteri Sanatları Topluluğu, Aşkın Ensemble, Aynur Doğan and Şevval Sam were also on stage.

2. Conclusions

Thus, the belief in the potential of new media and technologies to enhance conflict resolution and promote peaceful dialogue is certainly not cyber-utopianism. However, the development of such tools is and will remain merely as a means to achieve much greater ends.

So how is it possible to build new media communications architectures that encourage dialogue and nonviolent political solutions?

There are a number of observations and recommendations to guide media practitioners, conflict resolution professionals and NGOs on how the media can best play a constructive role in conflict and post-conflict scenarios.

For example, here are some of the guidelines of "The Strengthening Lifeline Media in Regions of Conflict "conference (http://www.mediasupport.org/documents/papers_and_articles/the%20media.doc):
- obtain a detailed understanding of the conflict;
- build partnerships with conflict resolution organizations/experts and other NGOs working in the field;
- be trained in conflict resolution;
- interventions should be long-term and sustainable;
- don't be too ambitious – "do the do-able";
- a participatory approach should lead local people to «own» the media intervention;
- choose credible media outlets;
- if possible, use a multi-media approach;
- avoid simplistic representations of "goodies" and "baddies";
- level the playing field by giving the powerless a voice.

In our view, it is important that experiences like those we have mentioned in our case study are researched in depth so that a body of knowledge can be accumulated in this important area of new media and conflict resolution.

The virtual networks are good as long as they eventually transform into real-life relationships (or are used to maintain previously established in-person contacts). The ability of new technologies and social media to contribute to conflict-resolution or establish long-lasting, meaningful relationships is also undermined by the fact that short virtual messages do not provide the time or space necessary for engaging in a more substantial conversation.

Citizen and social media's potential for conflict resolution remains strong, as long as they are recognized and utilized as tools to facilitate dialogue among troubled societies. Yet, such attempts should be carried out with great care and sensitivity so as not to compromise the integrity or the credibility of the initiative.

Seda Grigoryan

A View from Inside: Clash of Theory and Practice within

Ms. Seda Grigoryan obtained MA in Linguistic and Intercultural Communication majoring in European Studies at Yerevan State University. In fall 2009 was her first encounter with *dvv international* within its project of Adult Education and Oral History Contributing to Armenian-Turkish Reconciliation. Seda Grigoryan describes it as a turning point in her life since a new sphere was introduced to her and she discovered new interests and educational possibilities for herself.

When I first applied for this project aimed at contributing to Armenian-Turkish reconciliation, I had already formed my own idea of reconciliation, according to which even communication between Armenian and Turkish students was already a step forward.

The first camp in Dilijan, Armenia, was a nice place where communication and dialogue became possible between students from Armenia and Turkey. The further phases of this project demonstrated that we are not so foreign to each other, and in various situations we discovered that we "understand" the jokes that are usually specific to only one culture or environment and are usually not universal, yet we were pleasantly surprised that every time we made a joke, thinking that only Armenians or only Turkish people would "understand," it turned out that we have a similar and shared sense of humor. In another instance, when our Turkish friends visited Armenia, we were having dinner and one of our Turkish friends said that "We also have similar taste. We have similar tastes in our cuisines."

During our communication and interaction, each of us has so-called "culture studies" which is important for all of us, but we do not talk too much about it, usually only in silent observations. During our communication, however, we discovered much about each other's culture and the phrase "we also have it" became the most common phrase among us, and we took for granted that if we said: "We have this," our Turkish friends would say in turn: "We also have it" or vice versa. Recently a funny incident occurred: we were tasting guhta (biscuits), and our Turkish friends said: "This is really tasty," an Armenian friend asks: "Don't you have 'guhta'?," the Turkish one responds: "No" and the Armenian shouts with hands up: "Yeah! Finally! 'Guhta' is only ours... I can now say for sure that 'guhta' is Armenian".

The most valuable thing I gained from the two camps, and this is true for the other students of our Armenian team as well, was the personal friendship that we gained. I can say now that I have Turkish friends for whom I honestly care about as friends. But unfortunately, there is a topic that creates discomfort in the path of understanding each other: the genocide issue.

When I first decided to apply for the project, it never even occurred to me that the Turkish students who applied for the same project would have any doubts on either the event itself or its wording, mainly because I thought that otherwise, they would not have applied for a project of "reconciliation." Maybe I was naïve, but it never occurred to me. At the camp, and especially at the second camp because there were mainly a new group of Turkish students, I first felt the clash of my theory and practice in reconciliation. According to my theory of reconciliation within the scope of our project, I imagined it like two groups of students who agree on the subject to be reconciled upon and would try to take small steps towards bringing "reconciliation" to larger groups. The oral history method we were taught at the camp seemed such a powerful tool that could bring ordinary people into a "free-of-politics" sphere where they would be able to understand each other on the level of human feelings. Hence, the oral history research on personal memories of the past in Armenia and Turkey seemed to me a strong action to be taken in the path of "reconciliation".

The interview part of the project, when we were collecting oral histories, became a turning point for my personal perceptions. It was like a reopening of a wound which became even more painful now. While previously, I knew family stories of genocide survival, including where they came from, who survived and so on, my experience of interviewing through the oral history method personified the events of the genocide for me and revived scenes of it with people telling the family stories of their parents or grandparents, as related directly from them. And now those people were not only those Armenians survivors from Western Armenia, but they became much more personified, as the father of Vazgen Ghukasyan, the grandmother of Eleonora Ghazaryan, the grandmother of Anahit Hovhannisyan, the mother of Anahit Bardakchyan, and others. I could see the pain still burning inside when the interviewees were still telling the stories with their voice trembling, with eyes full of tears, with interruptions and emotional sighs. When the interviewees were telling the stories transmitted to them with so many details I was astonished and wondered how many times they could have heard the same story to remember them in such detail, and many of them would say: "My mother was always remembering... my father was always remembering that... my grandmother would always say that..." Then I thought: "What an interesting thing this post-memory is!" These people, who are the carriers of usually sad and painful memories of their parents, grandparents, great grandparents, preserve those memories giving the space to them by sacrificing their own. Like the part of their life which could be happy without traumas and painful events, and would be just remembered as a happy period or at least an ordinary one without any extraordinary event but which would be theirs, their own memories, ordinary ones but without traumas that wipe out not only many personal minutes but also happy moments as well.

Another aspect of reconciliation I have in mind is concern or at least interest of any kind within the parties involved. The students' small-scale projects were another opportunity to widen our circle of communication and to achieve more diversity of social and educational backgrounds. The students' project is another experience that was important and valuable for me. This was another layer towards uncovering my concept of 'reconciliation.' The nature of our interviews, as arranged by our international group of Armenian and Turkish students, supposed that the students would be the ones to be interviewed by people in Turkey and Armenia. When we were in Istanbul, the Armenian students were to be asked questions, any questions. And there were instances when people would not ask anything. I usually feel uncomfortable in a silent group but trying to somehow keep the aim of our project I was waiting for a question. But again it was me who broke the silence. Or I caught myself saying often: "What else? What else would you like to ask?" The overall picture I received from my experience with the Istanbul interviews was that relations with Armenia was a question of 'little importance' both for the state and for the individuals because the common sentence we heard was: "Turkey has many problems." "The Armenian issue is of little importance." The so-called "Armenian issue" as I observed was really politicized in Turkey because people in Istanbul would say: "Turkey has many other problems" and we were constantly asking: "What about you? What do you personally think or feel?" Another thing I noticed was the obvious difference of perceptions and awareness which might partially be the result of "unimportantness" of the issue or just "uninterestedness" in it. A very vivid example of that was when one of the Armenian students said: "1915 …" and a Turkish young man said: "What's that 1915 …? What happened then?" But this was not the case that the Turkish young man did not know anything at all about the events because we were talking about it and he was speaking about numbers of Armenians living in Ottoman Empire as documented by Ottoman archives. This was rather interesting to me because if he had been interested enough to find statistics and data on Armenians living in the Ottoman Empire he perhaps never tried to have a look at what Armenians themselves say about the period, because we have enough of "1915" in the Armenian life.

Another instance which according to me illustrates how politicized "the Armenian issue" is in Turkey was revealed to me during a conversation with a middle-aged religious man. He said: "I share your pain, but if I were the president I wouldn't recognize it, either." And when we asked him how he saw our future relations, he said: "It happened over two hundred years ago…. It is past… Let's forget the past and walk ahead." Did it happen two hundred years ago? And is it past? Is it a past for the people who still long to visit the village of their grandparents, to see their paternal house, and the happiest one who has the luck and the chance to visit and to bring a handful of soil, a stone of their house, flowers from their village that are so dear to him, or is so full of chaotic emotions and feelings that having visited his grandparents' village has failed to shoot for at least few minutes though he had the camera on in his hands? …They describe their lost house with so many details and when asked whether they could find their house if they ever happened to be in their village the answer is firm: "Yes, sure!" And the suggestion is: "Let's bury the past…" Is it a past and where to bury it?

After hearing these comments, an inner dilemma arose within myself: "Who am I to take steps towards reconciliation? I do not have family stories of the genocide. True, I also feel pain but the pain I feel is no match to theirs… do I have the right to speak on their behalf? Can they ever forget? And these people who know nothing about that and seem to be unwilling to know…"

After the Istanbul research, I felt like I was walking into a wall. What is "reconciliation"? What is the purpose of it if for one of the parties the issue is of "little importance," they are not interested in it? Or how can these people telling these stories forget? How much of them have they forgotten?

The Yerevan research was also an interesting and valuable experience for our Turkish friends. Because it was a recent event we have not had a chance yet to have a thorough discussion but I am pleased to have had the chance to present the thoughts of one of our Turkish friends as well: "In Armenia the first thing that was striking to me was the collective nationalism which I never experienced in any other country. In our interviews I did never come across any person in Armenia who questioned the high nationalism and potential dangers that may stem from it... After the interviews in Armenia it is hard for me to speak about the possibility of imminent reconciliation which seems hard considering the tough nationalistic attitude in Armenia..." Is it "collective nationalism" or could that be "collective trauma and pain"? Maybe that is the reason nobody even "questioned the high nationalism."

During the stay of our Turkish friends in Armenia, after an exhaustive day of interviews, one of our Turkish friends says jokingly: "We do not want any more interviews... We do not want to discuss "genocide" any more... We are tired..." Of course, this was a joke but I could feel that in Armenia our Turkish friends had too many questions on genocide.

What we all learned from our student project is that we came to appreciate every small change we could bring even in an individual who somehow began to re-think their stereotypes and began to question some of their previous thoughts. And one thing that is more than obvious is the fact that speaking and listening to each other is very important even if the issue discussed is painful and conflicting for the parties.

In conclusion, I would say that I highly appreciate this project which gave me the chance to gain my own experience but which also raised more questions within myself than provided answers. And for me, it was more of a research on trying to understand what "reconciliation" is and the possibility of "reconciliation" within the chosen societies.

Ismail Keskin

Nor&Eski and History for Life

Mr. Ismail Keskin has a BA at Boğaziçi University, he has been an Erasmus student at Panteion University (Athens) and also an exchange student with special bilateral agreement at University of Athens. He is an MA candidate in History at Boğaziçi University. Mr Keskin has taken part in various MA research projects and articles, some of which are: "Modern Genre Theory and Turkish Historical Novels of early 20th century," "Anabasis: March of the ten thousand into the Modernity" (Published in peer reviewed journal: "Tarih: Graduate History Journal" 2009), "Masks of the Identities, The case of Pan Turanism in Hungary, the challenge between "the east" and "the west"." He has been lecturing recently at the French Institute of Anatolian Studies Istanbul, in the frame of seminary "After the exchange: the integration of the refugees in Greece and Turkey: cultural, political and socio-economical perspectives", as lecturer of the 8th session on: "Rethinking the etymologies on "population exchange". Certain types of remembering as a way to forget (Listening first generation through oral accounts/Bithynia case)".

Waiting for the Barbarians
What are we waiting for, assembled in the forum?
The barbarians are due here today.
Why isn't anything happening in the senate?
Why do the senators sit there without legislating?
Because the barbarians are coming today.
What laws can the senators make now?
Once the barbarians are here, they'll do the legislating.
Why did our emperor get up so early,
and why is he sitting at the city's main gate
on his throne, in state, wearing the crown?
Because the barbarians are coming today
and the emperor is waiting to receive their leader.
He has even prepared a scroll to give him,
replete with titles, with imposing names.
Why have our two consuls and praetors come out today
wearing their embroidered, their scarlet togas?
Why have they put on bracelets with so many amethysts,
and rings sparkling with magnificent emeralds?
Why are they carrying elegant canes
beautifully worked in silver and gold?
Because the barbarians are coming today
and things like that dazzle the barbarians.
Why don't our distinguished orators come forward as usual
to make their speeches, say what they have to say?
Because the barbarians are coming today
and they're bored by rhetoric and public speaking.
Why this sudden restlessness, this confusion?
(How serious people's faces have become.)
Why are the streets and squares emptying so rapidly,

everyone going home so lost in thought?
Because night has fallen and the barbarians have not come.
And some who have just returned from the border say
there are no barbarians any longer.
And now, what's going to happen to us without barbarians?
They were, those people, a kind of solution (Cavafy 1992: 18).

Constantine Petrou Photiades Cavafy (1863-1932), a Greek poet who experienced a lifelong journey and enjoyed-suffered multiple identities, was warning his readers about the absence of barbarians. It could be perceived as a dilemma – reflecting the absence of barbarians as a negative thing – since barbarians are the ones whom everybody fears, and whom everybody struggles against. On the other hand, on a second thought, the threat of the barbarians is also what keeps masses obeying their rulers without question, because the ruler/ruler group protects the people from barbarians, and that task needs endless sacrifice.

So, barbarians could also be a good solution for rulers, who do not want to explain anything to the masses they rule, or who do not want the masses to interfere with their brave and corrupt deeds. To make the masses love their rule, without questioning what they love.

In this case, life without barbarians is a hard one, so today we came together here and we are trying to find out how to reconcile two societies. In other words, metaphorically speaking: how to live when barbarians are not coming anymore?

We have a serious challenge here. Because both countries have lost so much time waiting for the barbarians to come, delaying every single necessary step for peace and refusing any chance for reconciliation with the excuse of the approaching barbarians. Still, many people in both countries are living with the ghosts of the Barbarians.

Yet the ones "returning from the border and saying there are no barbarians any longer," namely, the peace initiators, have to be well aware of the disappointment of the barbarians' loss from the minds of the people is not an easy challenge to undertake. As mentioned in the poem, they, the barbarians, were a kind of solution: a necessary evil, as it is well defined by the term itself, an "evil" that is necessary most of the time. So, working on such challenging problems which are already turned into a chronic disease by time, needs very erudite research and a very careful approach to people and their traumatized memories. The memories that have never seen or experienced barbarians, have grown up with painful stories and always put in line with the abuse of that pain.

It is important to be clear here. We are not talking about the legitimacy of the pain or memory of the pain, not about the pain experienced by Armenians or Turks. Yet, we are talking about the abuse of pain by using it as an "absolute truth."

At this point, I would like to present briefly the project we are working on.

The name of our project is Nor&Eski (*nor* means new in Armenian and *eski* means old in Turkish). The inspiration for the concept of this project came during the Adult Education and Oral History Contributing to Armenian-Turkish Reconciliation Project's Antakya workshop which was held in August 2010. Antakya is an example of a city where you can feel the harmony of living together with its reflections on the material culture. This scarce example made me think more about the possible role of the material culture and history that is narrated through material culture on the process of reconciliation.

Approaching memory through material culture would be an effective way to gather and present some – with Elazar Barkan's term – "practical pragmatic truth," truth which can challenge nationalist propaganda, especially without directly negating national narrative – which can end up with a direct refusal of the approaching efforts – but rather deconstructing it (Barkan 2005: 234). We will turn back to practical truth issue and explain its use more, while talking about the application of the project.

Let us turn back to our project.

The name of the project "Nor&Eski" was revealed during the research on possible methods that can be used working on material culture. During a small scale Internet research on Yerevan, I have realized the abundance of district names that are starting with the "nor" adjective and end with city names from Asia Minor. This was actually a phenomenon which I was very used to seeing in Greek case, only with the difference of the adjective Nea – the word for new in Greek, instead of Nor. It would be a very fertile title for a short documentary film, especially as inspiration during the plotting the story.

So what is "Nor&Eski" project and what is it about?

Nor&Eski is a student project that is both a part and outcome of the "Adult Education and Oral History Contributing to Armenian-Turkish Reconciliation" project. The project team consists of six students from Turkey. The outcome of the project will be a short documentary movie, planned to be about 15-20 minutes long. Footage consists of both oral history interviews and the landscape plans in Turkey and Armenia, since one of the main objectives of the project is to show our audience what the other country looks like today...

The aim of the project can be summarized as following: as a team, we believe that reconciliation requires mutual knowledge and understanding between societies, therefore, it is necessary to reveal not only what had happened in the past, but also the current lives of the people, to show what is happening "there" now. Armenia and Turkey, two neighboring countries that have many bitter stories about the past, yet hardly know each others' present. This project aims to reflect the changing faces of the old and new experiences within the lives of the cities, characterized by the new lives of the newcomers flourishing side by side with locals and the old stories, old neighborhoods and neighbors within a city that is supposed to stay stagnant as it was in the "good old days."

To reach this objective, a short documentary film project of "Nor&Eski" ("New & Old ") is planned as history project which "flourishes life" instead of burdening life with monumental and antiquarian histories. By barrowing the Nietzschean conceptualization of the historiography, the project aims to follow the absolute truth, which is full of heroes and traitors as we have seen a lot in our secondary school history textbooks.

On the other hand, reconstruction needs parts from the construction that is deconstructed so not to be rejected by the immune system of the audience. So absolute truth of Rankean historiography could be deconstructed into practical realism in which, the domestic historian is working very eruditely on the research material within a framework of the professional values and methodologies of the international community, subscribed to international standards of historical research, yet on the other hand, also very well aware of the national/regional narratives. So, a historian who is well aware of the national and regional narratives without negating them, can reconstruct them so they can contribute to reconciliation by breaking the resistance of the society which has an absolute faith on the evil character of the counterpart, rejecting every single possible criticism of the self and memory sites constructed through education (Barkan 2005: 233).

So, our project team has chosen the region of Bithynia and its "nor" sister in Yerevan Nor Butaniya as research field for three reasons: first, Bithynia is very close to Istanbul, so we would make more than one field trip to the region without going too far into our budget, and second, it is a very chaotic region where there are always newcomers and lastly, for examining the advantages and disadvantages of "being a local historian" who knows the region geographically and historically in detail and has a broad network of acquaintances.

If we turn back to methodology, as a result of the abovementioned chaotic nature of the region, it is more precise to apply the term of regional narratives rather than the national one, since even in the smallest village of the region, where people are supposed to be from the same homogenous nation, there are many different identity complexities: i.e. old and new immigrants from Circassia, Abkhazia, Bosnia, Albania, Greece, Bulgaria and so on during the last century. Their relations with the locals of the region, called "manavs," also gave us invaluable data on the myth of homogeneous nation, since immigrants, who had never experienced living together with Armenians were mostly loyal to the discourses of the state they learned through education. Yet some locals, who did not cut their ties with their old Armenian neighbors and learned the story of "what actually happened there" not from secondary school text books, but from the people who experienced it, whose stories were not silenced or isolated since their version of the story was not totally supporting the state discourse, and their relations with the Armenians could not be appreciated by the system as a model.

The third party, old people aged between 80 and 100, who became trendy as a source of oral history and spoiled by the system tools such as television channels, newspapers or universities, as "living oak trees" of the country, would distort the stories, would use euphemisms about the relations between different social and ethnic groups in the neighborhood, would exaggerate enmities of the past as s/he is expected to do and so on. We had one such example among our respondents, who was around 90 years old, already had a documentary dedicated to his memories and had very different version of the stories about such issues as Armenians, Greeks and Jews as well as the early relations of the local people with the newcomers. As a *manav,* or local of the region, surprisingly, he was absolutely negative about the first, and extremely positive about the latter, quite opposite to what we used to hear from manavs. The effect of being a media figure was quite obvious since even his son opposed some of his views while we were talking about the footage afterwards, especially about his father's absolutely euphemistic statements about the early relations between locals and newcomers that came to the places of Greeks and Armenians.

During our field trips to Bithynia, we visited old Armenian towns and villages; we have talked mostly with the second generation. We had two types of respondents: local respondents or so-called *manavs*, and immigrant respondents or so-called *muhacir/macır* in Turkish. From those respondents, we heard a wide range of narratives about living together, massacres, plunders, treasure hunting, the arrival of newcomers and so on. These were stories generally heard from father or mother, in some cases, even from old Armenian neighbors who had visited them many years later.

During those interviews, as mentioned, we had respondents who duplicated the national myths about Armenians, massacres, relation between locals and newcomers. But on the other hand, we had also some respondents who gave us invaluable set of original data, which has a potential of turning into practical pragmatic truth that can challenge national histories.

I am concluding my presentation with an example from one of the most striking interviews we had in Yeniköy, the town which was the third biggest Armenian settlement in Western Asia Minor after İstanbul and Izmir, where approximately 13,000 Armenians were living.

Our respondent was a *Manav* from Yeniköy, which means a local of the town. They have found their old Armenian neighbors in the 1950s and kept relations until 1980s. I will project the translation of the text from power point and put the original record as a background sound. Thank you for your patience for the last presentation of the long day.

Project team: Ismail, Cansu, Burcu
Attendants: Somnur Vardar (Film Maker), Leyla Neyzi (Oral History Professor), Sibel Maksudyan (Independent Photographer)
Respondents: Mehmet T. (around 70-75 years old) and Ahmet T. (Mehmet's brother, around 65-70 years old)
Interview made in a mini-bus and by respondent's request, only sound recorder used.

Cansu: Please take a seat.

Mehmet (Respondent): Ok my dear, I'm alright, I'm alright.

Somnur: Please sit comfortably.

Mehmet (Respondent): I'm fine I'm fine. You ask and I'm gonna answer. I am gonna tell the things I know.

Ismail: We started to ask about Armenians.

Burcu: We wonder the old life here.

Mehmet (Respondent): We don't know the old life, too.

Burcu: Things like what you heard from your mother and father.

Mehmet (Respondent): You're doing this (referring our short documentary) about the Armenians right? Or...?

Burcu: Yes the part with Armenians as well.

Mehmet (Respondent): Armenians were coming from Van as a society (he uses the term kavim: from context it is hard to translate it as tribe, horde or clan).

Ahmet (Respondent's younger brother): close this (mini bus' door).

Burcu: Is it open, ha?

Ismail: Zafer Abi! Yes it's open.

Ismail: Zafer Abi Zafer Abi.

Ahmet (Respondent's Brother): Zafer.

Ismail: Close the door.

Ahmet (Respondent's Brother): Zafer close the door, honey.

Door closed.

Leyla: From Van.

Mehmet (Respondent): coming from Van.

Ahmet (Respondent's Brother): They're coming from Van.

Mehmet (Respondent): They were (Armenians) given a village here. This was a Muslim village with 30 houses. Our teenagers were going to war/wars (as recruits). There were no many males in the village, just elders. They took them (Armenians) as laborers to here, Yeniköy. Of course, it is hard to go olive picking in winter. It is very far from here. They say, there was an obelisk there, "Lets give a land to them from there (near to that Obelisk) they will establish a place for them. They say it will be easy to find laborers. They did it like this. Armenians were coming here... I'm telling these from what we have listened from Armenians' narrations (of old neighbor Armenians).

Ahmet (Respondent's Brother): These are the things that Armenians told us.

Mehmet (Respondent): We have an Armenian friend, he told these. I asked him once. There is a neighborhood now here, where people call as gypsy neighborhood. I asked him about the history of that neighborhood (to old Armenian neighbor, Agop): "Were there gypsy here? (Agop answered)" No, my son!" and he started to tell me this story (of Armenians) as saying that it was so and so (the story of Armenians that they were living there where is now called a gypsy neighborhood)...

(Listen:) This is the story (what Agop told me about the history of Armenians living here): They established their place here. Our guys (Manav: local Turks) were going for military service and dying as martyrs. This place has never exceeded 30 houses (as number of Manav/local Turk inhabitant).

Ahmet (Respondent's Brother): They were (Armenians) not going for military service.

Mehmet (Respondent): Minorities weren't obliged for military service at that time.

Ahmet (Respondent's Brother): They were not taken into Ottoman army.

Mehmet (Respondent): And they reached 13,500 population here. They had money but they couldn't buy any property/land because Ottomans did not sell them, did not give them title deed. After first and second Tanzimat (a reform and modernization of the Ottoman Empire that lasted from 1839-1876), they obtained this right. Then they bought all Yeniköy. Ours (manav/local turk) were poor, there was no one able to work. Women were unmarried or widowed. Their soldiers went to military service but didn't come back. Their children were still so young... And, they (Armenians) stayed here all the way till deportation (He uses term sürgün:excile/exodus). And Deportation was as...

(The rest of the story can be followed from short documentary Nor&Eski).

References

Cavafy C.P. (1992). *Collected Poems.* Translated by Edmund Keeley and Philip Sherrard. Edited by George Savidis. Revised Edition. Princeton University Press.

Barkan E. (2005). Engaging History: Managing Conflict and Reconciliation. *History Workshop Journal.* Issue 59, pp. 229-236.

Leyla Neyzi

Oral History as a Tool for Reconciliation? Remembering Armenians in Contemporary Turkey

Leyla Neyzi is an Associate Professor at the Faculty of Arts and Social Sciences at Sabancı University. Her publications include *Speaking to One Another: Personal Memories of the Past in Armenia and Turkey* (with Hranush Kharatyan-Araqelyan) (Bonn: *dvv international*, 2010); "Oral History and Memory Studies in Turkey", *Turkey's Engagement with Modernity: Conflict and Change in the Twentieth Century* (Celia Kerslake, Kerem Öktem, Philip Robins, eds. London: Palgrave Macmillan, 2010); "Remembering Smyrna/Izmir: Shared History, Shared Trauma." *History and Memory* 20(2) Fall/ Winter 2008: 106-127; "Strong as Steel, Fragile as a Rose: A Turkish Jewish Witness to the Twentieth Century." *Jewish Social Studies* 12,1 (Fall 2005): 167-189; "Remembering to Forget: Sabbateanism, National Identity and Subjectivity in Turkey," *Comparative Studies in Society and History* 44, 1 (January 2002): 137-158.

In this paper, I discuss the results of the oral history research conducted in Turkey as part of the project "Adult Education and Oral History Contributing to Armenian-Turkish Reconciliation" (Neyzi and Kharatyan-Araqelyan 2010).

As the research team in Turkey, our goal was to conduct oral history interviews with ordinary individuals to find out whether and how Armenians are remembered in their homeland almost one hundred years after the genocide. Our starting point was the conviction that remembering, narrating and sharing the past is an important step on the path toward reconciliation. While few witnesses of these traumatic events remain alive, the past is "remembered" through postmemory, including oral transmission from generation to generation (Hirsch 2008). Oral history can act as a tool for reconciliation because it makes it possible to set differing and possibly conflicting accounts of the past side by side as equally legitimate narratives which can be read together (Barkan 2009). Indeed, this was one of the major aims of our joint research in Turkey and Armenia. As our findings show, not only did the accounts of individuals from Armenia and Turkey differ, but there were also variations among the accounts from Turkey. I will focus in this paper on these variations, which I argue stem largely from the ethnic/religious (and political) affiliations of the individuals interviewed.

1. Methodology

Given its focus on reconciliation in the present, our research was planned so as to actively involve young people. Our team included project assistants, university students who attended the summer camp where we provided training in oral history methodology, and those taking my course on oral history at Sabancı University during Fall 2009.

We conducted our research in regions where Armenians formerly made up a large proportion of the population. In addition to the city of Istanbul, where most of the Armenian population of present day Turkey resides, these included central Anatolia, eastern Anatolia, and southeastern Anatolia. As memories of Armenians have been largely silenced and taboo in the public sphere in Turkey until recently, our topic was highly sensitive and challenging (Dixon 2010). In order to achieve trust and to get permission to record, we accessed potential interviewees through personal networks, including those of members of the research team. This proved to be an invaluable method, and we visited the home villages, towns and cities of students and research assistants and their acquaintances, getting to know potential interviewees by spending time as guests in their homes. Our trips frequently involved a tour of homes and neighborhoods in which we focused on material remnants and memories of place/space. Ethnographic fieldwork and participant observation provided the background for the oral history interviews.

Because we reached potential interviewees through personal contacts, we were able to get permission to interview and to record, although some interviewees did ask to remain anonymous (we chose to use pseudonyms in our publications). One of the major challenges we faced in the field was how to present our research topic to potential interviewees. Given the narrow confines through which the "Armenian problem" is represented in the mainstream media, we particularly wanted to avoid introducing the terminology of official history. We therefore spoke to potential interviewees about our interest in local and family history, cultural heritage, and material and other remnants of the past. We asked them to narrate what they knew about the history of their region, community, and family, and to recount their own life story. We deliberately tried to avoid directing our interviewees, hoping to elicit through close listening particular stories (as well as silences) concerning Armenians. Having conducted background research on both the localities and the interviewees themselves, we knew beforehand that it was highly likely that our interviewees would introduce issues of interest to us. The narratives thus produced made it possible to investigate both the ways Armenians are remembered as well as the frameworks and discourses shaping these memories and postmemories.

Overall, we were taken aback by the willingness of individuals to speak as well as by the degree to which memories of Armenians are retained in contemporary Turkey. The transmission of oral accounts from generation to generation has made this possible. In addition to stories (including legends, myths, dreams), postmemory is buttressed by material remnants such as ruins, buildings, objects and the landscape itself. Our research shows that despite the silencing and denial in official history, including school textbooks and the mainstream media, memory pertaining to Armenians continues to be transmitted orally over the generations. Our impression is that ordinary people in Turkey are extremely generous when they perceive a genuine interest in their life experiences and interpretations concerning the recent past. It is highly unfortunate that "orality" (the oral transfer of knowledge and experience) and local storytelling remain underutilized sources for historical research in Turkey, given that the history of Armenians in Turkey remains an "open secret". It is to be hoped that collaboration between postnationalist historians, oral historians and anthropologists will reverse the trend. While interviewing is always a challenge, I believe the time is particularly ripe for oral history research in Turkey, given the expansion of civil society, the palpable and growing interest in knowing and debating the recent past and the increasing willingness of individuals to speak in the public domain (Keyman 2008).

During 2009-2010, we conducted, recorded and transcribed interviews with around one hundred individuals from different social class, ethnic/religious, sex/gender, generational and geographical backgrounds. While each life story narrative is unique, I would like to briefly discuss some of the themes that emerged. While all interviewees spoke about Armenians, there were variations in the accounts of members of different communities. Our interviewees included Armenians as well as individuals of Muslim origin, such those who identified as Turks or Kurds.

2. Armenians

There is so little research on the Armenian community in contemporary Turkey that it seems that even those interested in the Armenians view this as largely a *historical* subject. It is high time more ethnographic and sociological research is carried out on the Armenian community, now largely but not wholly based in the city of Istanbul (Komsuoğlu and Örs 2009). Population estimates suggest a figure of around 70,000, though exact numbers are difficult to establish and the rise in intermarriage increasingly blurs the boundaries between communities.

Our interviews with Armenians demonstrate that although traditional fears remain, community members are more receptive to speaking in public, even when their interlocutors are Turks (our interviewers included both Muslims and Armenians). Not only were Armenians we approached willing to be interviewed (though not necessarily willing to be named or photographed), but they were surprisingly open in speaking about (and naming) the genocide, its effects on their own families, and their experiences with discrimination under the Turkish Republic. While this sea change is largely due to the democratization of Turkey in the last decades, a significant additional factor is the murder of Hrant Dink, which made him a martyr and an example to follow in the struggle for democratization and equal citizenship, especially for Armenian youth.

How did our interviewees speak about the genocide, the experiences of their own families, their own experiences under the Turkish Republic, differences and divisions within the Armenian community, and the meaning of Armenian identity in contemporary Turkey?

Dikran (not his actual name) is an Armenian man who owns a clothing store in the historic business district of Istanbul. Born in 1954 in Istanbul, he was 56 at the time of the interview. He clearly established 1915 as the point at which the stories of all Armenians in Turkey began: "Our histories closely resemble one another... None of us has a story without thorns... The lives of Anatolian Armenians are full of stories like this... going all the way back to 1915." For Dikran, experience is as good a piece of historical evidence as written documents: "Not everything has a written document. The document in this case is the person, it is me. My life, my past is the document. The Armenians who lived in Anatolia, who used to till the land, are no longer there." (For a similar view, see Nichanian 2009).

Like other Armenian interviewees, Dikran made the point that Armenian families were hesitant in transmitting their experiences to their children due to fear: "We couldn't talk about these things in the past. Our fathers would not tell us our stories. I used to think this mobilization for war was something that happened only in our village. It was only after Turkey became more democratic, and books began to be published about the genocide that I realized that what happened in our village also happened in Muş, in Van, elsewhere."

While Dikran regrets the fact that he knows little of his family's past, he clings to his roots through a sense of attachment to the land: "Our history is very short. I can only tell you about my grandfather. I have nothing in my father's land. They cut me off from the soil of my father's land... We are a people of this land. People ask us, 'where do you come from?' We came from nowhere, we were already here. Before the Turks came to Anatolia, there were Armenians, Greeks here, that is us. Sometimes you get offended for being called a foreigner."

Intriguingly, Armenian as well as Muslim interviewees waxed nostalgic about a shared past that was destroyed. In the words of Sarkis: "Until 1915 Anatolia had a highly developed civilization. These mistakes took the country way back economically. Today we would have been a country like America."

Armenian interviewees emphasized the fact that the roots their families reestablished and their economic achievements were continually undermined by discriminatory policies of the Turkish Republic. This resulted in outmigration as well as the habit of living one's life largely within the confines of the community. This meant attending community schools, socializing through the church and other community institutions, marrying within the community, and steering clear of politics and from being in the public eye. While this tends to be the norm, in some cases fear of discrimination led some families to encourage their children to assimilate, hoping that if they had Turkish names, spoke Turkish without an accent, received a good education and became middle-class professionals, they would have an easier time. For example, Selin, a 24 year-old young Armenian student we interviewed spoke of her revolt against her parents, especially after the murder of Hrant Dink: "There is a language spoken at home which I don't understand. My friends' families are different from mine. There is a problem which I try to figure out. I made a big scene at home after his death. I was mad because they left me without an identity."

Armenian interviewees concur that the murder of Hrant Dink had a transformative effect on the community. Selin insightfully suggested that Armenians reacted to the event vis-à-vis the reaction of the majority: "They were very surprised by the slogan 'We are all Armenians!' These reactions affected them more than his death itself. They became more brave when they saw Turks were protesting". While the murder confirmed Armenians' worst fears, it also galvanized the young in particular to continue Hrant Dink's struggle for democracy, rights and equal citizenship.

Concerning reconciliation, while Armenian interviewees are glad to be able to speak more freely in public, and believe the suffering of their community should be acknowledged, they also express the hope that they can continue to live in their homeland in peace. As Sarkis puts it: "This history is very painful. Even I don't tell my children a lot, for we don't want our children to feel rancour towards the society they live in. When I tell these stories I do not fill them with hatred, I fill them with love. If I tell with rancor, revenge or hatred, there is no meaning in telling. If there is a desire for revenge, this will go on."

3. Kurds

Among our interviewees of Muslim background, there were those who identified as Kurds. As historically Kurds and Armenians frequently lived in the same regions, the memory of Armenians is strong among the Kurdish people. The violence unleashed against the Armenians by the Kurds with the support of the Ottoman state (and the incitement of local religious leaders) is well-known (Klein 2002). Accounts of relations between Armenians and Kurds in the past often revolve around two issues: property and women (and children). The genocide meant that the Kurds who lived alongside Armenians stood to benefit from their land, homes, and any other property they left behind, including buried gold. In addition, surviving Armenian women (and children) were frequently incorporated into Kurdish and other Muslim families as free laborers and child-bearers. It is only in the last years that the taboo about conversion and being of Armenian origin has been challenged (Çetin 2004). Our research confirms that many Kurdish (as well as other Muslim) families descend from converted Armenians.

While the Kurds played a significant role as perpetrators during the genocide, the stance of the PKK has meant that the discourse, particularly of young, politicized Kurds vis-à-vis the Armenians is changing. Both political leaders and ordinary people are increasingly willing to acknowledge the Kurds' role in the genocide as part of a discourse that identifies with oppressed peoples and emphasizes the responsibility of the Ottoman/Turkish state as the instigator of this calamity. At the same time, some interviewees suggested that blaming the state did not absolve the Kurds of responsibility, as they acted willingly to benefit from the property belonging to the Armenians. Kurds' increasing empathy with Armenians as victims also stems from their own experience of victimhood at the hands of the Turkish state during the dirty war of the last thirty years which has led to great loss of life and has forced several million people to abandon their homes and villages.

One of our interviewees was Adil, a 26 year-old Kurdish man from Kulp, Diyarbakır. Adil recounted the story of an old man in their village who suffered at the end of his life from flashbacks: "He said, 'We rounded up all the Armenians from the villages around midnight. There is a very deep cliff at Eskar. We took them there and threw them down the cliff one by one. I can no longer sleep. Whenever I close my eyes, the children I threw off that cliff take hold of my hands and pull me towards the cliff". Adil also spoke about the Armenian land appropriated by his own family: "Much of our land used to belong to Armenians. Many of our fields have Armenians names. 'The Priest's Field': it is quite obvious". According to Adil, villagers fear that Armenians will return someday to claim their property: "Our village guard said to the guerillas, 'We know what you are after, you are all Armenians, you are going to take the land from us'. This is one of the reasons why people become village guards".

Adil suggested that, for some, a handy way of dealing with guilt is to identify with the victim: "Being so interested in my grandmother's Armenianness may be an attempt to overcome this sense of guilt. Taking on the victim's grievance and feeling that responsibility opens up a space of power. Being a victim is satisfying; it makes people pat you on the head." The fact that perpetrators of the past (who themselves may have descended in part from their surviving victims) have become victims in the present makes the relationship of the Kurds and the Armenians in Turkey exceedingly complex.

4. Turks

Muslim interviewees who identified as Turks tended to be the most challenging to interview. We took particular care in these interviews to avoid the discourse of official history and the mainstream media and to not mention the topic of the Armenians until it was introduced by our interviewees. Our interviews demonstrated that Turks tend to tell highly ambiguous tales, avoid discussing agency, speak in multiple voices and frequently contradict themselves. Most noticeably, we encountered a divergence between local history and national history as recounted by our interviewees. For example, interviewees would tell harrowing anecdotes concerning the experiences of particular Armenian individuals they or their families knew, while reverting to some version of official history when speaking about the Armenians in general. In addition, while Armenian or Kurdish interviewees were likely to use the term "genocide," very few interviewees who identified as Turkish used this term. The terms used included "war mobilization," "conflict," "the events of 1915," "deportation," and "massacre."

Nevertheless, the degree to which people retained local memories of Armenians was surprising. Interviewees told stories about particular craftsmen, neighbors and friends in detail. They also tended to represent the distant past as a golden era in which neighbors lived in peace. Interviewees also tended to contrast the modernity of Armenians with the primitiveness of Muslims, describing Armenians as intelligent, hard-working, disciplined, trustworthy, well-educated and generous.

Despite the fact that many expressed sorrow about what the Armenians had suffered, the issue of agency and responsibility was largely elided in the Turkish narratives. Silences and defensiveness frequently filled the gap. Necmi, a 70 year-old retired schoolteacher from the eastern Anatolian town of Divriği, said that when he was a child, the elderly women told him, "What was wrong came from above." He described how his grandfather, a local official, had saved an Armenian jeweler on the promise that he would take on his son as an apprentice. Kamil, a middle aged resident of the central Anatolian town of Akşehir, where Armenians and Muslims used to live side by side, mentioned the silences concerning Armenians that prevailed during his childhood in the 1960s: "It was as if somebody has forbidden it somehow. People don't want to talk about these things. I don't exactly know if they were afraid or what." Kamil blamed outside "provocations" for spoiling the good relations between the two neighbors: "These were decent and honest people. Only, bad stuff came in between, somebody derailed them, somebody indoctrinated them and the two people became enemies." Conspiracy theories, particularly associated with "outside forces" are a common way of dealing with (or avoiding) the issue of responsibility.

In some interviews, oral accounts directly reflected official discourse. For example, the representation of Armenians as perpetrators and Muslims as victims is most common in border regions where violent battles were waged over territory and both sides suffered as well as inflicting suffering. Zübeyde, a 69 year-old Turkish woman from Van recounted the losses in her family during this period. She told of how her family fled during the Russian invasion as well as of their return with the Turkish army: "They escaped on oxcarts. My mother remembers the wheels rolling over corpses. Many died from the smell." Acknowledging the violence unleashed by both sides, she described the way Armenians fled so that families like hers were able to take over Armenian homes: "They took their lives and went. They didn't take anything. They said, let's leave the house right now, just like that." Like others brought up on post-memories of war and violence, Zübeyde to this day expresses the fear that Armenians will return to reclaim their property, including the gold that the residents of Van believe remains buried underground: "They want Van since eternity. The Armenians always said, 'If we conquer the castle of Van, we will cover it from top to bottom with a red cloth to shade it from the sun'. " The obsession with buried treasure and the fact that digging for gold is a major pastime to this day demonstrates the degree to which the ghosts of Armenians continue to haunt those who have replaced them on the land.

5. Conclusion

While our research shows that the accounts of members of different communities concerning the recent past differ, it is important to note that conversion, dissimulation, intermarriage and the multiplicity of identities blurs the line between seemingly distinct Christian and Muslim communities. In their narratives, some of our interviewees spoke from exactly that margin, which, as we are increasingly finding out, is much less marginal than previously thought. As Ayhan, a 30 year old man from Sason, Batman put it: "What are we brother? We are three things. We are Kurds at home, we speak Kurdish. We are Turks at school, we speak Turkish. We are Armenians at the summer camp, we speak Armenian."

Concerning reconciliation, it is clear that while the memory of Armenians remains alive and well in Turkey, accounts of the past diverge widely. Among Muslims, young and politicized Kurds in particular seem more willing to publicly challenge official history, while Armenians are becoming bolder in speaking out about the experiences of their families in the past. The divergence between local experience/post-memory and official history means that narratives concerning the past are frequently fragmented and contradictory. It is to be hoped that as local memories are increasingly recorded and shared publicly, a new history based on the experience of ordinary people can be written.

References

Barkan E. (2009). Historians and Historical Reconciliation. *American Historical Review*, October 2009: pp. 899-913.
Cetin F. (2004). *Anneannem*. İstanbul: Metis Press.

Dixon J. (2010). *"Defending the Nation?* Maintaining Turkey's Narrative of the Armenian Genocide." *South European Society and Politics* 15(3): pp. 467-485.

Hirsch M. (2008). The Generation of Postmemory. *Poetics Today* 29 (1): pp.103-128.

Keyman E. Fuat. (2008). *Remaking Turkey: Globalization, Alternative Modernities, and Democracies*. Lanham, MD: Lexington Books.

K. Janet. (2002). *Power in the Periphery: The Hamidiye Light Cavalry and the Struggle over Ottoman Kurdistan, 1890-1914.* Unpublished Ph.D. Dissertation, Princeton University.

Komsuoğlu A. and Örs B. (2009). Armenian Women of Istanbul: Notes on Their Role in the Survival of the Armenian Community. *Gender, Place and Culture*, June 2009, 16(3): pp. 329-349.

Neyzi L. and H. Kharatyan-Araqelyan (2010). *Speaking to One Another: Personal Memories from Armenia and Turkey.* Bonn: dvv international.

Nichanian M. (2009). *The Historiographic Perversion.* New York: Columbia University Press.

Hranush Kharatyan-Araqelyan

On some Features of Armenian-Turkish Joint Memories of the Past

Hranush Kharatyan-Araqelyan is the Head of the Chair on Cultural Anthropology and Area Studies at the Yerevan State Linguistic University and is also affiliated with the RA Institute of Archeology and Ethnography. She is an ethnographer with a degree of Candidate of Sciences from the Institute of Ethnography of the USSR Academy of Sciences, Leningrad (Sankt Petersburg).
Her field of scientific interests include: Caucasian Studies (North-Western Caucasus, Caucasian Albania), social-cultural changes of Armenia in transition period, Armenian national culture (celebrations, festivals) ethnic and religious minorities, adaptation problems of refugees, migration processes, and the anthropology of memory, among others. She has published five books and more than 70 scientific articles, and is a member of the editorial board of several scientific councils and periodicals.

In 2009, out of 45 students who applied to participate in the project, "Adult Education and Oral History Contributing to the Armenian-Turkish Reconciliation," only ten were selected. They were students from different universities, specializing in different majors, who did not know each other before taking part in the project. It turned out later that each of the students more or less carried shared family memories of genocide in their families, although the selection committee, composed of employees of the German DAAD and *dvv international* (Institute for the International Cooperation of the Association of German Adult Education Centers), did not have such a requirement. Moreover, none of the students interviewed by the committee said they were interested in the project because of their family memories (later as well they insisted that their own family past played no role in their wish to participate in the project). However, while participating students had no idea about one another, it was discovered later that they had at least one commonality: in their families there were some memories of genocidal past (grandmother or grandfather on mother's and father's side and in some families the grandparents on both sides were children of genocide survivors). The geography of Western-Armenian past of our students is rather broad – Bursa, Adana, Urfa, Caesaria [Kayseri]*, Amasya, Kars, Igdir, Artvin, Ardahan, Trabzon, Erzurum, Basen [Pasinler], Mush. After participation in the first Camp in Dilijan, Armenia and becoming familiar with oral history methodology and use of memories and memoirs as a source for the study of recent history, after being involved in the actual fieldwork, some of the students applied the same method in their families and revealed interesting details of their family history and ties which they were unaware before. In other words, research process in Armenia made the researchers themselves to reproduce certain elements of the present-day life of second/third generation genocide survivors, while the research did not have such an objective. This includes restoration of family ties, separation of family memories from social memory.

---

*　In the square brackets are the present-day Turkish toponyms.

Interestingly there were no ethnically non-Armenians among training applicants in Armenias: all the applicants were ethnically Armenian and the Armenian team was formed exclusively from ethnically Armenian students. The selected applicants in Turkey were Turkish nationals, ethnically Turks, Armenians, and Kurds, and as it turned out later, at least two of the Turks had Armenian grandmothers. I can not say to what extent their interest in the project was conditioned by... or whether in general it was conditioned by the "Armenian past" or the Armenian identity. However, it was obvious that the interest and enthusiasm of the selected Armenian students did not diminish, on the contrary, it gradually increased. Up until now the Armenian team participates in the program with almost the same set of people, while there was a considerable turnover among the participating Turkish students throughout the two years of the project implementation.

In Armenia the materials were collected exclusively in the families of the genocide survivors. There was no alternative: the objective was to record memories of those who had a personal experience of interaction with Turks in their family history, so as not only they would talk about their social memories but also about their personal experience of their family history, their family narrative.

And these are almost exclusively next generations of genocide survivors.

Five out of 13 respondents of Turkish narratives included in the joint book "Speaking to one Another" published in 2010 are Armenians born in Turkey (Digran, Vera, Ayhan, Selin, Aram). Two other respondents have either an Armenian mother or a grandmother born in Turkey (Ruhi and Adil). Yet, another one has Armenian blood in his family tree (Mete). So, eight out of thirteen are either Armenians or have some Armenian ancestry. Not surprisingly they are interested in the Armenian issue and the attitude towards Armenians in Turkey. However their memories about Armenians and their personal life experience is probably somehow different from the mainstream memories and perceptions in Turkey. In their life these people have more or less interacted with Armenians. On one hand they partially bear the "Armenian burden" in Turkey, on the other hand their judgments have been accumulated from personal experiences. Their narratives are not so much "memories" and/or "post-memories" but rather stories of personal experience. They are far more "motivated" in the issues related to Armenians than the Turkish society in general. Thus, making judgments about memories of the Armenians in the Turkish society on the basis of narratives of these people will be at least one-sided. These narratives are more of an answer to the question on how and what the Armenians (or suspected Armenians) felt and feel in Turkey. However, the remaining five stories, as well as the three stories having an Armenian "trace" in families (by the identity of respondents-Turkish and Kurdish) to some extent accomplish the mosaic of the Armenian memories in the Turkish society. Turkish and especially Armenian material proves that 95-year-old events in present-day Armenian and Turkish societies are not only a historical past. Their consequences to a great extent are a part of the present day life. Particularly in Turkey a part of the present life are the misgivings for the "Armenians' return," the possibility of getting back their former property, the fear of revealing presence of the Armenian blood in their family past, as well as rejection of the Armenian blood and on the contrary the efforts of revealing Armenian identity in the difficult search for identity. More or less "a part of the present life" are the toponyms reminding of the Armenians, the houses forsaken by the Armenians, household belongings, etc. You come across these fears in narratives of the Turkish part of the book "Speaking to one another" (see "The fear of losing the town" – Turkish "Zubeyde's" story, "Sosi's green eyes: why am I different?" – Kurd Adil's story born in 1983 in Diyarbakır. Adil is telling, "We were living together, we didn't interfere with each other, then I don't know what happened, but we seized their property. For example, much of our land used to belong to Armenians. My grandfather spent fifty years in court cases. He ended up getting all the land, yet many of the fields in our village have Armenian names... There is this belief that the Armenians who were deported want to come back."). In the preface of the Turkish part of the book "Speaking to one another" Leyla Neyzi writes, "The stories of women and of property show that 1915 can hardly be relegated to the past, but remains very much part and parcel of everyday life in contemporary Turkey. What is particularly intriguing about the narratives of Muslims is the tendency, particularly on the part of the younger generation, to rediscover and identify with the Armenians in their own families. This desire to identify with the victim may be viewed as an outcome of contemporary identity politics and a means of dealing with guilt in a society which refuses to publicly acknowledge responsibility."

The materials of the Armenian part show that particularly the genocide survivors' "present is mostly in the past and the past is in the present." Especially in the areas densely populated with survivors the structure of life to a great extent reproduces the connection with the lost homeland; special efforts are made to transfer family memories, to make them public. The sources feeding the memories of the Armenian-Turkish shared past in Turkey and Armenia considerably differ. On one hand there is a considerable number of material resources, on the other hand-feelings, emotions, memories. In both countries the personal memories are complemented by social memories, moreover, the sources feeding them also differ. In Turkey, the bulk of social memory is probably higher in Western and Northern regions, where there were not many Armenians in the past and where both the participants and the witnesses of the events of 1915-22 were far scanty. The narratives here, if there are such, should have been fed by Turkey's official historiography and the media. The bulk of social memory in Armenia is among the local population – the so-called Eastern Armenians. Their narratives are based on the accounts of survived Western Armenians plus the official historiography, the ritualized publicity of the genocide memories (especially the annual commemoration of the Armenian Genocide), literature and the media. Unlike Turkey, where there are plenty of objects (Armenian villages, toponyms, cemeteries forsaken by the Armenians, destroyed, sometimes still standing Armenian churches, the former houses of the Armenians, where Turks and Kurds are living now, areas with Armenian names, the Islamized Armenians who changed their identity, kidnapped or found Armenian young girls who later became mothers and the children of which in this or that way with the fact of their existence reminded the surrounding people of the former existence of the Armenians, different household items left by the Armenians like a sewing machine, pan, etc) to maintain the memories of people living in the areas where the Armenian Genocide was implemented, memories of "Turkish past" in Armenia practically do not have such objects. *Ergir*[1] was left in Turkey, and the survivors in Eastern Armenia were left with their memories. These memories much more frequently and sometimes almost exclusively refer to them, to their village, town, to violence

---

1   The word Yerkir, which has several meanings in Armenian – "whole world", "part of the country, administrative region", "ground, soil" – in the dialect of Moush and Sasoun refugees also denotes "homeland". In Moush-Sasoun dialect this word sounds like "Ergir". People from Moush and Sasoun use word "Ergir" only in reference to the homeland.

experienced by many of their refugee-fellows, the escape hardships, deaths, children left on their way of migration and escape, at times the cases of help. However, frequently enough we come across memories generating from feelings of homesickness.

Our material on the Armenian memories is based on 35 interviews conducted in 2009-2010. Selection of the respondents/families was based on several criteria, including:

▪ Whose ancestors settled in the territory of the Eastern Armenia immediately after the genocide in the same settlement with other survivors, and their children were born, grew up and lived in an atmosphere full of relatively dense memories of the past (villages of Ujan, Ashnak, Norakert, Dashtadem, Shgharshik).

▪ To understand the amount and content of memories of past and their manifestations in a thematically heterogeneous environment, we have selected families/respondents whose ancestors, after the survival settled in Eastern Armenia but not in the settlements densely populated with genocide survivors, but next to the local population of Armenia, mainly not far from Yerevan or in Yerevan itself (cities of Yerevan, Gyumri, Geghashen, Parakar, Dalarik).

▪ Whose ancestors, before settling in Eastern Armenia, lived for a few decades in other countries (Lebanon, Egypt, Syria, Greece, Iran, etc.) and came to the Republic of Armenia during the years of the organized repatriation the 1940-1950s.

These selection criteria were important for us to understand whether the intensity of transferring memories from generation to generation and the material differ because of difference in settlements. And we can state that indeed, they differ. In the mostly refugee populated or exclusively refugee-populated areas, the life structure is completely different. The culture of their homeland, *Ergir, i*s reproduced here. Newborns here were born and even 100 years later continue to be born to the atmosphere of repeated narratives. Growing up, they inherit the dialect, the peculiarities of meals, songs, and dances. Everyone here knows the history of the other ones, and all were connected with each other and still are bound with kinship ties. There is almost no "isolated" history or memory: someone's story of their grandmother is the story of another one's aunt, for the third one – that of an uncle's wife, for the fourth one-the uncle's mother, for the fifth – that of a neighbor, etc. Here they perfectly know the name of "their village," the entire *Ergir* geography of inhabitants of their current settlement (generations of inhabitants from 36 and more than eighty villages of Sasoun are now living in Ashnak and Ujan respectively, in Norakert – from Sekh and Ov of Bitlis, Mkhkner, Sosrat and other villages of Van, etc.). In such areas not only the stories of their own family overlap and are recalled at length but also the stories of a neighbor, relative, fellow-villager, former fellow-villager, countryman. The narratives remembered and told here have been transferred/are being transferred with the same experiences, with the same feelings; sometimes the "heroes" of these stories are their present countrymen. Here at times even the social hierarchy existing in the lost homeland has been reproduced. At the same time they all together with the help of one another were searching, finding and/ or tried to find their lost relatives. Together they celebrated when a relative was found and mourned the losses, they talked to each other, they shared with their stories, retold about the same people and they all wailed and whimpered for the same people. The the settlements and churches where their relatives were burnt (it is consistently mentioned of people being burned mostly in the churches), as well as the lost ones were often the same. Their children were born and brought up in the world of these stories and feelings and, indeed, they have become the part, the participant of their narratives-narratives that mainly refer to lost homeland, but this homeland becomes the homeland of the next generations as well. At the same time, in the places densely populated by genocide survivors, personal narratives are more affected by generalization, as well as social and collective memory than the narratives in the areas of diffused residence. It seems that collective memory needed less specification as everybody knew the same things and here we often come across such general terms as "Turks," "Kurds," etc. The second group of our respondents differed from the first one in far more "individualization" of memories. The respondents of this group are more aware of their own family stories, they seldom recur to the lost homeland, their "Armenian-Turkish joint past" is more individualized, "focused" on people, individuals, sometimes they remember people's names from that past. At the same time the representatives of the present-day generation of these groups as compared to the first group are less emotional.

From the peculiarities of "memories" of the third group some nuances can be particularized. The forefathers of the Armenian respondents of this group were all from the territory of Kilikia or from northern regions of Turkey (Marash, Adana, Caesaria [Kayseri], Amasya, Adabazari, Mersin, Dardanelles [Çanakkale]); and they were mainly Turkish-speaking, their children heard their parents' stories in Turkish – a phenomenon that evidently had its impact both on the very memories and the mode of transfer of these memories. However, this phenomenon lacks materials and needs supplementary analyses for broader generalization. Yet, it is obvious that while this group actively transfers family memories it also extensively makes generalizations.

In all three groups, family memories of shared "Armenian-Turkish" past start and end with the interruption of that joint past-the genocide; and the narratives essentially include two basic themes: what were the losses and what was the violence experienced by their grandparents (this is what is recalled in minute details) and how the survivors could narrowly escape. Even those narrators, who instead of more frequently used terms "massacre," "slaughter," "stampede" use the words "migration," "exile" while telling their personal stories, often recollected and at length transferred to their descendants mainly violence accounts. These include the vicious murder of their father, mother, child, other family members or some other episodes of murder that gave them a severe shock or were forever stamped on their memory (they recollected even the hem of a mother's-in-law skirt burning in the tonir, the blue-eyed girl's dress swaying in the breeze, walking along the slope of the mountain with his brother and her screaming out "Turks, Turks" on meeting the brutal murderers, the fire of the hearth fizzling with the running blood of the father killed in bed, the gunshot-like explosions of the corpses lying and swollen in the scorching July sun, etc).

The length and weight of these phenomena may have driven away the memories of everyday simple relations with Turks or at least the importance of telling about those relations to their children. In case of the interviewer's persistent questions on the life of their family hundred years ago, the respondents sometimes recall only specific family details such as grandfather's or grandmother's education, a pilgrimage, the wealthy or poor life of their ancestors and so on. However even these stories were often full of their ancestors' fears of living in Turkey before the genocide. Active memories of our respondents, particularly those from Cilicia include specific cases of their grandfathers trying to "send" their children out of Turkey and to rebuild their further life in other countries-the USA, Egypt (G. Chugaszyan, N. Tajiryan), or how their grandparents in their childhood have been secretly taking food to their fathers, brothers hiding from the Turks in the mountains (G. Badalyan).

In present-day memories, relating the stories of their ancestors about hiding away young girls still remains active. We have even recorded a story according to which the organizer of the Armenian slaughter in Mush and Sasun was in love with a beautiful Armenian girl but he was turned down by her. According to this mythologized story a Kurd named Musa Bek falls in love with a beautiful Armenian girl Gulo. The Armenians, scared of Musa Bek's unceasing persecutions, applied to sultan for help. At the Sultan's request "Musa Bek was found guilty, and sentenced to hundred and one year imprisonment. They used to tell it so. As soon as the Young Turks started the slaughter Musa Bek was set free. He was set free and told to assemble troops and to treat the Armenians the way he wanted. Musa Bek massacred everybody. Those who slaughtered people in Moush, Khut and Sasoun were his gangs" (V. Ghugaszyan).

It is known that long before the genocide, girls were taken from Armenian families. The Armenians had already become accustomed to the idea and ways of hiding the beauty of their daughters or even disfiguring them. And in today's memories the stories about "taking away" the girls have been preserved in active memory; and not only the concrete Genocidal events are recalled but also the phenomenon in general. In the Turkish part of the book "Speaking to One Another" there are only cases about "taken away" girls in the period of genocide – Ruhi's mother of Turkish identity, Adil's grandma of Kurdish identity, Mete's grandma of divided Turkish-Kurdish identity).

It is noteworthy that those telling about violence usually use the word "Turk", "Turks" even if while telling it turns out that the one or those who resorted to violence was a Kurd/were Kurds or the identity of the murderer is unknown. This phenomenon, on one hand can be attributed to the influence of at least 100-year-old social memory, on the other hand, to the circumstance that in memories of people those who used violence were either the representatives of the Turkish army and the police or acted under their patronage. Although the army and the police had no "ethnic face," they were mainly identified with the national name of a concrete country. In Turkey, they are "Turks" especially during the genocide, when Turkey, engaged in war, not trusting the minorities living in its territory, formed its army and the police mainly from Turks or at least the Muslims. That's why the "Turks" ("the Turkish nation" "deduced" from them) becoming the hostage of the denial policy of the Turkish century-long authorities, still remain in Armenian memories the main defendant and the one responsible for the genocide.

Although our research is chiefly based on oral histories, we came across other ways of memory transfer and in general there are many other ways of transferring memories, such as written memoirs, various monuments related to the genocide and the lost motherland, regular celebrations of specific genocide-related phenomena, reproduction of

From Albert Mamikonyan's photo archive

toponyms and so on. Having visited just 35 families, our research group "encountered" numerous individual-private initiatives of preservation and recording of memories/among our respondents' families (Mihran Avetisyan's manuscript "The story of our family," the mother's story written by Almast Harutyunyan titled "40 days among the corpses" which has recently been published in a limited number of copies, Garnik Manukyan's narratives expressing homesickness for Van titled "A Call of Pain," "Flowers of Sipan mountain," the audio recording of Aregnaz Poghosyan's mother's story before her death, the publications and records made in Garegin Chugaszyan's family, shooting a film on Vasak Toroyan's visit to his native village, Albert Mamikonyan's and Nairi Tajiryan's family photo and handwritten rich archive, family trees, epitaphs, etc).

To this we should add other individual and collective ways of recording and transferring memories. The collective ways of transferring memories are different in terms of what to do and what not. For instance, until now survivors from Mush haven't celebrated "Vardavar"[2] as the brutal massacre in Mush were organized on the very same day of Vardavar; inhabitants of Ujan and Ashnak periodically commemorate the birthdays or death anniversaries of their heroes of self-defense battles-Andranik, Gevorg Chaush. The relatives of those heroes or the entire community have jointly erected statues and other monuments, and the school pupils are regularly taken to see these monuments to pay tribute to the memory of those who at the cost of life saved the life of their ancestors. The house-museum of Gevorg Chaush was built in Ashnak village; in the same village one of the hero's relatives turned a spacious room of his into a museum of Gevorg Chaush's memories; under the initiative of one of the villagers a monument to the memory of the Armenian Genocide victims was built. In Ujan village with financial support of the community Andranik's statue was placed, later – the statuary of the "fedayis"[3], the streets of the village were named after the names of people who played a major role in the survival of Ujan's inhabitants.

The statuary of the "fedayis" in Ujan village

It is important to note that if telling, writing, epitaphs, in one word the individual, family ways of transferring memories were rather active in the Soviet period when speaking about the genocide was forbidden, then the collective ways of transferring memories emerged in the sixties, when the authorities officially kept silent, but didn't actively pursue the "silent speakers." In any case not only were they the product of the official ideological campaign but they were also against the official silence, they were shaped in the conditions of opposition by the authorities and perhaps also for this reason their forms are of a considerable variety.

The first manifestations of monuments among the survivors in Armenia can be observed on the tombstones of the deceased bearing inscriptions which, as a memory of the past, contain information on the birthplace of the late.

it's written on this tombstone of the Zovasar village cemetery of Talin region:

BORN IN GELIE
MSUR VILLAGE OF SASUN
KIRAKOSYAN SEDRAK, SON
OF HOVHANNES 1895-1974

---

2   Traditional Armenian holiday full of water games.
3   Fedayee – fighter of the self-defense battles.

far left:
On this tombstone of Nerkin Sasnashen village cemetery of Talin:
THIS IS THE TOMB OF THE LATE AVETIS AVETISYAN, SON OF KHACHATUR, BORN IN 1882, IN MSHGEGH VILLAGE OF SASUN, DIED IN 1960

left:
VAZIR MOVSISYAN,
SON OF POGHOS
1909-1986
BORN IN SASUN
ARTSVIK VILLAGE

We often come across similar epitaphs in the thirties-seventies, particularly in cemeteries of the densely-populated settlements of the survivors. As time passed, the number of those born in "ergir" of course decreased. This tombstone of the cemetery in Nerkin Sasnashen village of Talin dating back to 1986, for instance, is one of the latest of gravestones of this type.

At times you come across some expressions of homesickness as, for instance, is the epitaph on the tombstone in the cemetery of Khachaghbyur village of Vardenis (bottom left).

Another "monumental" group of transferring memories is "the monuments of genocide" first built in the seventies and becoming more popular with time. They are mostly documents of collective memories. The data implied

far left:
Oh, our homeland Mush,
You're very sweet and dear,
Euphrates and Tigris rivers,
Were left as memories to us.

left:
Nerkin Bazmaberd village

right:
Nerkin Sasnashen village

far right:
Mastara village

right:
Ashnak village

far right:
Goris

by thesemonuments is very "stingy:" they include either some date, usually "1915" that is the accepted date of genocide usually accompanied by the date of the monument erection or they have the inscription "To the memory of the victims of genocide;" sometimes the information content of the "memory" of the monument can be inferred from sculptures, symbols.

The moderation of the Genocidal monumental culture is noteworthy. In monuments of local initiatives we practically meet no text information; moreover, we never meet the word "Turk." Of relatively "aggressive" symbolic monuments is, for instance, the one built in Talin region, adjacent to Mastara village under the local initiative, on which we see Soghomon Tehleryan[4] with his foot on Taliat's chest (see on the next page).

The official monuments built from the end of the sixties do not contain any text and aggressive symbols as well. Except the monument of Tsitsernakaberd perpetuating the "memory of the genocide victims," those scanty monuments that exist

---

4   Soghomon Tehleryan, who lost his family members during the Genocide, in 1921 in Berlin killed the minister of Home Affairs of the government of the Young Turks, one of the organizers of the Armenian Genocide Taliat Pasha.

far left:
Monument built in Talin region near Mastara village

top left:
The monument devoted to the victims of Genocide in Yerevan

bottom left:
The monument devoted to Mount Musa heroic battle

in Armenia are mainly devoted to self-defense events. These are, for instance, Sardarapat Memorial[5], the monument representing the self-defense of Nor Hachn,[6] the monument devoted to survival of the Armenians after the 40-day resistance of population of the Armenian villages (surrounding Mount Musa situated on the shore of the Mediterranean Sea) to the Turkish regular army.

The Armenian memorial culture related to the topic of genocide in case of both the local, community initiatives and

5   In May of 1918 in the territory of the Western Armenia, by the battle of Sardarabad the Armenian volunteers could prevent the forwarding of the Turkish regular army that had raided into Armenia from Turkey. The monumental complex has been built in the place of the battle.
6   In 1920 in Turkey, in the territory of Kilikia, on the slope of Mount Kermes the population of Hachn-almost 90 kms to the North-West from Marash, had been for 8 months resisting the Turkish regular troops.

YOU TRAVELER!

THIS LAND PIECE, ON YOU UNINTEN-TIONALLY STEPPED,

IS A LAND WHERE AN AGE HAD PASSED.

LEAN AND CAREFULLY LISTEN TO THIS MASS OF LAND,

IT IS THE CRUCIAL PART; THE HEAR OF A MOTHERLAND.

THIS MONUMENT IS PUT UP BY THE KARS GOVERNORSHIP ON THE 1992 IN THE MEMORY OF OUR INNOCENT CIVILIAN PEOPLE WHO HAD LOST THEIR LIVES DURING THE ARMENIAN TRIAL OF WIPING THE VILLAGE OF SUBATAN OF THE MAP.

AT THE END OF THE II WORLD WAR AND AFTER THE BREST-LITOVSK AGREEMENT WHERE THE RUSSIANS WERE DRAWING BACK FROM THIS REGION, THE ARMENIANS WHO HAD FOUND THE OPPORTUNITY TO DO ANYTHING THE VILLAGE CALLED SUBATAN GATHERED THE PEOPLE AND TOOK THEIR VALUABLE BELONG-INGS AND JEWELRY, PUT THE PEOPLE TOGETHER INTO THE HAYLOFTS, POURED KEROSENE, AND SET THEM TO FIRE, CUT THE HEADS OF SONS OF THE VILLAGERS WITH AXES WITHOUT SEPARATING CHILD, OLD WOMAN OR MAN, CLEAVED THE ABDOMENS OF OUR PREGNANT WOMEN STICK THE BAYONETS INTO THE UNBORN BABIES, LEFT THE COPSES AROUND TO BE TORN AND PULLED INTO PIECES BY THE DOGS AND TOTALLY 570 TURKISH HAD BEEN MURDERED BRUTALLY AND PAINFULLY.

the official-state projects strike the eye with its text moderation, the monuments are addressed to the memory of the victims or the success of self-defense. The main information is implied my means of ratification of dates. Their aesthetic shaping mostly imitates the khachkar of the Armenian tombstone culture sometimes accompanied by a primitive symbols of sorrow (mostly by images of a mother and a child). Sometimes you come across monuments with simple symbols (split destinies, lost homeland) and busts. The considerable part of symbols accompanying these monuments is either the eagle or the bell (in the given case-alarm signal) or the spring. If we compare them with the Turkish monumental culture of the same time period we'll see a remarkable difference. The monumental memory of the Armenian-Turkish joint past in Turkey refers exclusively to the period of genocide as well, but in them it "informs" with texts and characters that the Armenians here have massacred Turks. For instance, the obelisk on the way of Ani-Kars implies in written text that in that territory the Armenians have slaughtered and massacred the Turkish population, raped the Turkish girls, tore open the bellies of pregnant women, etc.

Summing up the given brief report on the Armenian memories and some features of their manifestation concerning the Armenian-Turkish joint past, we may infer that they are mostly emotional, they do not concern "the past of the joint life", and they are thickened around the events of the "past of the death" holding the period of Genocide in its axis and have a tendency to be transferred to the new generation.

The present material on the Armenian memories of the Armenian-Turkish joint past cannot become a tool of Armenia-Turkey rapprochement unless these memories reach adequate recognition in Turkey, unless an atmosphere of social and political respect towards them is established.

The interviews conducted throughout 2009-2010 in 35 families of Armenia show that the present-day generation of the genocide survivors practically is not ready for reconciliation with Turks. All our respondents-both the intellectuals and the villagers and ordinary town people think that the Turkish society is not ready for reconciliation as well. By their estimate the Turkish society wants the period of genocide to fall into oblivion, and in this case even the issue of forgiveness by the Armenians loses its sense. The act of apologizing and that of forgiving is a mutual serious process containing numerous components. For the one who apologizes, it is first of all the actual and serious awareness of the act of forgiveness and the phenomenon which may become the source of repentance, penitence, pain for the victim's sufferings, self-purification and other feelings. These are serious feelings bringing honor to the "apologizer," as to the Armenian Genocide, except a small layer of the intellectuals, judging by the materials of the Turkish part "Wish they hadn't left" of the book "Speaking to One Another" are missing in the Turkish society. By the estimate of the Armenian respondents, if the Turkish society is able to forget the hugeness of the crime and the sufferings of the victim, they actually do not need the Armenian forgiveness. This very philosophy is reflected in the title of the Armenian part of the book "Speaking to one another" – "Whom to forgive? What to forgive?"

**An interactive article
by Vanya Ivanova
and Matthias Klingenberg**

The History Network
of *dvv international*

For five years, from 2004 to 2008, **Vanya Ivanova** served as the manager of the History project in South Eastern Europe at *dvv international*, working in the field of interactive methods of handling and teaching recent history in the Balkans. Currently, Ms Ivanova contributes to the *dvv international* History network within the framework of the Reconciliation project between Armenia and Turkey. Ivanova is also a researcher at the New Bulgarian University's Center for European Refugees Migration and Ethnic Studies (CERMES), where she is conducting her Ph.D. research with a focus on return policies towards highly qualified migration in Bosnia and Herzegovina and Bulgaria.

Matthias Klingenberg was born on 16 September 1972 in Lower Saxony, Germany. He studied History and Political Sciences at the University of Heidelberg, with a specialisation on development theories and GDR-Soviet cultural relations. His work experience includes the educational and development sector for the Goethe-Institute, the German Academic Exchange Service (DAAD) and the Institute for International Cooperation of the German Adult Education Association (*dvv international*). He has served in several missions abroad, including Kazakhstan, Uzbekistan, and Tanzania. He currently serves as the leader of the Asia Team at *dvv international*'s headquarters in Bonn, Germany.

For several weeks now, together with Matthias, driven by the desire to contribute, to reflect and to systemize in an article the message, ideas, knowledge and experience of the *dvv international* History network, we have discussed via Skype, project meetings and e-mails how to do it, we have exchanged many structures, what is important, why it is needed, what we have accomplished so far, and thus, we have piled various paragraphs of different aspects of our work. This process of work was giving us new and new insights, but at the same time making it more difficult to gather it in a joint format. Why, you may ask? And the answer is simple, because although we have very many ideas in common and we are both inspired by the work we do, we are phrasing things in different ways, having our own styles of expressing and explaining our ideas. So, in a way, this creative process was a lot resembling our adult education non formal approach of work in the history sphere, where in the centre is the person/the individual with his/her personal background and story, personal motivation and willingness to bring a change in his/her personal and professional life (acquiring new skills and competences, when we talk about training; getting better understanding and awareness when we talk about reflecting the past; preserving the story of a family, a village or a particular place, when using biographical approach, etc.). Thus, we decided to continue this process, to be much closer to the work we do and the ideas we believe in, to do something creative and interactive, an article that follows the philosophy of "out of the box thinking" and in fact is resembling the most the title of the project and the publication in the frame of which we publish this article "Speaking to one another."

So, in the following pages, we would like to offer our answers and ideas of several important questions, presented in the form of a dialogue/an open talk that will give you an insight and information about who we are and what motivates us to do this work, what is the scope of the history network and how it was growing through the years, what expertise we have gathered and where you may read more about the work in the various regions, what learning experience we have generated so far and what are the challenges we have faced, what are the future possibilities and plans and how to reach us if you get inspired too.

We would like to start with our personal stories within the dvv international and more specifically how we get involved in the history network:

Vanya: For me this happened in October 2002, when I took part in a 10 days training seminar in Germany, organized by *dvv international* under the Stability Pact for South Eastern Europe. I was one of the three participants from Bulgaria, along with others from Albania, Bosnia and Herzegovina, Serbia and Montenegro (at that time) and Romania. We were trained in various interactive approaches of dealing with history through the events and experience from the German modern history. The training had a great format, a combination of input sessions, interactive discussion and many site visits and meetings with experts who work in the history educational and cultural sphere or just persons with great historical consciousness, vivid memories and great sense and attitude to the past. We have visited various places in Germany: the Old synagogue in Essen, Dortmund History Workshop, the Society for Christian-Jewish Cooperation in Dortmund, Weimar and its historical sites of the Weimar Republic, Buchenwald Memorial, the Thuringia-Hessen "Schifflersgrund" Border Museum. This part of the program gave us unforgettable experience, direct involvement in the work of the people and the institutions that we have met and visited, it brought us deep insights and an enormous variety of views on the topic. In the program there was enough time for reflection and evening discussions where everybody openly shared our perceptions of the days, making connections with the history of our countries and the controversies we also face.

At that time, I have just finished my undergraduate studies in history at Sofia University with a specialization in the contemporary history of the Balkans and, after four years, mainly spent in the university halls and in the library, where I have been absorbing a great amount of information, for which I was grateful about, I found out how much more learning, creativity and understanding there is in the interactive non-formal way of approaching, even when dealt with very sensitive issues from the recent past.

I came back in Sofia so much inspired. I wished myself to have the opportunity to continue working in this particular sphere and about a year later this opportunity appeared for me.

In August 2003, a regional meeting with some of the participants from the training in Germany happened in Sofia (at that time the *dvv international* regional office for South East Europe was based in Sofia) and I was invited to help for the preparation of it and to take part. The great news was that there was some additional funding to create a meaningful event in the region, using the experience and the learning from the previous year experience. After two days of debating we agreed on making a traveling exhibition. A traveling exhibition – firstly, that idea looked so much impossible – how shall we – representatives from nearly all the countries on the Balkans – agree on a joint topic, so to start preparing such an exhibition and then how to make it really traveling! The idea was good, but there was quite much skepticism as well, still it was not enough to prevail our enthusiasm and deep trust that in this way we will reach a larger audience of the people in our countries. A year later – the exhibition started traveling from Skopje (Macedonia), to Tirana (Albania), then in Sarajevo (Bosnia and Herzegovina), Belgrade (Serbia), Cluj-Napoca (Romania) and finally came at the end in Sofia (Bulgaria).

In the process of doing/preparing – the solutions were born, we have agreed not to have one single topic, but to choose different ones that are important for each of our countries for better understanding our present through going deeper in particular events from our common sensitive past.

This is how it started for me.

After that, the history project in South Eastern Europe became even bigger; I was coordinating it for five years covering activities in nearly all the Balkan countries with focus on interactive methods of teaching history in the classroom, working mainly with history teachers, because after assessing the needs and evaluating the feedback from the exhibition, we found out that the teachers are the ones who first have to confront the spontaneous questions of the pupils and students about "What happened in …?" "Why do these people hate the other ones?" "Why did people kill each other?" etc.

So, how to teach history, what to remember, what to forget, how to bring the positive and wise messages of the past to the younger generations, were just some of the questions that we have worked together with history teachers, experts, students in various places, cities and towns, memorial and cultural sites.

There was one unspoken understanding that we were reaching with every group in each seminar, and that was, that we need to remember all what have happened in the past (also wars, protests, genocide, death), but in a way that encourages greater understanding, removes stereotypes and reduces conflict.

One of the methods we have used was the oral history methodology. It was again in Germany when for the first time I have heard of it, and then we have devoted two years of the history project on the Balkans (2005 and 2006) in training history teacher of using it in the classroom, again with the aim of brining the personal story in the centre, supplementing political history, bringing the voices of the marginalized, generally provoking critical thinking and understanding the multi-perspective approach of teaching and learning.

The lessons learnt are questioned while being shared and in practice. What we have learnt in the History project of the Balkans I have had the privilege to present/to share in various events (conferences, trainings, seminars) in Berlin (May 2006), Yerevan (October 2007), Tashkent (May 2008), Issyk kul (July-August 2009), Bonn (June 2009), Phnom Penh (September 2010). In all these places projects connected with history and dealing with the past are taking place within the *dvv international* network, have taken place or will be taking place. In all these places there are practitioners in the history field who have similar stories like mine. In all these places important activities in terms of processing the past, identity and national building, confronting genocide and many other is present in the everyday life of the people and need special attention to deal with.

Matthias: My grandfather died in 1993, this was the year I finished my A-levels, and we were all in party mood, drinking, dancing and hanging out with our classmates. It was one day in May, the sun was shining and it was extremely hot for that time of the year – in the evening he died. Realizing his death took me some time – but then I knew what would be the heritage of that dead man to me. Before he died, let's say the last 10 years, he more and more opened up about his past – mainly about the war. He did not open up freely – it was me forcing him to dig deeper in his own burial site of memories.

At that time I was 21, I had gone through the whole war history, the holocaust and the German guiltiness for it several times in school and in all of the youth movements I had joined. But one question I could not let go: "What did my grandfather do in that war?"

This is the same question the first post war generation in Germany asked their parents. This questioning happened a lot in the sixties, and we all know that as a result it led to the 1968 Cultural Revolution in the West.

My grandfather, 25 years later, still hesitated a lot and did not want to tell all these sad and brutal stories to his young grandson. But I asked and asked and did not let him go without an answer. So he opened up about being at the beginning careful – talking more about war anecdotes and funny stories with his comrades. Then, after a while, talking about fighting, lying in the trench, about weapons, shootings and killings. The first real story coming now writing this up to my mind was about a deserter, who shot himself through a loaf of bread in the arm in order to get to the hospital and therefore away from the front-line. He was caught because they found breadcrumbs in the wound and then shot by an execution commando. Was my grandfather personally involved in that execution? I cannot remember. Other harrowing stories followed – also about the SS and the killings on their way back from Russia.

It was then the first time after almost fifty years that he had talked about these heavy past memories and I felt that it was for him like getting rid of a trauma.

This talking about the past, on the other hand, showed me a complete up to then unknown side of my grandfather and changed my perception on him enormously. Knowing this live story I much more understood habits, behavior and convictions of my grandfather and his generation. And it had a strong influence on my identity. As one of the results I started to study history. I felt and still feel closely linked to that family history and hence to the history of those people.

I nowadays have much more a feeling that I know where I am coming from and what the special responsibilities of that ancestry are. And I am explicitly not talking about guiltiness – I never could feel guilty for something that had happened before I actually was born.

I remember writing this my history teacher at secondary school saying "don't study history. It will be a much too boring conservative subject for you. Better study political sciences or sociology." She maybe said so, because she knew well, that I was mostly so much interested in history, because of my political convictions at that time. These were the times of the first and second Gulf War and our resistance against it, the times of the big anti-nuclear movement in Germany and me and my friends were part of it. All these social movements rooted for my understanding in that (above mentioned) 1968 Cultural Revolution and therefore in German contemporary history. It was at that time that I joined the Green Party as (for me) the only German political power clearly breaking with both totalitarianisms of the 20th century: Fascism and Stalinism.

I started studying history in Braunschweig specializing surprisingly enough on Ancient history. After some semesters I moved to Heidelberg and prolonged my studies at the oldest and as one can imagine, most conservative history seminary in Germany. Heidelberg was not really my choice – I went there because my partner at that time started her studies there. The change included also shift to contemporary, in Heidelberg called "new" history.

I was very lucky to find a professor, who was quite an opponent to overall business at the history seminary at the time. He had specialized on the French Revolution and social protest movements in general. I was studying West Germany's post-war protest movements. In the courses he held we were working a lot with historic sources. He always provided us a big variety of text materials which were illuminating the object of research from all possible sides. He always included personal stories of ordinary people and was stressing to us that these sources, if you want to get closer to the truth, are not worse the others, but sometimes more important than the official political ones of e.g. governments.

Both schools of history teaching, at my secondary school and at the University, were very much characterized by a "history from below" approach. Both teachers were also convinced of the same ideas, were coming from the same background of conviction; the conviction that history is more than the "history of events and big men." Both are passionate advocates of a history writing that includes the history of ordinary people and their strategies of coping with life. It can be called Social History. In my last semesters, I focused on East-German-History. Born and grown up some close to the German-German border it was always my wish to find out more about this regime and the people who had to life in it. I wrote my master thesis on Soviet-GDR cultural relations and a mass-organization called the German-Soviet Friendship Society (DSF). Therefore I did a six week stay in the Federal Archives ("Bundesarchiv") in Berlin. The archives of the DSF had at that time just been transported to the Federal Archives. They were in a very bad shape, not sorted and with no-one knowing where to find what. I just started to examine everything that I got into my hands. These were very often letters from the DSF to the Soviet contact officer which no-one after the end of the regime head read before. This letters gave a completely new "turn" to my up to then written pages, it changed my perception of the DSF. After the archives session I decided to talk with people from that period of German history. These were my first experiences with eye witnesses.

After my studies I was appointed for Kazakhstan by the Goethe Institute. After a year I went for Uzbekistan to work for the German Academic Exchange Service (DAAD) as a country coordinator. Very fast I got to know my colleagues Dr. Reinhard Krumm from the social-democratic Friedrich Ebert Foundation and Uwe Gartenschlaeger from *dvv international*. At a joint lunch we found out that all of us had studied history and that we all would like to realize a project in the field of history and development. Accompanied by Dr. Chris Guenther from the Goethe Institute we initiated the "German-Uzbek History and Identity Project Week," which from there on took place for 5 subsequent years. The idea of the project was as simple as necessary for this transition country: Uzbekistan after independency in 1991, a state based on an artificial national myth with no real national identity, led by a government mostly consisting of old Soviet cadres. What we wanted was to show that nation building cannot be done without (the history of) the people living in that special place. All participating organizations dealt with problem according to their own mission and vision. I was initiating collaboration with an Uzbek Mahalla (a traditional Uzbek administrative unit, like a district or quarter) and German Universities. We were thematizing the relation of power, architecture and identity. The main message was that Soviet Union intentionally destroyed ancient oriental architecture and replaced it by Soviet style houses in order to destroy the native identity and create the Soviet ideal human. The subtext said "Please be aware about what your actual regime does!"

Two years later, Uwe Gartenschlaeger convinced me to take over his position at the *dvv international*'s Regional Office for Central-Asia and Southern Caucasus. He had brought experiences with oral history and the biographical method from Russia and the Balkans to Uzbekistan. The office was already at time actively engaged in history work. They had adopted the method Talking Café from dvv's Russian projects and renamed them according to Uzbek traditions into "Tea-House-Talks." The idea here is to bring together older persons, contemporary witnesses, in a pleasant atmosphere to drink tea and eat *plov*, a Central Asian rice dish, and with the guidance of a facilitator trained by *dvv international*, encourage them to talk about their personal experiences and own history. Attending these events impressed me a lot: How participants opened up, how much empowered they were by the well-dosed facilitation of the dvv trainer.

The first bigger oral history project was actually a combination of the DAAD experience and oral history. In 1966, a powerful earthquake shook Tashkent – the capital. Soviet powers used the situation to destroy oriental Tashkent and they built the first ever "Soviet Master City" instead. One omnipresent legend is the altruistic help of work brigades coming from all over the Soviet Union. We interviewed up to fifty witnesses and published a book called "Tashkent Earthquake of 1966: Remembrances of Eye Witnesses." The whole edition was concluded within a week. We worked afterwards successfully on comparable topics with similar methods.

In 2008, I was invited to International Adult Education Festival in Krasnojarsk (Siberia). To be honest the whole event was not very interesting for me. But by chance it happened to be that I found myself in a seminary led by Mikhail

Rojansky about his "Siberian Almanac" which he had just published at that time. The almanac is about the "history of change" in Siberia after the end of the Soviet Union. Ordinary people present their place of home in a spectrum of the last 20 years. The almanac combines aspects of oral with social and local history and it is an impressive example for the "history from below" approach. I decided to invite Mikhail to Tashkent to invent a similar project for Uzbekistan. The work on the Uzbek almanac was a real challenge. We had to take into account so many local factors. Mentality in Uzbekistan is not used to open criticism, people tend to describe things much more positive as they experienced them, if forced to do so in public; to name just one difficulty. The outcome is a colorful kaleidoscope of today's Uzbekistan and the constant change the country and its people experience: Sometimes for the better, very often not.

The years 2007 and 2008 were also the starting point for Vanya's and my active collaboration. We invited Vanya to different workshops as an expert on Adult Education and Oral History.

I went back to Germany in early 2009. Just before on the yearly planning session my colleague Nazaret Nazaretyan from Armenia and I developed a project idea on the Turkish-Armenian reconciliation which got then happily financed by the German Foreign Office. We asked Vanya to help us implementing this project which mainly consisted of a summer camp for students from both countries, an oral history research led by these students and a book. Vanya agreed to join the team and after phase I we started to implement a much bigger phase II. This time coordinated by Ulrike Pusch.

This project was and is the biggest challenge to me. I learned a lot from these two years: Mainly because it is the first time for me to deal in such a deep way with genocide; but also because it became the biggest single project on history that dvv had implemented so far.

In autumn 2010, Vanya and I went to Cambodia for a fact finding mission on the Khmer Rouge Regime. At the moment we are preparing phase III of the Armenian-Turkish Reconciliation project and the 2011 Bonn Conference on Adult Education (BoCEAD) which will deal with Adult Education, Oral History and Reconciliation work.
Why the network is important for us? What makes it unique for us?

Not only *dvv international* is working with biographies and contemporary witnesses; projects on oral history are implemented by lots of institutions and agencies all over this planet. Same applies for youth exchange programs, reconciliation workshops and publications on it – all this is also done by others. This leads to the question: What are the unique aspects in the projects of the dvv history network *or*, to take it more personally, what it is unique in these projects for us?

Matthias: Very short, in a nutshell I could answer:
All project measures within the dvv history network have in common that the human being; the individual occupies center stage. It is the human being and its welfare itself wherefore these projects are implemented. This means – to

put it another way – the empowerment of people for the sake of themselves and their fellow human beings. Taking this idea into account as the main principle to follow, all other characteristics can be easily subsumed: People feel empowered in a comfortable, save and trustworthy atmosphere which enables them to share about their personal life experiences in way that helps listeners (and later maybe readers) to get a deeper insight into bygone life-worlds. This, in turn, enables the audience to get into an empathic dialogue with each other and the person telling its story.

Many of the participants feel a gain of inner strength and a remarkable change in their living quality, which sometimes even can be described as a process of (mental) healing. Often these changes are not only applying for the individual participant but for the whole community the interviewee lives in. Besides these aspects of individual and community empowerment – which are important factors in our development work and our struggle for a more democratic world – these measures and its outcomes have big impact on history writing, history perception and on the level of historic awareness. This facilitated reflection on own and others biographies; this dealing with the history of "normal" people is very useful for the processing of many societal processes which imply conflict, contention and discord.

Vanya: I agree completely with what Matthias has already said. I would like to add just several more things that I see unique for me as well.

Firstly is the idea of bringing change by improving particular skills and by being inspired to realize that you yourself can be that change. I believe in the power of being an example by doing your best, like Mahatma Gandhi says – "Be the change you want to see in the world". Through the history projects of *dvv international* people, who took part in the seminars, reflections and processing people get exactly this awareness in realizing that they could be such a change, for taking responsibility for the next generations and to their local communalities and societies that through their action they could serve for making a better future. This brings additional meaning in the life especially of the older generations.

Secondly, beside specific target groups we have (like history teachers, museum workers, adult educators, students etc.), our overall target group are the ordinary people in certain place and/or region who have experienced some life-changing events in their past, who are willing to share their stories to bring a different opinion on a certain fact, whose stories need to be preserved, so in this way who are transmitting their knowledge from a generation to a generation and who are enriching and adding light to events important for the whole society. The work, interaction, joint development with these ordinary people makes for me our work very important and unique.

Thirdly, this is our youth and adult education approach, our methods, the answer of the question "how?" For me personally, the way how you approach an issue is very central and needs specific attention. In each place where we have worked and work, we are searching for the right approach for the topic, for the methods that suit the most and for finding the partners with whom we can develop the strategy, who will bring us closer to the people and their stories, thus to implement our work in a efficient, empathic and enriching for all involved way. Sometimes this process could last longer than expected, sometimes it is even very difficult to adjust to the situation, to bring your expertise and

146

at the same time leave enough room for interaction, change, and improvement. And this is exactly the process how partnerships are built and how people grow together.

What inspires us to continue? Which are our golden moments?

Matthias: I could here describe numerous of such "golden moments" which I experienced in the last five years. Let me exemplary provide you with the latest:

Within the project "Adult Education and Oral History Contributing to Armenian-Turkish Reconciliation" which the network runs for two years now (2009/2010) a book under the title "Speaking to One Another" has been published. The book consists of scientifically processed interviews carried out within the project by students in both target countries. Ten students from each country were trained in a 10 day summer camp in Turkey and its equivalent in Armenia to work with contemporary witnesses. Afterwards these students, facilitated by well-experienced scientists, went into the field and interviewed people on their relation towards Armenians, respectively Turks. As all direct survivors of the 1915 genocide are naturally not alive anymore these interviews are mainly post-memories or even post-post-memories. While reading the book it becomes visible that the Armenian and Turkish part differ a lot from each other; this is not too astonishing as Turkey is representing the perpetrator's and Armenia the victim's society. The annex to the Armenian interviews shows a list of all interviewees with photo, name and biographical remarks on forefathers being eye witnesses/victims to the genocide. Turkish recipients preferred to stay anonymous – both approaches are very good "mirrors" of their societies or better: "mirrors" of how their society deals with the 1915 events: a fight for acknowledgement and compensation on the one side and a mixture of repression, relativization and guilty conscience (which is becoming stronger in the last years) on the other side.

Ashnak village is situated approximately 60 km north-west of the capital of Armenia, Yerevan. Ashnak lies only about 30km from the Turkish-Armenian border and is mainly inhabited by ancestors from Sasun (a district in the Turkish Batman province / South-East Anatolia). Their forefathers were refugees from the genocide and did choose Ashnak for resettlement because of its closeness to the border: until today residents of the village talk in a nostalgic way about the return to their homelands.

The motivation of village people to talk with our interviewers is for sure complex, but it can be taken for granted that the perspective of "Turks" reading these narratives after publishing of the book was a main stimuli for the villagers. Most of them living with an orally transmitted picture of "The Turks" from their forefathers as most of them never had met a Turk in real. It is not only that they never had talked to Turks before but also that their view of Armenia, the Armenians and the 1915 Genocide and, in addition, the picture of Turkey and "Turkishness" is a completely one-dimensional one. Important to say that same can be guessed for the other side: means Turk's view of Armenia. Both countries live still in their explanation of the past which is more or less not influenced by story of the other conflict party. Both "stories" serve national interests and at least imply strong aspects of mythology and creation of legends.

Within the project a one-day conference, titled "Prospects for Reconciliation: Theory and Practice" was held in Yerevan and organizers decided to take the Armenian, Turkish and international participants to Ashnak village the day after the conference. In the authors perception it was quite a challenge for the villagers: Getting the printed version of their own memories, and that even in Turkish and English language and realizing that these books will be read on the other side of the insuperable believed border, moved villagers into a condition between euphoria and uncertainty. Uncertainty caused a lot by the fact that the situation was absolutely unique for them and therefore not relatable to anything they knew. Turkish citizens as part of the group were not less emotionally touched but reactions were much more hidden. This happened to change later on that evening.

After half hour of handing over books, exchanging on the content in front of the memorials for the victims of genocide and World War II the group went to a local house wherein the occupant positions a small exhibition of wooden carvings in honor of Gevorg Chaush, an Armenian partisan leader. For sure the author is not able to relive the feelings of the Turkish participants: But taking into account that Chaush is seen as a terrorist in Turkey, the people never the less were overwhelmed by the simple and sympathetic devotion of the exhibiter. To complete the picture the author may share his personal feelings being a "third party" in this situation; he needs to confess that was not so much touched by the situation and more shocked by the naïve and uncritical worship of this villager. Obviously all involved parties, Turks, Armenians and foreigners, perceived this culminating situation quite differently.

The evening drew to an end in the nearby cottage, where the group got invited to by a local host. No need to describe the Armenian hospitality: There were overfull tables, music, dance and poems and speeches. Armenian language was translated into English, Turkish and even Kurdish. Poems and speeches were about lost lands, the big escape, heroism and the genocide itself. The evening did not fail to have the desired (or not desired?) effect: The Turkish representatives – even mostly coming from an urban and scientific elite – were heavily touched by the scenery and the openness of the Armenian hosts. It needs to be remarked that this was nevertheless not an "uncritical" evening: the Armenian speakers found a perfect mix of honest hospitableness and well-packed criticism which was, interesting enough, well received by the Turks.

The overall message was clearly understood by everybody: The Armenian villagers wanted in the first place acknowledgement. Acknowledgement of was had been done by the ancestors of the Turkish guests to their forefathers. Other "standard" claims of the Armenian side, such as reparations and the return of land, were indirectly articulated but in a more nostalgic and not concretely political way. It was clear perceptible that the Turkish side felt, maybe for some for the first time, quasi physically touched by the feeling of regret. The evening in Armenia showed also how similar both cultures are, or even that both sides rather belong to one culture. There is no difference between a Turkish and an Armenian coffee except for the name.

For sure such "golden moments" are not foreseeable or could be planned, but it is important to construct the project the way, that there is enough space for them to happen.

Vanya: The visit to Ashnak village in Armenia was a special experience for me too, especially because of the fact that the stories of the people were brought back to them in the form of the published book. My experience with making interviews, using oral history method, interacting with the local people is very much fulfilling. Giving back the result of this process to the people makes it very special for them too. The book that came out as a result from the first phase of the Turkish-Armenian projects is very important for all of us who are working in this rapprochement process, but this couldn't be possible without the genuine stories of the local people in both the countries. People – as the ones we have met in Ashnak.

Exactly such moments of closing the cycle of the process and making a new opening on a next level are very important in my opinion. Such a closing of the process within the work of the history network on the Balkans could be exemplified with the following: for one year teachers coming from all the Balkan countries were trained in oral history. In their school work they used the method with their pupils interviewing eyewitness in the classroom. They have thought their pupils how to use the method outside the classroom too, how to interview their parents, grandparents, neighbors on certain issues that cover some topics from the history curriculum, when learning about contemporary history. The results gathered by the pupils coming from different countries, Albania, Macedonia, Bulgaria, etc. were presented within another Youth Balkan Forum in Veliko Tarnovo, Bulgaria and were published in a book that was presented to the respondents too.

What is our learning experience?

Vanya: Both of us with Matthias, we have our lists with learning points, they are pretty much similar, but said in different ways. We have reached them through our own experiences.

There are no stronger bridges than the bridges among people, beyond ethnicities, religions and nationalities.

It takes time to create deep and meaningful relations/partnerships, but ones established they serve a lifetime.

It takes time to break down stereotypes. The way to do it is through creating space for people to meet, to talk, to learn.
- History teaching plays important role in developing personal, national, European, world identity. That is why it is worth investing in the ways of teaching and learning.

Matthias: The following list is for sure not exhaustive, but in order to answer the question I tried to put them – for me! – most important lessons learnt together. This is a very personal list and some of the bullet points may also be controversial, self-evident or even hypothetic:
- Bringing people together is always pushing things in a positive direction.
- Learning *about* each other, learning *with* each other broadens the common ground for respect and understanding.
- Adult Education empowers people. All processes start within the participant. The individual as part and actor of a social group stands in centre of all interventions.

- Past causes present, present causes future, past causes future. This "universal truth" is valid also for the individual and his individual past (Biographic approach).

- History is a combination of many "smaller" histories. The more "small" histories, e.g. personal life stories, enter the history writing the closer it will come to "historic truth". "Historic truth" is a rapprochement to factual truth.

- History writing is very often interpretation for the present but should be interpretation for the sake of a better future.

- Big history needs to be supplemented by history from below. People's history has to have the same significance as political history (!).

- Human being's perception, decision-making and processing is based on own experiences and "learned" experiences. The remembrance – as a form of individual history writing – has a big influence on the future decisions of people. The better this personal history writing is working, the better decisions will be taken for the sake of the future.

- Learning is not only an important tool to understand the world better but also to strengthen one's personal psychological health. Learning is therefore not only positive in a cognitive (Erkenntnisgewinn – the gaining of cognition) way, but also allows people to reach higher levels of empathy, balance and stability. All these are important preconditions for being responsible citizens.

- Societies are a "puzzle" of individuals living within a certain widely agreed convention. The educated (lifelong) learner (as described in above) contributes in a positive way to a democratic and free society of active citizens.

... and I am still convinced that the German writer and journalist Kurt Tucholsky was wrong as he said:

"Humans never learned from history, and they never will in the future"
(Kurt Tucholsky, Die Weltbühne 1926)

What challenges we face?

Matthias: There are numerous challenges in all of our projects and there will be many more (I fear) in all future measures. I would say that most of the challenges are very specific and differ a lot from context to context. Nevertheless I tried to formulate some general things which, I think need to be taken into consideration when running a history project. Most of what is written below is not really new and is also applying for many reconciliation and history projects not part of the history network:

1. Parties and Interests involved

Which parties are on which levels involved and are able to have a deteriorating or improving impact on the conflict. Which interests are represented by these parties? Differentiation between categories of parties: direct conflict party (e.g. Armenia and Turkey), indirect conflict party (Azerbaijan), involved third party (USA, EU, Russia, Switzerland), actors working on the conflict etc pp. (international organizations).

2. Politics, Policies and Polity in affected societies, states, "units"

The institutional, procedural and contentual dimensions of target society(ies) are of big influence on the form of the actual conflict. Differences in these three dimensions between conflict parties have very often strong impact on the conflict itself.

3. Society(ies) and population(s)

The social contract (*contrat sociale*) of each society involved and the differences between the social contracts of the involved direct and indirect conflict parties have enormous influence on the perception of the conflict on all involved sides. All factors related to the analysis of populations and inhabitants of societies – such as demographic factors but also such simple factors like the size of the societies (e.g. correlation between inhabitants and territory in the involved societies) are of high importance for the handling of the conflict and the reconciliation process. All socio-economic realities and all differences in these realities between the conflict parties have high impact. Also factors like level of freedom (of speech), diversity and pluralism.

4. Religion(s), Ethnic groups and Culture(s)

Religion, Cultural differences and belonging to a certain ethic group can play an important role, be the or one of the initial reasons for the conflict or may be a pleaded / "well placed justification" for the conflict. Several if not all factors presented here can be strongly influenced by religion, ethnic and cultural self understanding of individuals and parties involved. It has to be carefully considered where and when within the reconciliation attempt common parts of the involved identities or differences are accentuated.

5. History, history writing, the perception of history and the level historical awareness

Different societies, ethnic groups and individuals have different approaches and traditions of history writing; this is valid for the scientific but also for the popular history discourse (e.g. postmodern vs. Rankian school). In addition to that (and that seems to be even more important) the idea of history anchored within the population connecting with a certain tradition of historical tradition have an often underestimated influence (e.g. oral tradition vs. literate tradition). As most of all conflicts have historical roots, the right tools to bridge these differences in the perception of history itself can be crucial. Influenced by all above mentioned factors, plus the actual past (e.g. the Nazi-past of Germany) societies, states or other "units" may trend more to the repression or the processing of the past. As the German examples shows well the trend rather to process than to repress the past is not only intended by internal but a lot by external factors. Without the pressure of the allied powers on post-war Germany it is not so likely that West-Germany would have started to come into terms with its own painful past. Certainly this kind of "pressure" can also be applied by internal forces (also in the opposite direction in order to suppress any processing of the past), e.g. as an instrument to save the governing regime against "internal enemies".

6. Learning traditions, customs and convictions

As we are working in education it's important to ask about the actual learning situation in the regarding context. Some advanced methods of Adult Education, which were developed e.g. in a very progressive pluralistic open and free society in the west, are maybe not suitable for a more traditionalized, religious or closed society: Methods have to be adjusted according to the actual realities in situ. It may be sometimes helpful to empower participants to adapt to a new learning situation but it is as important not overburden them. The learning situation is defined by big variety of elements and the learning situations in two (or more) conflict parties may be very much different from each other. If we take e.g. the factor religion into account and we look on its influence on the learning situation it becomes very easily clear what is meant: The role and participation of women can be completely different at the two conflict parties (e.g. Muslim vs. Christian/Secular).

7. The role, perception and self-perception of the conflict processor

Conflict processors are people, groups and organizations working in the role of a mediator, project coordinator and/or trainer in the reconciliation undertaking. These actors are often not directly affected by the conflict. Many of them are foreigners to the conflict (region). This can be seen on the one hand as an asset and on the other hand as a liability. An asset because the actor has (hopefully) a more neutral position and is more neutrally perceived by the conflict parties; the strength of being neutral may on the other hand also be a weakness, because it may misbalance the work on the conflict. This needs to be explained: E.g. the conflict between Armenia and Turkey, where the unequal appraisal of the 1915 massacres are the main cause for the conflict. For Armenia it was genocide, Turkey is rejecting this appraisal. If the project processor tries to be neutral in this conflict he loses credibility on the Armenian side and indirectly also on all other involved "sides" as the facts definitely show that this was genocide. Therefore "Neutrality" is not a value itself – it has to be carefully considered within each conflict situation. Neutrality is very important and a must in more "even" conflicts where the conflicting parties cannot be divided so easily into victims and perpetrators. Coming back to the factor of "being a foreigner": it is important to realize that this "third party" is very often introducing a once more different set of the above described factors (point 2 to 6) into the conflict scenario. That means you may have three decisive different mind-sets in the reconciliation project. It is not only essential to analyze well the involved conflict parties but also to self-analyze yourself if you are in the role of being a "foreign" actor in the reconciliation process. What are you interests? Are you there because your personal history is closely linked to one of the conflict parties? What are your political and religious convictions? And so on.

8. Different concepts of reconciliation, conflict resolution and rapprochement

The different understandings of reconciliation, conflict resolution and/or rapprochement are not only based on the differing interests of the parties but once more also by cultural, social, ethnic, religious and historical reasons. Misunderstandings of the actual goal to reach and the way towards it are not only connected to language (wrong translations, etymologically different origins, unknown semantic differences between concepts in different languages etc.) but also by above mentioned factors. It is crucial to define very clearly what actual is the common understanding of the goal you want to reach together.

Last but not least: If the two conflict parties are so different in so many ways it should be considered to design the project in a unsymmetrical way; which means, that there is no need to implement the completely identical measures parallel in both countries.

Vanya: Matthias has explained the essence of challenges and has systemize them in a explicit way, I could only say that I pretty much agree with him and to go a step further in answering to the question what helps us in times of challenges.

For me, two things are very important when such challenges occur. The first is to go back to the source. The source could be different things in the different situations – it could be the conflict itself, the information about it, the people involved, the method used. Examining it again and again, establishing a direct contact with the people involved, forgetting who you are, but doing your best to walk in their shoes and understand their background motives, their situation, it always gives further learning how to continue.

The second important thing is the team, the people with whom you do the job. I am very grateful and I consider myself lucky with all the colleagues I have worked so far. The possibility to have colleagues, to work together with people with whom you have similar views, with whom to speak your mind, your ideas, your approach, and have the skill to hear their opinion too, brings the work on a next level.

And all this what we have said with one aim: to inspire the ones involved to take their fate into their own hands in order to live together in peace, because each one of us carries within us this responsibility.
Some of our fruits so far:

Remember for the Future. History project of South Eastern Europe (2004-2009)

Project website: http://www.historyproject.dvv-international.org/ Some of the publications:

Ivanova V. / Stoycheva V. (2010). Adult Education and Interactive History Teaching in the Balkans. *History and Identity: Insights into the dvv international History Network.* Klingenberg, M. (ed.). (International Perspectives in Adult Education No. 64/2010). *dvv international* Bonn, 2010, pp. 9-27

Stoycheva V. / Ivanova V. (2010). Adult education and interactive history education in the Balkans. *The deeds of Asenevtsi and Biodiversity.* Faber: Veliko Tarnovo, pp. 137-154. (in Bulgarian)

Ivanova V. / Stoycheva, V. (ed.). (2009). *A Portrait of a Neighbour*. DVD.

Ivanova V. / Stoycheva, V. (ed.). (2009). *History Project 2008. Balkan Stories – Good Practices of History Teaching in South Eastern Europe. Teachers' Guide. dvv international* - SEE Regional Office - Sarajevo

Ivanova V. (2008). For the Sake of the Future, *Bulgarian Diplomatic Review*, Issue 2/2008 (In Bulgarian, English and Russian)

Ivanova V. (2007). Oral History. Discovering Personal and Public Spaces from the Past, Male Female Spaces on the Balkans. *Balkan Forum of Young Historians*, Veliko Tarnovo, pp 30-36 (In Bulgarian)

Ivanova V. (2006). Diverse Approaches towards a Diverse Past. History project in South Eastern Europe. *LLinE / Lifelong Learning in Europe*, vol. 3, Helsinki, Finland, pp 174 - 177

Ivanova V. / Stoycheva, V. (ed.). (2006). History Project 2006. Enjoying Teaching – Oral History in the Classroom. *Teachers' Guide*. IIZ/DVV SEE Regional Office

Ivanova V. / Kien-Peng Lim (ed.). (2005). *History Project 2004 "Remember for the Future"*. The Traveling Exhibition Catalogue. IIZ/DVV – Regional office Sofia

Ivanova V. / Kien-Peng Lim (ed.). (2004). *History Project 2004 "Remember for the Future"*. Teaching Methods, Ways of Interaction and Reconciliation in South Eastern Europe. IIZ/DVV – Regional office Sofia.

Publications in Central Asia (extract):

Project's Website: www.istoriya.uz

Klingenberg M. (2008). Remember for the Future. History as a Topic for Adult Education (together with Uwe Gartenschlaeger, Olga Agapova and Vanya Ivanova). *Strohschen, Gabriele: Handbook of Blended Shore Education.* Chicago, S. 167ff.

Klingenberg M. (2009). Oral History, Contemporary Witnessing and History Projects in Central Asia. *Hinzen, Heribert (Hrsg.): 40 Years dvv international* (Adult Education and Development 72/2009), S. 247ff

Klingenberg M. (2008). Neue internet-gestützte Angebote der Zeitzeugenarbeit in Deutschland. Zum Beispiel die Onlineplattform *einestages.de* des Nachrichtenmagazins DER SPIEGEL (New Internet-Based Offers for the Work with Contemporary Witnesses. For Example the Online-Platform einestages.de of the News-Journal DER SPIEGEL).

Günther, Hussner, Klingenberg, Lapins Bomsdorf, Inomjonov (Hrsg.): Geschichte und Identität IV: Regionale Integration und Geschichte. Taschkent 2008, S. 142ff.

Klingenberg M. (2007). Kann man aus der Geschichte lernen? (Can one learn from history?) *Klingenberg, Landgrebe, Schutowa (Hrsg.): Geschichte und Identität: Migration und Nationales Selbstbewusstsein in Kasachstan.* Astana 2007, S. 86ff.

Klingenberg M. (ed.). (2008). Taschkenter Erdbeben 1966: Erinnerungen von Zeitzeugen (Tashkent Earthquake 1966: Memories of Eye Witnesses). *dvv international* – Regional Office Tashkent

Klingenberg, M. (ed.). (2010). *Uzbekistan: Through Space and Time* (In Russian). *dvv international* – Regional Office Tashkent.

Publication in Armenia and Turkey:

Neyzi, L. and Kharatyan-Araqelyan, H. (2010). *Speaking to One Another*: Wish they hadn't left / Whom to forgive? What to forgive? *dvv international* Bonn

Project's websites: www.learningtolisten.de & www.speakingtooneanother.org

Publication in Germany:

Klingenberg M. (ed.). (2010). History and Identity: Insights into the dvv international History Network. (International Perspectives in Adult Education No. 64/2010). dvv international Bonn

Publications available for free at: klingenberg@dvv-international.de and vanya.ivanova@oral-history.net

Hranush Kharatyan-Araqelyan

The Summing up of the Workshop "Prospects for Reconciliation: Theory and Practice"

The question of normalization of political relations between Armenia and Turkey and the social relations of the Armenian-Turkish nations that have caused quite a stir, stimulates new developments both inside the countries and within international political discourse. The public opinion of the two countries is only partially expressed by them. The reason for this, most likely, was the complete political silence on the Armenian Genocide perpetuated at the beginning of the 20th century and the policy of silencing public opinion, as well as for various reasons the policy to avoid making the question public both in Armenia up until 1965 and in Turkey until the end of the 20th century. As a result, the societies of both countries as well as the Armenian and Turkish peoples perceive the possibilities of Armenia-Turkey rapprochement, normalization of Armenian-Turkish relations in quite different dimensions. For the overwhelming majority of the present-day Turkish society, perhaps, the Armenian approach to the matter deeply stirring the feelings of the Armenian society is a surprise that the occurrences of 1915-1920 are not a historical past; and for the Armenian society it is totally incomprehensible that the past, which is not remote, could fall into oblivion. The concerned interest over the Armenian Genocide in Turkey was long ascribed mainly to the Armenian Diaspora, which was shaped as a consequence of the genocide. Although from the 1960s, in Soviet Armenia, they spoke out regarding the subject of genocide, however, among Turks, it is more frequently perceived as a consequence of pressure from the Armenian Diaspora.

In the last decade, after nearly a 90-year period of silence, the events of 1915-1920 became not only the subject of international, political and public arguments and discussions, but also the pivotal problem of the political agreement between Armenia and Turkey. The expert discussions on this matter at times encounter the problem of "historicity" – the expert practice has much more experience to discuss ongoing actual conflicts, whereas, the events of not a distant past are not always considered urgent or topical and they are discussed or recurred to in a "historical" dimension. The remoteness of the events, however, in fact does not "eliminate" the urgency of the problem.

The discussion topic of the given workshop was in this very context: taking into account the relative remoteness of the Armenian Genocide, what solutions the formation of Armenian-Turkish relations may have, what role the political proposals play in this matter or what role separate groups of society may play, taking into consideration the memories existing in societies, circumventions of memories, silences.

From the beginning of the 2000's, the question of the possibilities of the establishment of the Armenian-Turkish relations, more frequently with the help of international or separate states or civilian partners, has become the subject of searching, and inner-public and inter-public discussions of some part of scientific intellectuals and other groups of societies of both countries. It seemed that the "protocols" signed by both countries on 10 October 2009 in Zurich should contribute to the political shaping of this process, but they were not ratified by the states, thereby opening a new door for explanations and predictions of the political disposition of political elite of the two countries. With the help of research conducted by the method of oral history of family memories of individuals in both societies, we tried to understand the memories of individuals in both societies about the common life of the past and the present-day perceptions of each other; and during the workshop entitled "Prospects for Reconciliation: Theory and Practice" held on 27 November 2010 in Yerevan, the materials of which are represented in the given compendium, we will try to understand and look for possible ways out of this situation through expert discussions or experts' theoretical and practical views.

The speeches and discussions of the workshop can conditionally be divided into several statements of a central question:

▪ The analyses on Armenian-Turkish political relations throughout the last decade (Alexander Iskandaryan, Armenia-Turkey Reconciliation: Motives and Impediments);

▪ The analyses on the civil and public discussions of Armenia-Turkey Reconciliation throughout the last decade (David Hovhannisyan, The Process of Normalization of Armenian-Turkish Relations: the Official and Societal Dimensions; Diba Nigar Göksel, Reconciliation Initiatives: Emerging Patterns in Turkey)

▪ Historical and legal dimensions of the conflicts resolution (Elazar Barkan, Reconciliation beyond Subjective Histories);

▪ Possibilities of legal regulation of the Armenian-Turkish relations (Elazar Barkan; Yeghishe Kirakosyan, Armenian-Turkish Reconciliation: the Reality and Possibilities)

▪ Discussion of concrete patterns on easing of conflicts (Hasan Samani, Association for Historical Dialogue and Research (AHDR) and Reconciliation through History in Cyprus; Evren Ergeç, Creating Global Understanding on Peace among Young People through Youth Work);

▪ Offers of solutions drawing us nearer to Armenia-Turkey reconciliation (Garegin Chugaszyan, Old Conflicts and New Media: The Role of New Media in Reconciliation; Hans Gunnar Adén, Cultural Identities: Stumbling-Blocks on the Way to Reconciliation; Harutyun Marutyan, Can Collective Memory of Genocide Lead to Reconciliation? A view from Yerevan).

During the workshop, developments in Armenian-Turkish political relations throughout the last decade were introduced as a question of unequal self-interest. Although in the conception of the work meeting, it was demonstrated that "indeed, for the governments of both countries it is important to establish normal relations," however, the presenters from the Armenian side set forth some claims that the establishment of normal relations with Armenia for the Turkish authorities is not of much importance, moreover, it is observed as anachronistic (Al. Iskandaryan).

Besides the fact that the normalization of relations with Turkey for Armenia is required for the possibility to settle domestic economic problems, and for Turkey, relations with Armenia are essential for its foreign political projects, to become one of the most influential actors in the Southern Caucasus, if not the first one and to keep on with the political movement of pan-Turanism (the project of unity of all the Turkic peoples), but for the time being, it is a matter of perspective, both countries are not free in manifestations of treatment to each other: the Turkish one considerably depends on the conduct, expectations and requirements of Azerbaijan, while the Armenian one on the Diaspora, the "product" of the genocide. There were no objections to Iskandaryan's statements; moreover, they were partially confirmed by David Hovhannisyan's arguments. In his speech, entitled "The process of normalization of Armenian-Turkish relations: the official and societal dimensions," there was a remark that "Turkey has frequent relations with a number of countries with which there exist numerous controversial questions, that of territorial nature as well (for instance, with Greece, Syria, Iran, etc)," however, they, unlike the Armenian case, do not hamper the establishment of diplomatic and economic relations. David Hovhannisyan thinks that "Turkey does not observe Armenia as a state with which, inter alia, it can normalize and improve relations step by step, build a joint safety system, collaborate on the border zone, unanimously participate in settlement of regional issues and so on". Citing the active operations of Ankara in all Turkish-inhabited conflict zones starting from Bosnia and Kosovo to the Northern Caucasian Republics and analyzing the steps taken by the political leaders of Turkey towards re-integration and unity of Turkish-speaking nations and countries, David Hovhannisyan inferred that Armenia is a major hindrance to these projects, and, thus, Turkey will remain committed to maintaining tension for a long time and to wait for the proper occasion to eliminate this obstacle. By Hovhannisyan's estimate (the leader of the Armenian party of the Armenian-Turkish Reconciliation Committee created by the initiative of the US State Department), the committee's activity, breaking numerous taboos and stereotypes served as a sort of "provocation" in the societies of the two countries for the open discussions related to the genocide. The matter, above all, concerns Turkish society, as for the first time after long silence, the occurrence of the beginning of the 20th century captured the public attention. The contacts and discussions in various formats of public and national diplomacy became more frequent. Summing up his work experience within the framework of Armenia-Turkey rapprochement projects, Hovhannisyan inferred that "Armenia and the Armenians continue to perceive Turkey as a source of immediate harm and danger which is not sincere and candid in manifestation of its goodwill. The reason is in search and found in the genocide recognition/non-recognition issue as the historical memory dictates to struggle for such solutions the implementation of which will let us exclude the recurrence of a catastrophe, exclude the genocide."

The views of both sides on the possibilities of Armenia-Turkey rapprochement and the formation of common values were very noteworthy as well. In Diba Nigar Göksel's speech, "Reconciliation Initiatives: Emerging Patterns in Turkey," a special emphasis was placed on the necessity of unity of public activists for democratization of both countries. Diba Nigar Göksel's experience shows that the Armenian partners of Armenia collaborating with the Turks on this matter are led by the pre-hypothesis that "Turkey will never become democratic" as a consequence of which the effectiveness of activists of Turkey's democratization becomes diminished. The response of this question among the summit's speeches can be found in the following formulation of David Hovhannisyan, "from the point of view of the Armenian-Turkish relations, genocide recognition will mean drawing nearer the value system based on a similar evaluation of the past which will serve as a basis for creating common future in the same region." Göksel does not suggest forgetting the past, on the contrary, she calls on the Turkish side to discuss its past openly and transparently, but thinks that the abrupt turn in the evaluation of the past by the Turkish side is a matter of lasting time, whereas the problem of the joint contribution of democratic values is on the agenda today. In this connection we may supplement the foresaid statement with Marutyan's and Kirakosyan's speeches, where the problem of differences between social experiences of both nations prevails, which is also an inevitable threat to the prospect of formation of joint values. Here as well, there is a world of difference in Turkish and Armenian approaches: according to the Turkish approach, history is important, but the present should not be conditioned solely to the past, whereas the Armenian approach keeps on with the notion that "the formation of joint, common values of the present and the past is impossible without a joint evaluation of the past," also because the Armenian side assures that the present-day Turkish society, particularly the conduct of the ruling groups as compared to former Turkish authorities as to the Armenian question does not make a considerable difference.

If the political will is not sufficient for reaching Armenian-Turkish reconciliation, then the search for its solution is moved to the legal and civil dimensions. During the workshop, those who spoke about the legal dimensions most frequently used the words "truth" and "justice." Trying to realistically analyze the expectations of people and societies from these words, Professor Elazar Barkan mentioned that "there are very many different kinds of truth. Even without getting into philosophical discussions about truth, relativism and realism, we can make references which we easily recognize in our daily lives to the provisional scope of truth. Consider for example the difference between judicial truth and historical truth and the daily subjective truth in which each of us takes refuge when disagreements occur." On this matter, Professor Barkan suggested not hastening with the judicial truth as the court is led by laws, evidence, testimonies, protocols, procedures which not always prove the truth, whereas the verdict of the court, even if it is wrong, is recognized as the truth. "The judicial truth is very much final: once the truth has been decided in the court it's the final truth, historical truth in contrast is a matter of dialogue."

Professor Barkan agreed that even if the genocide can be surveyed as a historical phenomenon, then there also exists a modern conflict between Turkey and Armenia: Turkey's orientation of the Nagorno-Karabagh conflict which in its turn connects the memory with the impending danger and the negation of the genocide. "In the conflict between Turkey and Armenia there are the historical conflicts (the question of genocide) as well as the contemporary (Azerbaijan) one which is shaped by fears stemming from historical memory. In these cases the divided memory and the lack of acknowledgment shape current relations, more than, for example, trade disputes, territorial ambitions, or electoral politics."

Professor Barkan discussed the problems of legal and social justice, cited differences of social memory and awareness of people, offered to treat the historical memory seriously, "in the mechanism of the conflicts resolution the presence of historical memory is a serious picture and whether it is resolved by me I think I would call upon funding agencies, foreign ministries and other institutions not to avoid the historical memory and to use it." Professor Barkan assures that the social dimension of the conflict resolution requires great efforts, patience and time. Professor Elazar Barkan, the founding director of the Institute for Historical Justice and Reconciliation (IHJR) at the Salzburg Seminar, marked the direct connection between the acknowledgement of violence of human rights and conflict resolution. The fear of disaster and memories will not vanish unless they get a sincere treatment. They will emerge again and again as the memories are transferred from generation to generation. This phenomenon, according to the analyst, is noticeable not only in the Armenian-Turkish relations but also in those of the countries of the Eastern Asia as well as in the Balkans. Thus, in trying to reach a conflict resolution, we should take into account not only the past, which is not so distant, but also the memories of brutalities. "Greater familiarity takes a long time, it is not just to write, it is not just a text that a scholar-an objective scholar can produce, but it is something like the building of a community and in this communities it is very hard to see solutions of this process especially if the matter concerns education, teachers, the community level, scholars."

The second speaker discussing the legal dimension, Kirakosyan, found that, "in this specific instance, we have the elements of different types of justices – historical, restorative and retributive, which make the case a unique one" put special emphasis on the developing "restorative justice." "From the restorative perspective, retributive punishment is seen as insufficient for reestablishing a peaceful social coexistence, in contrast restorative paradigm is only concerned with the future, it is not concentrated on the guilt of the offender. Restorative justice is more oriented at making the offender conscious of the harm caused, admitting responsibility and trying to repair harm." She also mentioned that it "is crucial for the Armenian-Turkish reconciliation process, as in this case, we need a very balanced approach in order to achieve the actual reconciliation." In any case, by Kirakosyan's estimate, Turkey first of all, should recognize the genocide, the possibility of which she saw only in case of Turkey's membership in the EU.

During the workshop, the efforts of the civil society towards Armenian-Turkish reconciliation and the discussions of its results also proved the difference in the parties' approaches to the conflict and the duration of the process. In most speeches and questions, it was demonstrated that each of the societies has it myths and the collective identity of each of them hampers the initiation of joint programs, and moreover, their implementation (Hovhannisyan, Marutyan, Kira-kosyan, Göksel). The lasting absence of Armenia-Turkey contact and the social experience of its own, a very low level of mutual trust, the stereotypes formed towards each other only increase the number of obstacles. Here we can also add the demographic differences of both countries, the differences between levels of the society awareness, whereas in large Turkey, few people are aware of the Armenian-Turkish conflict, even in the active north-eastern part of Turkey, and it is very hard for the public sector to form an effective critical mind, whereas, the whole population of Armenia, including the whole Diaspora, are very much concerned about the matter and, one way or another, have their impact on the process, the level of priority of the Armenian-Turkish rapprochement issue both for political authorities and in public perceptions. If for Armenian society and Armenia, it is one of the most urgent and primary questions, then for Turkish society and Turkey, it is not even a secondary one. According to Turkish experts, the Armenian side does not estimate adequately the efforts of Turkish intellectuals engaged in discussions of the Armenian question and treats them with mistrust and uncertainty, thus, diminishing not only the effectiveness of these efforts, but also indirectly influencing the number of those much concerned about the Armenian question. By consistently working exclusively on the legal recognition of the genocide, the Armenian partners miss even the social and other aspects of possibilities of the genocide recognition and sometimes strengthen the less-informed population of Turkey against them. Here we can also add the lack of a high-level of democratization of both countries which, in its turn, influences the efficiency of civil actors engaged in Armenian-Turkish reconciliation.

Moreover, Klingenberg's and Ivanova's candid articles, not entered in the work of the discussions agenda, but that are included in the given compendium, embrace the mentioning of the statement that "the past is the cause of the present, the present is the cause of the future, the past is the cause of the future" and are far too modern. The socio-cultural revolution of the sixties of Europe, which Klingenberg mentions, was the consequence of the philosophical search for understanding the history of a non-distant past and youth movements, a sincere wish of individuals. Perhaps here, we must look for differences between approaches of the Armenian and Turkish partners to the Armenian-Turkish reconciliation issue.

In the end part of the given summary it is necessary to mention that Ismail Keskin's article entitled "Nor & Eski and History for Life", seems to be abruptly interrupted with a fragment of a conversation with a respondent. Actually it's Ismail Keskin's choice. Those interested in his article should wait for the end of his project.

What can be done?

The more accentuated contributions of the work group discussions stated that:

1. Armenian-Turkish rapprochement is not the establishment of diplomatic contacts and the opening of frontiers; it is, above all, the acquisition of mutual trust which is possible only in case of equal awareness of the past, its acknowledgement, expiation, forgiveness;
2. The new tool that should be widely implemented in the reconciliation process is the intensive work regarding writing short narratives through historical dialogue, with the help of people, scholars and others that are involved with the process. That can be initiated by the civil society; diplomatic circles or the government;
3. To attach greater importance to the factor of individual and social memory, to enlarge the scope of awareness with their help;
4. To enlarge the framework of activity on social and reparative, restorative justice;
5. To try to increase the mutual trust of the Armenian and Turkish partners engaged in Armenia-Turkey rapprochement issues, to initiate joint programs only in the presence of mutual trust;
6. In the absence or lack of mutual trust between the Armenian and Turkish partners, as well as at the bidding

of differences between the local features to try to initiate non-synchronous programs serving for the solution of the problem;

7. To give an opportunity for Armenian researchers to work in Turkey and for Turkish researchers to work in Armenia. It will considerably increase the trust towards the materials;

8. To transfer some part of these projects from the "field" of "actors" (the intellectuals and experts to a level of wider social class), see the example of the Ashnak village given in the Klingenberg-Ivanova joint article;

9. To try to use television (the widest informative tool of both countries) for the purpose of "historical dialogue" right through the dialogue, involving in this dialogue both historians and the carriers of family and social memories, with the help of simultaneous interpretation;

10. To widely use new technologies, particularly the Internet, in order to increase the scope of awareness and public discussions;

11. To study traditions, beliefs of people and the values of the current life, to widely inform the population of both countries, desirably with a joint text;

12. To translate the present scientific literature and literature, especially the memoirs containing information on each other correspondingly into Armenian and Turkish.

Mr. Hans-Jochen Schmidt, Ambassador of the Federal Republic of Germany in Armenia

Prof. Elazar Barkan, Columbia University, Co-director Human Rights Concentration School of International and Public Affairs, Founding Director of the Institute for Historical Justice and Reconciliation, USA

Mr. Hans Gunnar Adén, Former Ambassador of the Kingdom of Sweden in Armenia, Azerbaijan and Georgia

Dr. Harutyun Marutyan, Leading Researcher, Institute of Archaeology and Ethnography, National Academy of Sciences, Armenia

Mr. Alexander Iskandaryan, Director of the Caucasus Institute, Armenia

Dr. David Hovhannisyan, Head of the Center of Civilization and Cultural Studies, Armenia

Dr. Yeghishe Kirakosyan, Assistant Professor at the Yerevan State University, Assistant to the Prime Minister, Armenia

Ms. Diba Nigar Göksel, Senior Analyst, European Stability Initiative, Turkey

Mr. Hasan Samani, Association for Historical Dialogue and Research, Near East University, Cyprus

Mr. Evren Ergeç, Head of International Relations Department, Community Volunteers Foundation, Community Volunteers Foundation, Turkey

Mr. Garegin Chugaszyan, Executive Director, Information Technologies Foundation (ITF), Armenia

Ms. Seda Grigoryan, Participant of the Project *"Adult Education and Oral History as Contribution to Turkish-Armenian Reconciliation"*, Armenia

Mr. Ismail Keskin, Participant of the Project *"Adult Education and Oral History as Contribution to Turkish-Armenian Reconciliation"*, Turkey

Prof. Leyla Neyzi, Professor at the Sabancı University, Turkey

Prof. Hranush Kharatyan-Araqelyan, Head of Chair of Cultural Anthropology and Area-Studies at the Yerevan State Linguistic University (YSLU), Senior Researcher at the Institute of Archaeology and Ethnography, National Academy of Sciences, Armenia

Mr. Matthias Klingenberg, Head of Asia Department, *dvv international*, Germany

Ms. Vanya Ivanova, Coordinator History Network, *dvv international*, Bulgaria

Ms. Ulrike Pusch, Project Manager "Adult Education and Oral History as Contribution to Turkish-Armenian Reconciliation", *dvv international*, Germany

Mr. Nazaret Nazaretyan, Head of Office, *dvv international*, Armenia

The activities of the workshop have been organized by the **Ms. Gayane Shagoyan**, *"Hazarashen"* Armenian Center for Ethnological Studies (Armenia), instrumentality of **Mr. Ragıp Zık**, *"Anadolu Kültür"* (Turkey).

With the help of the photos and small comments published at the end of the compendium the march of the 2-year activities of the project *"Adult Education and Oral History as Contribution to Turkish-Armenian Reconciliation"* is displayed.

Summer school in Dilijan, 10.13.2009, Photo by Gohar Movsesyan

Students meeting in Antakya, 08.18.2010, Photo by Ragıp Zık

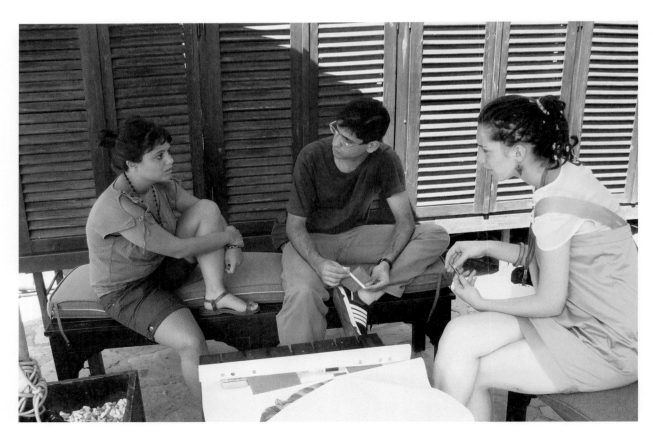

Summer school in Antakya, Kabusie, 08.21.2010, Photo by Hranush Kharatyan-Araqelyan

Conference in Yerevan, 11.27.2010, Photo by Gohar Movsesyan

Meeting at the German ambassador's residence, 11.27.2010, Photo by Gohar Movsesyan

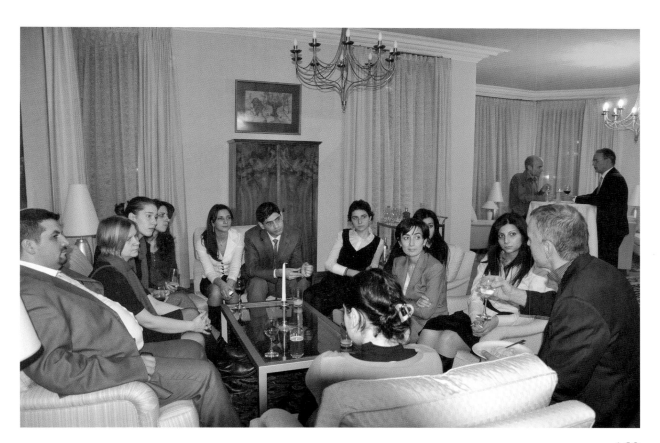

With interlocutors from Ashnak, 11.28.2010, Photo by Gohar Movsesyan

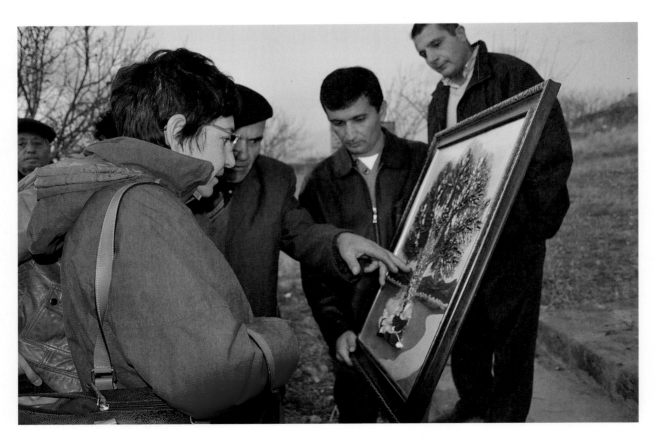

With interlocutors from Ashnak, 11.28.2010, Photo by Gohar Movsesyan

Students in Iznik, 10.03.2010, Photo by Sibel Maksudyan

Exhibition in Istanbul, 12.17.2010, Photo by Ragıp Zık

Exhibition in Diyarbakır, 01.07.2011, Photo by Önder Özengi

Exhibition in Istanbul, info desk, 12.17.2010, Photo by Ulrike Pusch

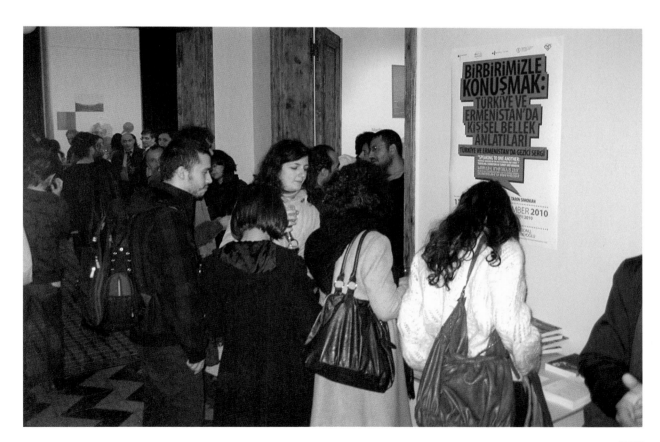

Exhibition in Diyarbakır, 01.06.2011, Photo by Önder Özengi

Exhibition in Vanadzor, 01.16.2011, Photo by Gohar Movsesyan

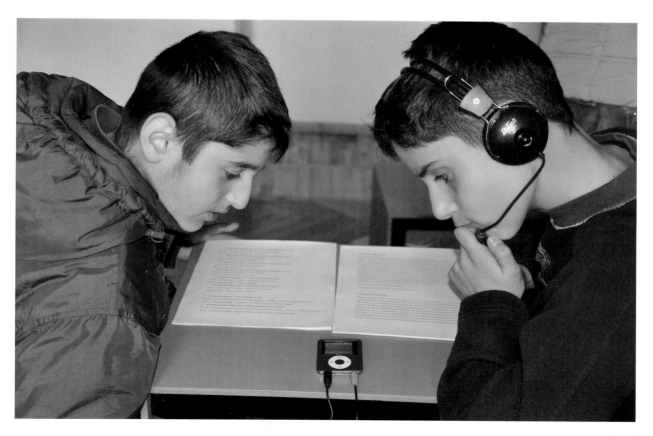

Exhibition in Ijevan, 01.22.2011, Photo by Gohar Movsesyan

Exhibition in Yerevan, 01.29.11, Photo by Gohar Movsesyan

Exhibition in Yerevan, 01.29.11, Photo by Gohar Movsesyan

Exhibition in Yerevan, 01.29.11, Photo by Gohar Movsesyan

Final meeting in Istanbul, 02.18.2011, Photo by Gohar Movsesyan

National project result, 02.18.2011, Photo by Gohar Movsesyan

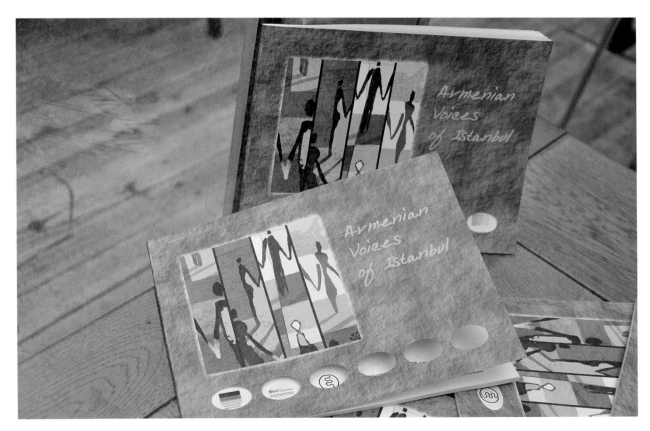

Study tour, Berlin, 02.08.2011, Photo by Nane Khachatryan